CONCEPTUALIZING EGO STATES IN TRANSACTIONAL ANALYSIS

Within this book, Grégoire reviews and extends the founding concepts of ego states in Transactional Analysis, starting with Eric Berne's foundational thinking about ego states and then examining and integrating the evolution of subsequent models and thinking.

The ego state theory describes extensive aspects of human existence, exploring phenomena belonging to very diverse dimensions, for example, the person, their inner being, their relationships, their past and present, amongst many others. A conceptualization of the three ego states is newly presented within this book as systems which are constantly in mutual interaction, each with its specific psychological functions: the Child experiences subjectively, the Parent internalizes aspects of the external family and social worlds, and the Adult allows contact with reality. This complex but necessary process is always in evolution and lasts throughout the phases of growth, permeating every aspect of the internal, external and relational life of the person. The book also further explores emotions, grief, groups, relationships and empathy through the lens of ego state theory.

Providing a greater comprehension of Berne's texts and the multilevel concept of ego states, this book will be a valuable resource for transactional analysts, both in practice and in training.

José Grégoire is a psychotherapist, an EATA Certified Clinical Transactional Analyst and a Teaching and Supervising Transactional Analyst. Besides his work as a therapist, teacher, supervisor in TA and translator of the French TA review *Actualités en Analyse Transactionnelle,* he has worked in an interdisciplinary therapeutic team for the therapy of persons wanting to cure addictions.

INNOVATIONS IN TRANSACTIONAL ANALYSIS: THEORY AND PRACTICE

Series Editor: William F. Cornell

This book series is founded on the principle of the importance of open discussion, debate, critique, experimentation, and the integration of other models in fostering innovation in all the arenas of transactional analytic theory and practice: psychotherapy, counselling, education, organizational development, health care, and coaching. It will be a home for the work of established authors and new voices.

NEW THEORY AND PRACTICE OF TRANSACTIONAL ANALYSIS IN ORGANIZATIONS: ON THE EDGE
Sari van Poelje and Anne de Graaf

GROUP THERAPY IN TRANSACTIONAL ANALYSIS: THEORY THROUGH PRACTICE
Anna Emanuela Tangolo and Anna Massi

RADICAL-RELATIONAL PERSPECTIVES IN TRANSACTIONAL ANALYSIS PSYCHOTHERAPY: OPPRESSION, ALIENATION, RECLAMATION
Karen Minikin

REVITALIZATION THROUGH TRANSACTIONAL ANALYSIS GROUP TREATMENT: HUMAN NATURE AND ITS DETERIORATION
Giorgio Piccinino

WORKING WITH DREAMS IN TRANSACTIONAL ANALYSIS: FROM THEORY TO PRACTICE FOR INDIVIDUALS AND GROUPS
Anna Emanuela Tangolo and Francesca Vignozzi

CONCEPTUALIZING EGO STATES IN TRANSACTIONAL ANALYSIS: THREE SYSTEMS IN INTERACTION
José Grégoire

https://www.routledge.com/Innovations-in-Transactional-Analysis-Theory-and-Practice/book-series/INNTA

CONCEPTUALIZING EGO STATES IN TRANSACTIONAL ANALYSIS

Three Systems in Interaction

José Grégoire

LONDON AND NEW YORK

Designed cover image: © Getty Images

First published in English in 2025
by Routledge
4 Park Square, Milton Park, Abingdon, Oxon OX14 4RN

and by Routledge
605 Third Avenue, New York, NY 10158

Routledge is an imprint of the Taylor & Francis Group, an informa business

© 2025 José Grégoire

The right of José Grégoire to be identified as author of this work has been asserted in accordance with sections 77 and 78 of the Copyright, Designs and Patents Act 1988.

All rights reserved. No part of this book may be reprinted or reproduced or utilised in any form or by any electronic, mechanical, or other means, now known or hereafter invented, including photocopying and recording, or in any information storage or retrieval system, without permission in writing from the publishers.

Trademark notice: Product or corporate names may be trademarks or registered trademarks, and are used only for identification and explanation without intent to infringe.

Published in French by NORPPA 2019
Translated by Muriel Treharne

British Library Cataloguing-in-Publication Data
A catalogue record for this book is available from the British Library

Library of Congress Cataloging-in-Publication Data
Names: Grégoire, José, author.
Title: Conceptualizing ego states in transactional analysis : three systems in interaction / José Grégoire.
Description: Abingdon, Oxon ; New York, NY : Routledge, 2025. | Series: Innovations in transactional analysis : theory and practice | Includes bibliographical references and index. |
Identifiers: LCCN 2024011216 (print) | LCCN 2024011217 (ebook) | ISBN 9781032735764 (hardback) | ISBN 9781032657677 (paperback) | ISBN 9781003465003 (ebook)
Subjects: LCSH: Transactional analysis.
Classification: LCC RC489.T7 .G74 2025 (print) | LCC RC489.T7 (ebook) | DDC 616.89/145--dc23/eng/20240319
LC record available at https://lccn.loc.gov/2024011216
LC ebook record available at https://lccn.loc.gov/2024011217

ISBN: 978-1-032-73576-4 (hbk)
ISBN: 978-1-032-65767-7 (pbk)
ISBN: 978-1-003-46500-3 (ebk)

DOI: 10.4324/9781003465003

Typeset in Times New Roman
by KnowledgeWorks Global Ltd.

CONTENTS

Editor's preface		*vii*
Foreword		*x*
1	Three perspectives on ego states	1
2	Ego states as personality systems	12
3	What is the purpose of each system?	18
4	Growth and personal development	30
5	The Child: The system that experiences life	47
6	The Parent: The system that internalizes	60
7	The Adult: The system that integrates reality	72
8	From disjunction to integration	86
9	Emotions	99
10	The sense of Self	108
11	Integration and relationships	117
12	Co-creativity and relationships	127

13	Communication within the relationship	142
14	The practitioner and the interaction perspective	148
	Conclusion	159
	Afterword: Ego states in Transactional Analysis	*161*
	Bibliography	*174*
	Acknowledgements	*182*
	Index	*183*

EDITOR'S PREFACE

José Grégoire's *Conceptualizing Ego States in Transactional Analysis: Three Systems in Interaction* was first published in French as *Les états du moi: Trois systèmes interactifs* in 2007 (Editions d'Analyse Transactionelle) and republished in 2019 (NORPPA). This book has long had an important influence within the French-speaking TA communities, recognized there for its important contributions to TA theory. Sadly, it has taken more than a couple of decades for it to find its way to English publication. One might ask why we are publishing a book nearly 25 years old within the series "Innovations in Transactional Analysis". Finally having arrived in this wonderful English translation, I have no doubt as to the innovations it brings to transactional analysis and, hence, to this series. As editor of this series, I have become aware of numerous innovative texts that await translation into English. It is with pride and pleasure that I welcome *Ego States in Interaction* to the Routledge "Innovations" list.

Now retired, Grégoire practiced as a transactional analytic psychotherapist, supervisor and trainer for nearly 40 years. Before his involvement in transactional analysis, Grégoire earned degrees in mathematical sciences, philosophy and the history of religious theory. The depth of his scholarship is richly apparent here, as he delves deeply into Eric Berne's foundational theory of ego states, laying the ground for a radical extension and revision of Berne's original work. Berne's own thinking about ego states was in many ways a work in progress, often containing apparent contradictions as his thinking evolved over the course of a decade, so typical of a creative thinker. Tragically, his writing and teaching came abruptly to a halt by his untimely death at age 60 in 1970. His final two books, *Sex in Human Loving* (1970) and *What Do You Say Hello?* (1972) – a compilation of manuscripts he was working on at the time of his death – were published posthumously. The three "schools" of TA (Barnes) emergent at the time of Berne's death shared an emphasis on the structural and historical/repetitive nature of ego states, while proposing radically different styles of therapeutic intervention. Those closely associated with Berne at the time of his death became advocates for "classical" TA, which sadly concretized many of his ideas. In the half century since Berne's death, second- and third-generation transactional analysts have proposed various (and often competitive) models of ego states in nature and function.

Grégoire returns to Berne's writings about ego states with eyes both respectful and critical. He takes up the subsequent models of ego state theory in a manner equally thoughtful and critical, as he seeks to integrate these various theoretical and clinical models into a comprehensive theory, written in such a way that readers are invited to explore their own thinking and practice. Grégoire rightly criticizes Berne for his preoccupation with distinguishing transactional analysis from psychoanalysis, which had the inadvertent and unfortunate consequence of concretizing what was, in fact, a rather complex investigation of the nature and functions of ego states. Grégoire offers the example of Berne's wry comment about realizing that "each individual is three different persons, all pulling in different directions…so it is a wonder that anything ever gets done" (1970, p. 103), which made it all too easy for psychoanalytic critics to dismiss TA as a "pop psychology". He goes on to argue that "Berne is so fascinated by the degree to which repetitive ego states sometimes resemble their origin that he seems to refer to personality systems as three persons in one individual". The tension throughout Berne's model(s) of ego states between an emphasis on the repetitive aspects of ego states (as well as games and scripts) and the more forward/generative/developmental functions of ego states is a recurrent theme in Grégoire's reflections on Berne's writings. This was – perhaps inevitably – a tension that filtered through much of the debate about the nature of ego states in the decades since; this is the tension that Grégoire seeks to creatively synthesize in the pages of this book.

Grégoire wrestles with the theoretical debates within the evolution of TA theory. There are those who conceive of the Child ego state as an archaic, fixated structure within the mind. Grégoire, while acknowledging that the person's very first learnings through infancy and early childhood are founding strata of the Child ego state, argues that the essence of the Child is the home of one's subjective experience, lived and living emotional realities, quite capable of being engaged with and influenced by here-and-now experience. He posits the Parent ego state as the essential complement to the Child, i.e., the memory and carrier of the experiences and beliefs granted through one's encounters with significant Others. Often cast with a negative, limiting valence within much of the TA literature, here in Grégoire's conceptualization, while the Parent ego state may at times be problematic, the Parent system situates one within the world of Others, situates the individual within one's cultural, social and relational worlds. Grégoire characterizes the Adult ego state as one's capacity to recognize and engage with reality, referring to the Adult as the "reality system", a necessary (though sometimes disappointing or frustrating) complement to the Child and Parent. It is "the job", the function, of the Adult ego state system to cope with the reality that life often falls short of both Child hopes and wishes, as well as the demands and expectations of the Parent. While this may at time seem like a hapless function, it is vitally necessary. Key to Grégoire's vision is the capacity of the ego state systems in the ongoing interaction and influence of each system upon the others. The mid-section of this book then engages in the description and reflections on the diverse theories within TA with regard to ego states. At times, Grégoire offers critique, but more often he seeks synthesis, and in so doing models his premise of the interaction and influence of one system upon another.

Grégoire situates his elaboration of ego state theory within a frame juxtaposing structures and systems, the notion of structure, i.e., something organized and bounded, held alongside a sense of systems, more fluid and interactive. What I have found radical in Grégoire's articulation of his understanding of the nature of ego states is his conception of ego states as *systems* within the psyche, both underpinning and informing psychological development. Each ego state is, on the one hand, a specific and rather unique aspect of psychological organization and perception (structure) while at the same time living, changing and interactive, mutually influencing system of experience and knowing. Ego states are reframed here as three fundamental psychological/perceptual systems that interact with each other and with the world at large, subject and author of one's experience. As such, the ego states may at times, especially under stress and uncertainty, infiltrate the present day with the beliefs and potential rigidities forged in past experiences and yet, at the same time, have the vitality of living systems capable of seeking and incorporating novel experiences and fostering developmental maturation. This, to my mind, is Grégoire's stunning extension of ego state theory into a model that is thoroughly engaged with our contemporary interests in the relational and social fields that can inhibit, inform or enliven our capacities for psychological and emotional robustness. In so doing, to my reading, he anticipates – in a text written 25 years ago – the contemporary shift from the epistemological emphasis that had dominated psychoanalysis and early models of transactional analysis with an emphasis on history and the question of "why?" to that of an ontological perspective that asks "how?" and leans into the future.

Berne developed transactional analysis as a method of psychodynamic psychotherapy, and as such, there was a nearly inevitable emphasis on the fixated and repetitive aspects of the past – the psychotherapeutic viewpoint tending to look to history. Since then, TA has found rich and important applications in the fields of personal development, education and organizational consultation in which the primary orientation is more overtly towards the future. Grégoire argues that in any field of application, it is the central task of the professional to open spaces for reflection and learning, writing that the interactional systems perspective he develops in this book "gives room to the past without confining itself to repetition and is open to the present, and the future to be built; it keeps within sight access to autonomy and creativity for the person, the group, or the institution".

The evolution of theory, especially within its foundational premises, demands what can be a daunting, even painful, process of letting go of cherished ideas. Through the pages of *Conceptualizing Ego States in Transactional Analysis*, José Grégoire invites the reader to question and let go. But in that letting go, he does not leave the reader in a void but offers a rich and enlivening re-conceptualization of these foundational concepts in transactional analysis, a leaning into the future.

William F. Cornell

FOREWORD

The ego states theory describes extensive aspects of human existence. It does not describe them all, because some belong to other theories, present or future, and a great number will undoubtedly never be described theoretically. However, it gathers and relates phenomena belonging to very diverse dimensions: the person, their inner being, their relationships, their past and their present, their deep tendencies and their manifestations, their communication and their action, their body, their thought, their affects and their imagination.

Theoretical clarifications are like spotlights projecting a light beam that originates from a specific angle and illuminates one area only, big or small. This is especially the case in psychology. Not surprisingly, therefore, theories have a history. In each era, theorists have their own perception of practical necessities, of the prevailing theoretical conjuncture and of their theory's requirements; with them in mind, they adjust the beam's position or width or direct it towards still unexplored areas. To understand what our research on the ego states theory is aimed at, here is a brief recall of its evolution's main stages.

Eric Berne

It all starts with Eric Berne: although the term "ego states" comes from Paul Federn,[1] Berne gives it a meaning, or rather a series of "blended" meanings, which are fundamentally innovative[2]:

- *Meaning 1:* An ego state is *"the total behavior and experience* of the individual at a given moment"[3] with all their internal and external aspects. Berne condenses these into "feelings and behavior"[4] or "feelings, thoughts and behavior".[5] This concept is well suited for describing a person's successive reactions.
- *Meaning 2:* Berne divides these experiences associated with behaviours into *three groups*: some come straight from the person's childhood (Child ego states), others reproduce parental figures' experiences (Parent ego states), and others are presumed to be "adapted to the current reality"[6] (Adult ego states). These categories, as we can see, are especially suitable for the identification of repetitive experiences.

- *Meaning 3:* The term "ego states" also designates structures, which Berne calls *"personality systems"*[7] or *"psychic organs"*. He introduces them to account for the constitution, organization and implementation of the three ego states. Each system is always present and acting simultaneously; each provides an irreplaceable contribution to the person's development and activity. These concepts allow the analysing of non-repetitive dynamics.

After a creative phase, from his first articles on ego states in 1957 and 1958[8] to *Transactional Analysis in Psychotherapy*[9] published in 1961, Berne became more interested in other concepts; he only occasionally returned to the ego states theory. His work shifted towards fine-tuned behaviour observation with psychological games,[10] then returned in force to the intrapsychic with the concept of script.[11]

"Meaning 2", which directs thinking towards repetitions of past experiences, remains predominant for Berne. During his lifetime, in theoretical presentations, "Meaning 2" already overshadowed "Meaning 3" (even though the latter, crucial to analyse many dynamics, never disappeared completely). This is especially the case in TA's first presentations: in the second version of Berne's book *A Layman's Guide to Psychiatry and Psychoanalysis*,[12] the chapter about transactional analysis, written by J. Dusay at Berne's request, speaks only of "Meaning 2".

The "classical TA" period

After Berne's death in 1971, this trend became more pronounced in the so-called Berne school. A significant element appears: the ego states "descriptive model"[13] (so-called functional). The heuristic clues[14] that Berne mentions in *Transactional Analysis in Psychotherapy*[15] to identify repetitive ego states[16] become a general list of "options", i.e., of possibilities for the person's reactions in the here and now. In the 1970s and 1980s, this list, fully valid for its own purpose, will take on more and more importance in TA theory and practice, to the point of sometimes overshadowing the structural model, which will lead to reactions later.

During this time, a sort of "classical" and stereotyped TA image jells. We call "classical TA" this sequence of formulas extracted from Berne's texts; this becomes even more important when it is defined as the official program of introduction to TA.[17] It includes, in addition to the descriptive terms now gathered under the name of "functional model",[18] a structural model whose elements are exclusively defined by "Meaning 2". Classical TA sets side-by-side concepts describing repetitions of the past (the structural model) with elements designed to look for behavioural options (descriptive terms), leaving a gap in the *formulation of* the theory about what is happening intra-psychically in the present.

The redecision school,[19] whose theory is centred on the concept of impasse, i.e., intrapsychic conflict between personality systems, and the reparenting school,[20] where the central place is given to the relational concept of symbiosis, both use classical TA nevertheless.

Unconscious and transference are concepts absent from classical TA; however, transactional analysts from psychoanalytic training or inspiration have already begun their integration with TA, as shown by the publications of C. Moiso[21] and M. Novellino[22] on transference and counter-transference concepts, or M. Haykin and M. and K. Woods[23] on splitting, a notion which comes from object relations theory. Many others, no doubt, have asked themselves practical and theoretical questions about how concepts of psychoanalytic origin could be integrated into TA. But this would only come to light in the following period.

Transition and debates

Classical TA's predominance ended around 1988. *TAJ*'s January issue about ego states includes several important articles[24] that highlight the structural model (defined in "Meaning 2") both in Berne's thinking and in the understanding of psychological dynamics. In retrospect, it is mainly a return to Berne and a reaction to an unduly expanded use of the "descriptive model". But the argumentation shows that the wind is changing: R. Erskine introduces the concept of unconscious defence mechanism and makes it the very foundation of the Child and Parent ego states.

Over the following years, the debate on the ego states theory splits transactionalists intotwo groups. On one side, a traditional group, represented by C. Steiner and S. Karpman[25] among others, proclaims its attachment to Berne's "accessible" presentation of classical TA and displays an increasingly radical aversion and opposition to any psychoanalytical concept. On the other side, many authors are increasingly critical of the type of relationship such a theory induces between the practitioner and the client (or the group). They criticize its exclusive focus on the preconscious and conscious, on external observation, on verbal explanation and on the possibly "decisive' intervention".[26] Some see it as a way to avoid taking into account unconscious experience and bypassing a real in-depth commitment to the relationship; others see it as a source of power games.[27] All affirm the need to pay attention to unconscious dynamics if one really wants to help patients.

Since classical TA supporters did not recognize how valid this opening could be, nor how complementary with their own values, the debate became stuck on an "either/or" attitude, with some emphasizing the need to take the unconscious into account, and others fidelity to Berne's theoretical style or to the intentions attributed to him. It is presumptuous to rely on Berne's supposed personal reactions on this point because, despite his virulent attacks on the psychoanalytical *institutions* of his time[28] and the assertions of some practitioners[29] personally involved with him, a closer analysis of Berne's written works reveals that *the thinking they convey is "neither focusing on the unconscious, nor excluding the unconscious".*[30]

In such a context, many transactionalists belonging to recent TA trends have chosen Erskine and Trautmann's ego states theory as a tool and a symbol of this opening to psychoanalytic concepts and a practice inspired by them. However, as far as ego states are concerned, this theoretical formulation was probably neither necessary nor inevitable,[31] as we will see.

TA's recent trends

Here are some recent TA trends,[32] to which we will often refer:

- R. Erskine and R. Trautmann's *Integrative Psychotherapy* is a theory based on the new concept of "integrated Adult" and on the reduction of Child and Parent ego states to defence mechanisms; in practical terms, it is centred on respectful inquiry, attunement and the therapist's personal commitment.[33]
- M. Novellino and C. Moiso's *"transactional psychoanalysis"* highlights transference and counter-transference analysis, and unconscious communication.
- More recently, H. Hargaden and C. Sills' *relational TA*[34] focuses on bringing largely unconscious relational processes into the interpersonal sphere in order to change them through the relational process.[35]

In their view of development, these authors are inspired by D. Stern.[36]

- In a similar direction, G. Summers and K. Tudor's,[37] *"co-creative TA"*, describes the therapeutic relationship as a joint creation between the person and the therapist.

These four trends adopted Erskine and Trautmann's ego states theory as a working tool.

- W. Cornell integrates contributions from various neo-Reichian, transactional and psychoanalytical trends in an approach centred on relationship, body and healthy development.[38] His thinking includes non-psychotherapeutic fields of application.[39]

Not all recent transactional orientations are psychoanalytically inspired:

- D. Stern's concept of "interactions' generalised representations" applied to ego states[40] is not; this concept makes it possible to understand the person's development in an evolutionary perspective through increasingly extended ego states combinations.
- Neither is the constructionist or narrativist trend, whose leader is J. Allen[41]; it focuses on the narratives or elements of narratives that the person has developed about their existence.

Choices and values

Here are some of the choices made in writing this book:

- First choice: work with a theory *based on healthy functioning and healthy development* rather than on pathology.[42] This implies highlighting personal development mechanisms, which classical TA leaves aside in favour of repetition mechanisms, which must be situated in a wider context.

- Second choice: avoid the trap of making TA a simple duplicate of other theories, because these theories undoubtedly have much to offer us. In the long run, *integrating two theories* only makes sense between two elements that do not coincide with each other and *each of which retains its own specificity*. There is no need to be locked in the antinomy between the conscious and the unconscious: the ego states theory must make room for both dimensions.

These choices are part of a conception of psychotherapy which, despite the importance it necessarily gives to working through early or archaic obstacles, also includes support for empowerment, actualization of resources and release of creativity. What W. Cornell describes stands along the same lines: according to him, clients need interventions, thinking and relational attitude of their therapist to be open to multiple levels of intervention and able to go back and forth between different topics and processes, such as daily life concerns, intrapsychic conflicts, transference and counter-transference.[43] That suits an integrative conception of psychotherapy[44] and opens the theory to applications in the fields of education, counselling and organizational intervention.

For all these reasons, we chose the TA concept of personality systems ("Meaning 3") for this book. They include both unconscious and conscious aspects throughout the development process and, as such, comply with the criteria detailed above.

We hope this book will invite readers to re-engage personally with *seminal theoretical texts*, by Berne or by other theorists. For this reason, most chapters end with a collection of commented texts, which the reader can skip if they wish, but which form an integral part of the book's reflection. Without this, texts are reduced to ready-made formulas, taken out of context, and their strength is lost. It is better to be aware of where we deviate from what the founders thought; it is better to ask ourselves why we do so than to assume that they thought as we do by relying on a few words to which it is all too easy to attribute the meaning that suits us. For Berne, and many others for that matter, could well take up the words of a classic author: "Sir, I write books, not sentences!".

TRANSACTIONAL TEXTS

In the second part of most chapters of this book, various former transactional texts are summarized and commented on, to put the ideas asserted in the first part of the chapter in concordant or contrasting relation with them, and to include these ideas in the broader context of TA theory. Most notably, some controversial or forgotten texts of Berne's are analyzed.

Notes

1 FEDERN, P., 1952.
2 These three meanings, and the theoretical perspectives from which they derive, are discussed in Chapter 1.

FOREWORD

3. BERNE, E., 1961, p. 48.
4. BERNE, E., 1961, p. 1. Berne will detach thought from feeling only in his last book: BERNE, E., 1972, p. 11.
5. BERNE, E., 1972, p. 11.
6. BERNE, E., 1961, p. 52.
7. This expression, which comes from Berne (BERNE, E., 1961, p. 18 "systems of the personality") will be used throughout this work in preference to "psychic organs", which connotes Berne's hope that one day, "zones" corresponding to the three organs will be found in the brain: see SCHLEGEL, L., 1993[ES].
8. BERNE, E., 1957b, 1958.
9. BERNE, E., 1961.
10. BERNE, E., 1964a.
11. BERNE, E., 1972.
12. BERNE, E., 1968.
13. In the literature (but probably not in the collective creation process of the San Francisco Transactional Analysis Seminar, see HOSTIE, R., 1987), the starting point is Steve Karpman's article "Options"; KARPMAN, S., 1971. Karpman himself does not intend to create a new "model", but a new pedagogical way of introducing patients to the structural model (Meaning 2).
14. Heuristic: which helps to discover.
15. BERNE, E., 1961.
16. See BERNE, E., 1961, pp. 51–53. In his last book, Berne rightly calls them "descriptive terms" (BERNE, E., 1972, p. 13). In this text, he does not use the term "model", nor the terms "function" or "functional".
17. This formal introduction is called "TA 101". It is a quick overview of transactional theory and is mandatory for anyone wishing to engage in recognized training.
18. It is not in fact the function, the specific contribution of personality systems, but the "functionings" that may be manifestations of them.
19. See GOULDING, R., and GOULDING, M., 1978. GOULDING, R., and GOULDING, M., 1979.
20. See SCHIFF, J., and others, 1975.
21. MOISO, C., 1985[ES].
22. NOVELLINO, M., 1984, 1985, 1987.
23. HAYKIN, M., 1980 [ES]. WOODS, M., and WOODS, K., 1981 [ES].
24. CLARKSON, P., and GILBERT, M., 1988. ERSKINE, R.G., 1988 [ES].
25. E.g., C. Steiner's position in: STEINER, C., and NOVELLINO, M., 2005 and the letters from S. Karpman in *Script*, 1998–1999.
26. The expression is from BERNE, E., 1972, p. 365.
27. See the critique by BARNES, G., 1999a, 1999b, 1999c, which draws its inspiration from Bateson but not from psychoanalysis.
28. BERNE, E., 1972, p. 365.
29. F. English's contribution, for example, is a completely different way of understanding and interpreting Berne's thought. ENGLISH, F., 1977[ES].
30. GREGOIRE, J., 2007a [ES], p.11, and passim.
31. See on this point GRÉGOIRE, J., 2007b [ES].
32. See GREGOIRE, J., 2007c.
33. See ERSKINE, R.G., and TRAUTMANN, R., 1996.
34. HARGADEN, H., and SILLS, C., 2002.
35. SILLS, C., 2004, p.26.

36 STERN, D., 1985.
37 SUMMERS G., and TUDOR K., 2000 ES.
38 See CORNELL, W.F., 1988, 1998, 2000. CORNELL, W. F., 2003 ES.
39 CORNELL, W.F., and HINE, J., 1999.
40 STERN, D., 1985. GILBERT, M., 1996ES. HINE, J., 1997 ES.
41 See ALLEN, J.R., and ALLEN, B.A., 1997.
42 See CORNELL, W.R., 1988.
43 CORNELL, W.F., 2006.
44 PAGÈS, M., 1993.

1
THREE PERSPECTIVES ON EGO STATES

The concept of ego states in Berne and his successors consists of various articulated meanings because several perspectives are joined together, which happens very often with psychological theories. Although these perspectives have many points of contact, they do not coincide with each other, and they do not relate to one another; they are usually neither equivalent nor incompatible. In Berne's case, neither are they linked to distinct stages in the development of his approach, as is the case with Freud.[1] On the contrary, they intertwine; part of the history of transactional theory is the result of the divergent interpretations this situation has generated.

The sequential or descriptive perspective

First the *sequential* perspective: it is used to describe phenomena from the point of view of their sequence. In an imaginary theatre play, this perspective would be appropriate for a series of disconnected monologues: one actor leaves, the other returns. The fact that a play entirely made of such juxtapositions would be missing a sense of direction to the point of chaos makes us sense that the sequential perspective is meant more to describe sequential occurrences than to explain their mutual links.

Berne uses this perspective especially when he analyses ego states in patients' reactions. Ms "Primus",[2] for example, moves between three quite different "states": sometimes she behaves like a little girl and giggles nervously, sometimes she delivers information clearly, sometimes she is absorbed in listening to imaginary "voices".

Berne is interested in these three specific types of reaction because they correspond to the three great types of ego states he listed and named, respectively, Child, Adult and Parent. In the purely sequential perspective, these three terms still have a vague meaning: "Child" means that Ms Primus' first attitude *seems like* that of a child, Adult means that her behaviour in the second phase *is what one would expect of* an adult, and Parent means that the "voices" deliver orders and judgements as some parents would.[3]

Ms Primus' successive "ego states" can be said to be strongly contrasted and of diverse types, and to replace one another in an abrupt and transition-less way. The sequential perspective is the one that naturally comes to mind to describe such a succession of phenomena. We can also see why it can be equivalently called *descriptive*: faced with a succession of manifestations that appear "in bulk" and whose underlying link has not yet been unravelled, the first step is to describe them. The second step is to classify them, starting with an intuitive criterion: here, their likeness. As Berne states, this likeness is only a gateway towards a more precise and enlightening criterion, i.e., their starting point; it follows that the descriptive perspective leads to the next one, the origin perspective.

In the sequential or descriptive perspective, the light that theory brings can be *more or less wide* in the sense that the term "ego state" does not always designate precise and concrete behaviours at a given moment but sets or modes of reaction. Berne and Mr. Segundo used to distinguish between two terms, "the lawyer" and "the little boy", which included for them a great number of concrete manifestations of Adult and Child.[4]

In this context, the identification of each ego state, or *diagnosis*, is based on two sources: the person's observable behaviour (behavioural diagnosis) and the social impact that their/her behaviour and reactions have on others (relational or "social" diagnosis).

Interventions at the sequential level seek to change the sequence when it is unsatisfactory, for example by looking for alternative behavioural options.[5] Overall, the approach focuses on the behavioural and cognitive dimension; it enables the person to make an initial sorting out of what they are experiencing, if only by learning to classify their own reactions into at least three categories. It can involve emotional awareness and learning, as in emotional literacy.[6]

While the implementation of this perspective requires a relationship of acceptance and trust, it does not involve the analysis of transference and countertransference which, in principle, are not used as a source of information. Of course, the practitioner has to free themself from aspects of their own script that might hinder the process; this said, the alliance is more like the relationship between a service user and a specialist. Nevertheless, the sequential perspective serves as a gateway to the other perspectives; in any case, this is necessarily where the first contact with the person takes place.

Berne was interested in the sequential or descriptive perspective as a gateway to the repetition perspective. For him, the transition from one to the other is mainly made through "descriptive terms", for which today we use "normative, nurturing, adapted, rebellious and free".[7] There is another attitude directed towards reality, unnamed by Berne or classical Transactional Analysis (TA), but which they designate by the name of the corresponding ego state: "Adult".[8] Originally, these descriptive terms are always hypothetical[9] diagnostic clues for an initial identification of repetitive ego states. They take a more or less systematized form only in Berne's last book, together with their corresponding diagram,[10] though Berne does not mention it as a systematic tool in the rest of his book. It is only later that these terms will be used as a list of "options"[11] in the here and now.

The origin perspective: Evolution or repetition

The second perspective is the *origin* perspective. It focuses on the antecedents of the present situation. If it were a theatre play, it would be one with many "flashbacks", where each character tells of past events that explain why they are there and what they came to do. As viewers, we do not yet have a single narrative but fragments of narratives which we expect to come together at some point through interactions between the characters. The comparison with a theatre play lays the ground for the idea that the origin perspective shows the same fragmentary character and calls for a more global perspective, i.e., the interaction perspective.

In real life as in a play, the origin perspective is usually an *evolution perspective*. Usually, if Madame's maid says how naive and foolish she was when she was hired as a young maid, the audience discovers later that things have changed a lot since then and that perhaps she is now in fact running the house. Berne rarely uses such an evolutionary perspective with ego states.[12] But he puts a great importance on one of its forms, the repetition perspective, as do most psychoanalytical and psychodynamic trends. Among all the diversity and multiplicity of experiences, this perspective selects a very particular category, because of the key role it plays in psychological problems: re-enacting past experiences. In the case of Child ego states, these experiences belonged to the person; in the case of Parent ego states, to one or more parental figures. In this approach, the aspect of progressive evolution is considered absent or negligible. The maid, after 25 years, is still naive and foolish. You might think this play would not be particularly good and you would be quite right: the repetition perspective usually concerns experiences which, because they are repetitive, impoverish existence and inhibit creativity.

In the repetition perspective, the Child and Parent ego states are much more precisely defined than in the sequential perspective. The Child ego states are no longer simply those that *seem like* a child's behaviour, but those that reproduce the internal reactions and behaviours of the specific child that person once was. Similarly, the Parent ego states are no longer simply those that *seem like* a parental attitude, but those that reproduce the behaviours or behavioural type of other real persons, mainly parents or parental figures. Berne very often goes from one perspective to the other and insists on how important that is[13]: "The person who stole chewing gum was not called the Child for convenience, or because children often steal, but because he himself stole chewing gum as a child with the same gleeful attitude and using the same technique. (…) The Parent was not called the Parent because it is traditional for philanthropists to be 'fatherly' or 'motherly', but because he actually imitated his own father's behavior and state of mind in his philanthropic activities".[14]

Even though Berne presented the three ego states symmetrically in this passage, his definition of the Adult ego states *does not refer to their origin*: "The Adult was called the Adult, not because he was playing the role of an adult, imitating the behavior of big men, but because he exhibited highly effective reality-testing in his legal and financial operations".[15] This is because the concept of Adult ego state has a particular status in the repetition perspective, due to it being defined "by default" as an ego state unmarked by repetition: "Since the Adult is still the least well understood of the three types of ego states, it is best characterized in clinical practice as the residual state left after the segregation of all detectable Parent and Child elements".[16] Interestingly, Berne immediately adds: "Or it may be more formally considered as the derivative of a model of the neopsyche".[17] This represents a shift towards the interaction perspective, which we will address shortly.

Since classical TA presents the ego states theory from the repetition perspective, this difference has become very significant. For Erskine and Trautmann, it becomes the central opposition on which their ego state theory is based: the evolution perspective is implemented only for the "integrating Adult", whereas the Child and the Parent are reduced to the repetition perspective.

Like the sequential perspective, the repetition perspective applies not only to experiences that have taken place at a particular time, but also to larger or smaller sets of reactions, provided they generate reproduction rather than creative use. In this case, the emphasis is on the fact that the person is now exhibiting the same general patterns of reaction as when they were a child of this or that age (Child ego states) or the same patterns of reaction as their parents or parental figures (Parent ego states). According to Erskine, these general patterns comprise "needs, desires, urges, and sensations; the defense mechanisms; and the thought processes, perceptions, feelings, and behaviors"[18] related to a past stage of development (Child ego states) or emanating from another person (Parent ego states).

The origin perspective adds two new dimensions to the behavioural and relational (or social) *diagnoses*: the historical diagnosis, which seeks information about the person's past, and the phenomenological diagnosis, which is based on the person's phenomenological experience or at least on their emotional experience of it when they remember. In the "phenomenological experience", the person feels as if they are in a particular moment of their past at the same time as in the present, as if the two experiences are overlaid or superimposed. Penfield, who was Berne's Neurophysiology Professor at McGill University in Montreal, had induced such experiences in the laboratory by electrically stimulating certain areas of the cortex in epileptics.[19] What interests Berne above all is that the same result can be obtained in the therapeutic relationship, as shown by Ms Enatosky's experience[20] (see the collection of texts at the end of this chapter).

Berne insists that all four dimensions are necessary[21]; he starts from the outside layer, i.e., from the behavioural diagnosis towards the phenomenological diagnosis. Erskine[22] reverses this order: he states that the patient's experience comes first, both chronologically and by order of importance; that leads him to give first place to the phenomenological diagnosis, a term which then gains a broader meaning for Erskine than for Berne, for whom it simply refers to "reliving" a past situation. This key position emphasizes the need to avoid a one-sided emphasis on behavioural diagnosis and to give priority to the person's core experience.[23]

As for *interventions*, the repetition perspective leads to working through either the Child or Parent repetitive experiences, or the relationship from which they emanate. In *Transactional Analysis in Psychotherapy*,[24] Berne describes the stages of this work as he thought it should be: become aware of the repetition process (decontamination of the Adult), work on options in the present to obtain "social control"[25] and then, if the patient wants it, lift the Child's confusion.

The re-decision perspective, on the other hand, has generated many other more emotional and more creative methodologies. In the parenting approach or in the re-parenting school,[26] the identification of past events leads to a corrective experience[27] which cannot "heal the past", that is impossible, but which can symbolically clear the current incapacitation which is the consequence of this past.

Relational TA, "transactional psychoanalysis" and co-creative TA contribute to this perspective through the central idea that the source of psychological problems is to be found in childhood relational failures; they state that, when these are archaic, they can only be truly accessed by opening up to the unconscious dimension and to the analysis of transference and countertransference, which are essential tools to understand what is happening and, above all, what has been happening for the person. This requires a more open and committed relationship than previous approaches. Erskine and Trautmann[28] have summarized its characteristics within the following three terms: respectful inquiry, attunement and personal commitment.

The interaction perspective

A play is rarely reduced to monologues. Usually, characters meet on stage and interact. Then, you consider several characters and the impact they have on each other. This is what we call the *interaction perspective*. It is not in any way opposed to the two perspectives seen above; the audience comes to it as soon as the characters meet to speak and interact, and even when a character believes themself to be alone on stage while another character comments on their actions or words *in an aside* delivered side-stage or upstage, or when two characters compete front-stage to tell the audience disparate or contradictory things.

Berne goes one step further than the previous perspectives with the interaction perspective: he considers that each ego states type emanates from a different internal "organ", in a similar way that visual perceptions emanate from the visual system, auditory perceptions from the auditory system, and so on. He identifies three "psychic organs" or "*personality systems*"[29]: the Child system, the Adult system and the Parent system; the Child system generates Child ego states and reveals itself through them, and so on. In some texts, Berne calls the Child system the "archaeopsyche", which emphasizes its archaic aspects; the Adult system is called the "neopsyche", which emphasizes its aspects related to more advanced development; finally, the Parent system is the "exteropsyche", which emphasizes its orientation towards the internal and external reactions of others.

These are *structures*, i.e., theoretical concepts which do not correspond to directly perceptible or observable entities, but which give coherence and continuity to observable manifestations. The apparently chaotic succession of ego states observed in Ms Primus becomes coherent when one supposes that the human being possesses these three systems and that, in her specific case, they alternate their manifestations without being coordinated.

The theatre analogy allows us to consider the vast range of possibilities there are. In a play, characters observe each other, talk to each other, quarrel, avoid each other or form alliances. Conspirators hatch their plans together; Faust seduces Marguerite, while Mephistopheles leads the game; Dante speaks with the damned under Virgil's protection; Zeus reconciles Neptune and Athena... The same is true of personality systems. Their interactions can be described metaphorically[30] as: forming alliance, holding back, influencing, antagonizing, manipulating, monitoring, informing others, mediating, etc. Berne sums up all these possibilities under the term "influence".[31]

On the practical level, the interaction perspective opens the *diagnosis'* outlook by moving from the question "*which* ego state is operating in the person in this or that situation?" to the question "how does *each* of the three systems – Child, Adult and Parent – contribute to the person's internal and external reactions?" Particular attention is given to the systems that do *not* take centre stage, but which exert their influence "backstage". According to Berne, these ego states in the background may be unconscious: "Ego states manifest themselves clinically in two forms: either as completely cathected coherent[32] states of mind experienced as 'real Self'; or as intrusions, usually covert or unconscious, into the activity of the current 'real Self'".[33]

Corresponding *interventions* are therefore not only acting on one of the three systems; they aim at a better overall functioning of their reciprocal influences. They consider both the limiting and the resourceful aspects of these systems and their contents; they can be oriented either towards the cognitive-behavioural dimension or towards working on the past. The relationship they require depends on which direction the approach is taking, but it generally implies abandoning the position of the external observer or specialist for a personal commitment that is as open as possible. It implies being ready to intervene at multiple levels.[34]

The fact that the repetition perspective dominates TA's usual presentation, and several recent trends, should not blind us to how valuable the interaction perspective is. Much more than the repetition perspective, it is open to the description of healthy development and creativity, and it considers, in a better way, the complexity of the facts when leaving the field of strict pathology. Furthermore, it directs the practitioner's gaze towards the active systems in the background and makes them more open to the identification of less apparent dynamics, including unconscious dynamics. The interaction perspective is the focus of this book; the other interactions are well documented in TA's publications.

THE THREE PERSPECTIVES IN TRANSACTIONAL TEXTS

The sequential perspective

The sequential perspective, being descriptive, dominates the "descriptive" side of Berne's and TA after Berne: drama triangle,[35] the ego states' descriptive model (called the "functional model"), options,[36] mini-script,[37] behavioural life positions,[38] etc. The sequential perspective is useful to sort out observed manifestations according to the practitioner's chosen framework: the three types of ego states described above, their social manifestations described by "descriptive terms",[39] or any other descriptive approach.[40]

Berne particularly uses the sequential perspective when he wants to describe:

1. the to-and-fro between modes of reaction, both contrasting and of different types, as in the case of Ms Primus;
2. the external side of communication, in the particular case of simple transactions[41] where, at the external level, participants implement simultaneously only one type of ego state;
3. the successive stages of psychological games and scripts when identifying formulas;
4. the fluctuations of dominant ego state types, either in the person's awareness[42] or in their external action.[43] This last case suggests that the sequential perspective refers to another perspective in order to make it clear: if actors replace one another front-stage, it is because, backstage, they do not cease to exist but wait for the opportunity to come back on stage. This perspective is the interaction perspective.

The origin perspective

Berne rarely uses the *evolution* perspective, except when he described the evolution of the group imago[44] in one of the rare texts where, freed from his fascination for pathology, he portrayed the development of a healthy phenomenon (see more on that subject in Chapter 13 about relationships).

Berne is more inclined towards the repetition perspective. Ms Enatosky's case[45] admirably illustrates the phenomenological experience:

> Ms Enatosky also complained of periodic insecurity about walking, which she described as "walking high". (…) When she discussed her walking symptom, Dr. Q[46] remarked: "That's the little girl, too". (behavioral diagnosis) She replied. "Oh, for heaven's sake, that's true, a child walks that way. As you said that I could see a little child. You know how they walk and stumble and get up. It's hard to believe, but that makes sense to me. As you say that, I feel I didn't want to walk: a little girl in rompers who would rather crawl or sit. I feel funny now. They pull you up by your right shoulder and you're outraged and want to cry. You know I still have pains in my shoulder. What a terrible feeling! My mother worked when I was very small and I didn't want to go to the day nursery and I wouldn't walk, and they forced me".[47]

Classical TA defines the structural model's various elements in line with the repetition perspective. These are the ones the patient must understand to engage in a decontamination process:

> A Parental ego state is a set of feelings, attitudes, and behavior patterns which resemble those of a parental figure. (…) The Adult ego state is characterized by an autonomous[48] set of feelings, attitudes, and behavior

patterns which are adapted to the current reality. (...) The Child ego state is a set of feelings, attitudes and behavior patterns which are relics of the individual's own childhood".[49]

The interaction perspective

While classical TA and some recent approaches are based on the repetition perspective, Berne uses the interaction perspective very frequently, except of course during the work on decontamination and past events when the repetition perspective is quite appropriate. Berne implies the interaction perspective in many of his concepts and writings when he describes the systems as happening concurrently; this implies a perspective in which the Child, the Parent and the Adult systems perceive and act concurrently, whether chaotically, antagonistically or in a coordinated or integrated mode.[50]

The main aim of the following list is to show how the interaction perspective and the systems happening simultaneously is TA's basic structure:

1. the *"intrusions"* of one system, especially the Child system, during another system's activity[51];
2. the concept of *"boundaries"*[52] between systems;
3. the *"three persons in one"* metaphor. Its most provocative form in *Sex in Human Loving* depicts a situation where the three ego states act in an uncoordinated way, but this is only one of the possibilities:

   > It is most fruitful to think of the human personality as being divided into three parts, or even better, to realize that each individual is three different persons, all pulling in different directions... so it is a wonder anything gets done[53];

4. the reminder to the *practitioner* to be aware of the three systems' presence, each of which responds to anything they may say or do[54];
5. complex forms of communication, such as double or angular transactions or "bull's-eye" transactions,[55] or what Berne calls "permission transaction"[56];
6. mental states involving the simultaneous presence of two systems, including the *phenomenological experience.*

The extent of interaction between systems increases with the following concepts:

7. *influences* between systems: Berne does not limit them to those of the Parent system on the Child system[57] but extends them to all systems[58]; contamination and exclusion must be included[59];
8. the *internal dialogue* metaphor;
9. the assertion that "the relationship" between the Child and Parent systems "is usually a replica of the *original child-parent relationship* which the individual experienced"[60];

10. *psychological games* and *"rackets"*,[61] where one system "sabotages" the action of another according to its own tendencies, or at least satisfying its hidden motives without taking centre stage;
11. Berne's theory of *relationships*[62];
12. Berne's *regression analysis*,[63] which implies the simultaneous and conscious implementation of the Child and Adult systems.

Let us add to this list the *Transactional Analysis and Psychotherapy's* key chapter about "the psychic apparatus",[64] which Chapter 3 will focus on. It constitutes a masterly synthesis of the whole ego state theory within the interaction perspective.

Some non-Bernian concepts, such as *impasse*[65] or *frame of reference*,[66] also reinforce the interaction perspective. For example, according to Schiff, "(…) the Parent, Adult and Child are connected structurally and integrated functionally into a whole which is characteristic of the overall person. 'Frame of reference' refers to this overall structural and functional matrix".[67] It seems quite difficult, if not impossible, to practice TA without the interaction perspective!

Notes

1 For Freud, the two "topics" (firstly unconscious/preconscious/unconscious; then id/ego/superego), plus the reflection on the opposition between life drive and death drive, constitute three different perspectives, but they are clearly separate and linked to different periods of his research. See LAPLANCHE, J., and PONTALIS, J.B., 1967, art. "Topiques".
2 BERNE, E., 1961, pp. 11–14. An anecdote: the names Berne gives to their patients are disguises for numbers in various languages: Primus, Segundo, Troy, Quatry, Quint, etc. Enatosky, which we will meet soon, refers to enatos, i.e., ninth, in Greek.
3 That is, an internal or influential Parent. What appears in Ms Primus is the Child ego state under the influence of the Parent.
4 BERNE, E., 1957b, pp. 121–127. BERNE, E., 1961, pp. 14–15.
5 KARPMAN, S., 1971^{ES}.
6 STEINER, C.M., 1984. STEINER, C.M., and PERRY, P., 1996.
7 "Normative" is a non-literal translation; it removes the easily pejorative aspect of Berne's terms such as "prejudicial" or "critical". Furthermore, Berne does not say "Free Child", but "Natural Child". Finally, it is only in his last work that Berne distinguishes the "rebellious" Child from the "free" or "natural" Child. See BERNE, E., 1972, p. 13.
8 These terms have been systematized and gathered in what has been called the "functional model of the ego states" after Berne. He calls them simply "descriptive terms" (BERNE, E., 1972, p. 13).
9 They must be confirmed by the historical and phenomenological elements of the diagnosis.
10 BERNE, E., 1972, p. 13.
11 KARPMAN, S., 1971^{ES}.
12 He nevertheless uses it in two very important cases: the evolution of the group imago (BERNE, E., 1963, pp. 220–226) and of the script (BERNE, E., 1961, p. 86; BERNE, E., 1963, p. 227–230; BERNE, E., 1972).

13 This to-and-fro between the present and the past is part of TA's originality and strength: it combines interest in the dynamics emanating from the past with attention to the concrete manifestations in the here and now.
14 BERNE, E., 1961, p. 15.
15 BERNE, E., 1961, p. 15.
16 BERNE, E., 1961, p. 52.
17 BERNE, E., 1961, p. 52.
18 ERSKINE, E., 1994 [ES], p. 91.
19 BERNE, E., 1961, p. 1.
20 BERNE, E., 1961, pp. 117–120.
21 BERNE, E., 1961, p. 51.
22 ERSKINE, R.G., 1991 [ES].
23 ERSKINE, R.G., and TRAUTMANN, R., 1996.
24 BERNE, E., 1961.
25 See p. 17, note 5.
26 Re-parenting is a regressive approach concerning the whole of the person's development, whereas parenting concerns a particular point and does not require regression, at least not prolonged regression.
27 See SCHLEGEL, L., 1998[ES].
28 ERSKINE, R.G., and TRAUTMANN, R., 1996.
29 BERNE, E., 1961, p. 18.
30 Metaphorically, because they are not persons, but structures internal to the person.
31 For example, BERNE, E., 1961, p. 20, p. 52, p. 188.
32 "Coherent" here means "endowed with cohesion" rather than logically "coherent".
33 BERNE, E., 1961, p. 48.
34 See page 13.
35 KARPMAN, S., 1968.
36 KARPMAN, S., 1971 [ES].
37 CAPERS, H., and KAHLER, T., 1974.
38 ERNST, F., 1971b.
39 BERNE, E., 1972, p. 13
40 SCHMID, B., 1991, shows that there are always multiple descriptive grids applicable to a given set of phenomena.
41 Single transactions are opposed to double transactions, where at least two communication channels are implemented simultaneously, which implies the interaction perspective. To consider a transaction as simple is often a simplification.
42 This is what Berne calls "real Self" (BERNE, E., 1961, pp. 20–21): this concept describes the type of ego states in which the person recognizes themself and whose manifestations they attribute to themself by saying "I".
43 This is what Berne calls "the executive". BERNE, E., 1961, p. 19.
44 BERNE, E., 1963, pp. 220–226. See CLARKSON, P., 1991b, 1991c.
45 BERNE, E., 1961, pp. 117–120.
46 Berne uses this name when referring to himself in his case descriptions.
47 BERNE, E., 1961, pp. 117–118.
48 In *Transactional Analysis and Psychotherapy,* TA the term "autonomous" does not mean autonomy in its true sense, which Berne will elaborate later (BERNE, E., 1964a, pp. 178–181), but the fact that the contents of an ego state do not come from outside. The Child in their free manifestations is also said to be "autonomous". BERNE, E.,

1961, p. 53: "The natural Child is manifested by autonomous forms of behavior such as rebelliousness or self-indulgence".
49   BERNE, E., 1961, pp. 51–53.
50   The different modes of interaction between systems are discussed in Chapter 8.
51   BERNE, E., 1961, p. 48.
52   BERNE, E., 1961, pp. 29–30.
53   BERNE, E., 1970, p. 93.
54   BERNE, E., 1961, p. 184.
55   That is, which simultaneously reach the recipient's three ego states. BERNE, E., 1961, p. 186.
56   BERNE, E., 1972, p. 376.
57   BERNE, E., 1961, p. 52, p. 193.
58   BERNE, E., 1961, p. 18, pp. 189–190. At the end of *Transactional Analysis in Psychotherapy*, Berne also introduces the term "programming" to describe influences. BERNE, E., pp. 189–191.
59   BERNE, E., 1961, pp. 27–28. On the relationship between contamination and influence, see ibid, p. 190: "contamination has been described in spatial terms", influence theory in "functional" terms, i.e., in terms of process.
60   BERNE, E., 1961, p. 18.
61   BERNE, E., 1964a, 1964d.
62   BERNE, E., 1961, pp. 96–101.
63   BERNE, E., 1961, pp. 176–182.
64   BERNE, E., 1961, pp. 188–193.
65   GOULDING, R., and GOULDING, M., 1976[ES]. MELLOR, K., 1980[ES].
66   SCHIFF, J.L., SCHIFF, A.W., and SCHIFF (SIGMUND), E., 1975.
67   SCHIFF, J.L., SCHIFF, A.W., and SCHIFF (SIGMUND), E., 1975.

2
EGO STATES AS PERSONALITY SYSTEMS

From the interaction perspective, Child, Adult and Parent are seen as three systems acting both simultaneously and in mutual interaction. What does this mean? Firstly, they are systems: in other words, they are sets of elements, with links between these elements and diverse but organized processes. Secondly, they are *living* systems. These are defined by their ability to change their own processes according to their interactions with the environment in which they develop.[1] The three systems, each according to its specific mode, react to the whole of the internal and external life of the person, bring their contribution to it and evolve in accordance with it.

Berne called these systems "psychic organs" or "personality systems".[2] The first term is a metaphor, a comparison between psychic structures and material organs. Berne may have hoped that areas corresponding to Child, Adult and Parent systems would one day be found in the brain[3] and, indeed, the existence of specialized areas in the brain has since been amply confirmed. However, it has also been discovered that many functions essential to human existence do not depend on any one brain area, but on complex, circular interconnections between several areas. Nevertheless, let us explore what this organ metaphor suggests.

The organ metaphor

Perception modes

Our body has sensory "organs" and "systems": the eye is the sight organ, the ear is the hearing organ, etc. The eye itself is not enough to see; it is only a part of the visual system. Its function is to enable us to benefit from information about objects' light parameters. The term "*function*" is defined by what information the organ or the system can bring to the organism that is essential or important for its survival and its evolution and that no other part of the organism could.

This concept of function only makes sense when there are several systems, each collaborating with the others in its own way; the visual system does not perceive sounds, nor does the auditory system perceive light stimuli. It follows that we can only have a more global perception of what is happening around us by combining and integrating information from the different systems. D. Stern notes that from the very first manifestations of the child's psychic life, they are already capable of "amodal perception",[4] which does not depend on any sensory system and constitutes the beginning of integration between systems.

Memory

In addition to sensory and motor organs, we need memory to keep track of earlier experiences to be able to use the information they hold later. In fact, what we call "memory" covers many different processes: short-term and long-term memory, factual and narrative memory, implicit and explicit memory (analysed in more details later).

Evolution and organization

The phase of perception and memorization is followed by a phase of evolution, elaboration and organization. Why are we much better at climbing stairs today than we were the first time we did it? Because each time we learn from our earlier experiences in their various aspects, whether cognitive (how to recognize a staircase), affective (stairs are associated for me with pleasure, fear, etc.) or strategic (I do not go up an escalator as I do a flight of stairs, etc.).

This is not a simple accumulation process: learned strategies need to be adaptable, sometimes even inhibited to be replaced by others.[5] If faced with an escalator for the first time, I need to inhibit the strategy learned for a flight of stairs, because it cannot be applied the same way. This said, there is no need to "reinvent the wheel" at every change of strategy: on the contrary, I take advantage of what I have learned to adapt earlier strategies. Besides, replacing one strategy with another one does not destroy it: it is simply put aside until needed.

Action

All these elements, however, would be useless if we did not also have motor organs, which allow us to move our body and its various parts according to our needs and the information transmitted by all the above. When you watch a child learning to walk, you can see how this process is both complex and extraordinarily efficient once it is setup. Our sensory life arises from the environment that our perception put our body in contact with; in turn, during the organization and evolution phase, our sensory life revolves to the environment through the action we have on it.

Our physical equipment can manage all this, none of which is superfluous. In addition, each organ is coordinated in multiple and circular ways with other organs, so that the distinct phases are linked together by multiple feedback loops: for example, we perceive more easily what we expect to perceive.

The psychic organs

Berne writes about "psychic organs" or "personality systems". Like body organs, each psychic organ has its own domain, so that in principle they are as different

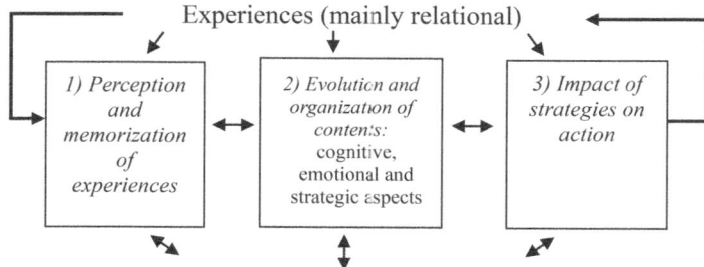

Figure 2.1 General schema showing how mutually interconnected psychic systems, analogically to physical systems, shape and orient our internal reactions and external actions through various interdependent processes.

from each other as the eye, the ear or the nose are. This is a fact we tend to forget as we are used to representing them by three equal and superimposed circles.

It would be meaningless to talk about these personality systems and their interactions if all three served the same purpose or had identical tendencies. Just as the human body has a visual system and an auditory system, but not two visual systems, Child, Adult and Parent systems each have their own function, their own specific contribution. That will be the subject of the following chapters.

Like the eye or the ear, the psychic organs *receive* information: "Just as the various organs of the brain and the body react differently to stimuli, so do the different systems of the personality".[6] But, each according to its own function, psychic organs can also *memorize, organize*[7] and direct one's *actions*. In a similar way to our sensory systems, their constituting processes start from the environment and return to the environment – with a capital difference though: our psychic life's "environment" is above all made of *relationships* which reinforce or impede all aspects of the process.

These elements, like those detailed for physical systems, can be synthesized, see Figure 2.1.

We know this is so because this happens during most of our healthy experiences: we cannot deny that we perceive, memorize and organize mental contents which shape our action. We have the necessary tools to make this possible. Yes, this diagram is quite complex, but that is how life itself works; we implement it with great ease and without realizing it at every moment of our physical and psychological life. In Transactional Analysis, the language used to analyse these conditions of *possibility* is that of personality systems.

Three interacting systems

Several systems within an organism implies coordination. This is everyday experience: even a simple action such as climbing stairs involves coordination between the visual and the motor systems, with an optional contribution from the auditory system when footstep sounds help.

The same applies to Child, Parent and Adult systems. When they are disjointed, i.e., not coordinated, existence becomes chaotic. Their coordination, however, should not be so tight that all tension between them is lost. This would prevent us from perceiving the range of information on one situation that these systems can provide from various standpoints; this would probably lead us to wrongly favour one of them at the expense of the others.

When there is influence, there is also modification and therefore evolution, except for repetitive ego states. The three systems, the Child, the Parent and the Adult, are hauled on the great river of the person's development (as analysed in Chapter 4).

PERSONALITY SYSTEMS IN TRANSACTIONAL TEXTS

Perception

The quote below, from *Transactional Analysis in Psychotherapy*, analyses the diverse and concurrent perception of the three systems. It shows how Berne weaves both interaction and repetition perspectives, revealing how closely related the two are in his mind.

> Just as the various organs of the brain and of the body react differently to stimuli, so do the different systems of the personality. The exteropsyche is judgmental in an imitative way, and seeks to enforce sets of borrowed standards. The neopsyche is principally concerned with transforming stimuli into pieces of information, and processing and filing that information on the basis of previous experience. The archaeopsyche tends to react more abruptly, on the basis of pre-logical thinking and poorly differentiated or distorted perceptions. In fact, each of these aspects perceives the environment differently, in accordance with its function, and hence is reaction to a different set of stimuli. (...) The three aspects also react on each other. The Parent may become excited (i.e., distressed) by the Child's fantasies, and the Child is particularly sensitive to inhibitory stimuli from the Parent. This relationship is usually a replica of the original child-parent relationship which the individual experienced.[8]

"A different set of stimuli" means different aspects of the same world. The perception of each personality system is dependent upon and directed by its function (detailed in Chapters 5–7).

Memorization

When Berne considers ego states in the memorization phase, he often emphasizes the global aspect of a memory with all dimensions within its experience:

> (Berne quotes Kubie) "The recall is essentially total, involving far more than he is consciously able to recapture, approximating that totality of recall which can sometimes be achieved with patients under hypnosis".[9]

The latent ego state is another notion relating to memory as it waits for an opportunity to manifest itself, either centre stage or via irruptions within the activity of another ego state:

> ...the intrusion of a single element or a set of elements from a latent ego state into an active one should bear the characteristics of the intruding ego state.[10]

Evolution

In an important but seldom used text,[11] Berne lists the psychic organs' four characteristics (the second and third concern the evolution of systems):

> The significant properties of these organs are as follows:
>
> 1. executive power: each give rise to its idiosyncratic patterns of organized behaviour (...);
> 2. adaptability: each is capable of adapting its behavioral responses to the immediate social situation in which the individual finds himself (...);
> 3. biological fluidity: in the sense that responses are modified as a result of natural growth and previous experiences (...);
> 4. mentality, in that they mediate the phenomena of experience.[12]

Executive power means the ability to decide or influence the person's behaviour (action phase); adaptability covers the ability to elicit different manifestations according to circumstances (elaboration phase); biological fluidity means the ability to evolve both with development and experience (evolving aspects of systems); mentality recalls the close link between the person's experience and the systems (phenomenological aspect).

Berne links these four characteristics with the ego state diagnosis, as they are the systems' manifestations:

> The complete diagnosis of an ego state requires that all four of these aspects be available for consideration, and the final validity of such a diagnosis is not established until four have been correlated.[13]

Impact on the action

Quoting the continuation of the same text is enough:

> It should now be clear that [the characteristics of ego states] manifest themselves in any act, attitude, or way of experiencing.[14]

Mutual influences between systems

Berne introduces the term *influence* in the context of decontamination, specifically for the Parent system's influence on the Child system. The perspective is the diagnosis perspective: the Parent ego states (in the repetition perspective) can be diagnosed not only directly, but also through the presence of the Adapted Child. For example, Ms Primus' voices[15] are primarily an Adapted Child manifestation (as a child listening to her father), but one can also deduce the intrapsychic presence of a Parent ego state.

When the Child or the Parent systems influence the Adult system, Berne examines the case of contamination[16] in *Transactional Analysis in Psychotherapy*. In this case, without any preliminary examination, the Adult accepts contents coming from one or both systems.

In the seminal text on the transactional psychic apparatus (discussed in Chapter 3), Berne looks at influences going from any system to any other system. He stops considering influence from the repetition perspective and acknowledges it as a normal and positive system function.

Notes

1. See VARELA, F., 1980; BATESON, G., 1972, 1979.
2. BERNE, E., 1961, p. 6, p. 18.
3. See SCHLEGEL, L., 1993[ES].
4. STERN, D., 1985, pp. 51–52.
5. See HOUDÉ, O., 2004.
6. BERNE, E., 1961, p. 18.
7. BERNE, E., 1961, pp. 189–191.
8. BERNE, E., 1961, p. 18.
9. BERNE, E., 1961, p. 2.
10. BERNE, E., 1961, p. 48.
11. See, however, the commentary by TUDOR, K., 2003[ES], pp. 213–215.
12. BERNE, E., 1961, p. 51.
13. BERNE, E., 1961, p. 51.
14. BERNE, E., 1961, p. 48.
15. BERNE, E., 1961, p. 14.
16. BERNE, E., 1961, particularly pp. 27–29.

3
WHAT IS THE PURPOSE OF EACH SYSTEM?

If there are several systems in an organism, they are necessarily *specialized*: the visual system specializes in the processing of light information, the auditory system in the processing of auditory information, etc. This is what is literally called the *function*[1] of the system: it is its "speciality", its specific contribution to the organism's survival, development and action that it alone can provide. Clarifying its role and place in the overall structure is necessary to understand the system itself.[2] This chapter examines the function, the specific and unique contribution of each personality system to the ensemble. In other words, it answers the question: what is the purpose of these three systems?

Systems are structures: they cannot be perceived directly but can be inferred[3] from their manifestations. When I look at a landscape, I can see the landscape, I cannot see the visual system; I know there is a visual system because it accounts for my ability to see the landscape and countless other images. A structure is what enables coherence and continuity; an object without structure is amorphous or about to disintegrate. In living organisms, structure evolves: it survives only by interacting with and adapting to its environment[4]; this implies that structure is sensitive to its environment and keeps a trace of it (a memory) that may modify its subsequent reactions.

The structural dimension is opposed to that of *manifestations*. The visual system's manifestations are the fact that I can see a thing at a time: a landscape, a street, an office, an object. These manifestations are multiple and changeable, but they all belong to the same system.

One consequence of the above is that, *from the interaction perspective, we cannot give a restrictive list of manifestations from one personality system only*. The three systems always act together, and each "scans" all experiences through its own dimension. Experiences do not belong to a single system, but each system perceives and registers it according to its own function in the primary sense of the word. One cannot say: "I can see a colour, therefore I am in the visual system and in no other", because that would mean "therefore I cannot hear a sound or perceive a smell". One can see, hear and smell simultaneously. The same is true of the personality systems: from the perspective of interaction, we are never "in" one of them; we are always in relation with all three at the same time.

The functions of the Child, Parent and Adult systems

According to the text about the transactional psychic apparatus, which will be discussed in detail at the end of this chapter, the three systems appear to correspond to three essential dimensions of existence. Therefore, they exist with us from the very beginning, although an extensive evolution connects their earliest, pre-verbal forms to their most complex forms, where language is superimposed on them.

The function of the *Child* system is to enable us to remember, organize and benefit from *the subjective aspect of our experiences*, when they are sources of reward or frustration, pleasure or pain, satisfaction or disappointment. From birth – even from conception – to death, we need the Child system because, from the beginning, we have or rather we are a body and a psyche with physical and social needs and experiences that we perceive very early on in a subjective mode where the emotions, imagination and desires are intertwined.

The function of the *Parent* system is correlative to the function of the Child system: it allows us to memorize, organize and benefit from someone's else reactions, especially if they are "important" to us. In social situations, our subjective reactions (Child system) only make sense *in relation to someone else*, and relationships, whether early or recent, are omnipresent in our existence. Even in our solitary experiences, we carry within us the "psychic presence"[5] of someone else. We live in a world both relational and social, and need to consider other people's judgements, reactions and customs. We need to be able to refer to them even in their absence, not only to know how "things are done" without having to "reinvent the wheel" at every turn, but also to assimilate the cultural or ethical rules which govern life in society.

The function of the *Adult* system is to memorize and organize the dimension of our experiences which seems to us to exist *out of both our own subjective reaction and other people's reactions to them*; it opens up a "panoramic" view[6] in which we can see both our and others' experiences with their connection and their difference. We generate and use Adult ego states throughout our life. They are indispensable for two reasons. First, we live within an objective reality ordered by its own regularities, subject neither to our own subjective movements nor to others'. Second, from the moment our life becomes intersubjective, we can only come into contact with someone else – a person different from ourselves – through this lucid and "panoramic" position. Without it, we would be alternately "overtaken" by our own subjective reactions (Child dimension) or dominated by someone else's (Parent dimension).

From this perspective, the three ego state systems seem to tie in with general dimensions of existential being[7] such as "I am a separate person with a body and an internal reality" ("being-there" – Child dimension), "I live with others who were there before me" ("being-with" – Parent dimension), "I live in the world, and the other person is outside me" ("being-in-the-world" – Adult dimension). Consequently, each is a vital resource for the person's survival, development and creativity.

WHAT IS THE PURPOSE OF EACH SYSTEM?

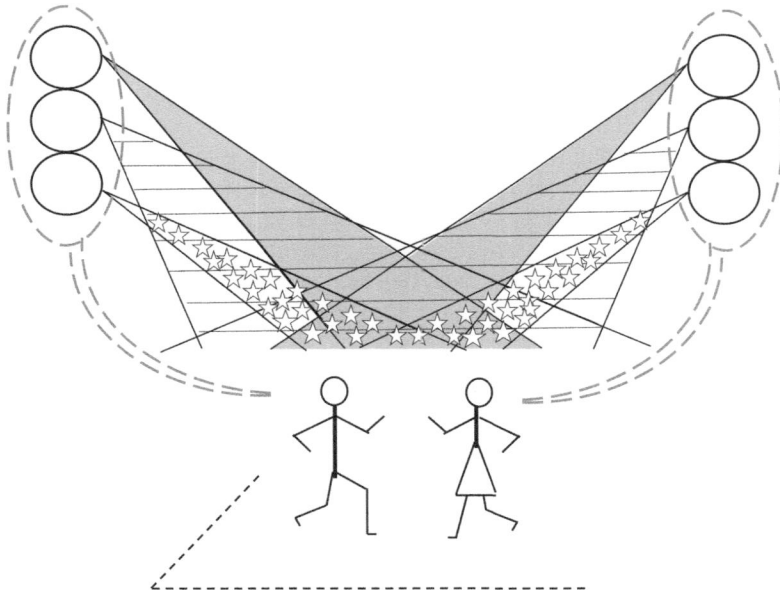

Figure 3.1 An encounter between two persons. Each perceives simultaneously the situation from the specific point of view of their three systems of personality and reacts accordingly.

Figure 3.1 shows a more concrete representation of the three systems' place in a concrete social situation

Any diagram needs explaining.[8] Two characters, a man and a woman, meet. They are not represented with three circles but with outlines to see the difference between what goes on in the outside world and in the intrapsychic one, including personality systems. Like in comic books or manga, each character's mind is pictured by a "speech balloon" with their three personality systems:

- The *Child system* projects onto the encounter a "beam" (area with stars) of questions and expectations focusing on the subjective dimension: what gratifications can I expect? Will the encounter be pleasant or unpleasant? What are my subjective expectations and fears? Comparing my collection of past experiences, what could be pleasant or unpleasant to repeat? Could there be something friendly, romantic, sexual, etc.?
- The "beam" from the *Parent system* (grey area) is directed first towards the other person, then towards a more social dimension: how will the other person judge me? How do others behave in such circumstances? What judgements have I been given about what is allowed or forbidden?
- The "beam" in the *Adult system* (area with horizontal lines) has a wider opening and points to a more objective dimension: What is his/her name? How did our last meeting go? How long has it been since I last saw him/her?

To *get a complete picture* of what happens in such an encounter, *one needs all three systems*. A system on its own can only give a partial vision defined by its function, which is not enough to grasp all the dynamics at play. In this respect, these systems are like the colour photographic plates of the pre-digital era which were made of several layers, each with a basic colour. One layer was not enough to get the full picture; they had to be juxtaposed. The same is true of personality systems: taken in isolation, each one carries only a representation of the person's experience, which is partial, meaning both in complete and biased – because each one records only its "colour", that is to say, what is related to its function. It is only by taking all three into account that a more accurate picture of the experience can be obtained.

THE FUNCTIONS OF THE THREE SYSTEMS IN TRANSACTIONAL TEXTS

Berne's text on the psychic apparatus

Berne's seminal text on personality systems is at the end of *Transactional Analysis in Psychotherapy*.[9] Its terminology is unusual and makes it somewhat difficult to absorb; but it is one of the very few texts where Berne features the interaction perspective without focusing on pathology and repetition perspective.

Berne identifies three levels: the "phenomena" level, i.e., ego states (manifestations); the "psychic organs" level, which he calls "organisers"; and the "determinants" level, meaning the "factors which determine the quality of the organisation and phenomena, that is, they establish their programming".[10] Determinants, in other words, are forces that impact on our ego states and psychic organs. Berne, who was very interested in cybernetics, calls their impact on our existence "programming". One could compare determinants to a river current, organizers or psychic organs to dikes that steer the current in this or that direction, and ego states to mills, turbines or irrigation channels that use the river's channelled energy.

The threefold programming

Berne asserts that our psychic life is dependent on both situational determining factors and intrapsychic determining factors. The latter include two types: those originating from biology and drives, and those originating from the internalized influence of others.

> 1. Probability programming arises from autonomous[11] data-processing, based on past experience. (...) Because the neopsyche is concerned with data-processing, it may be regarded as the organizer for probability programming.[12]

Berne starts with situation-related factors, which force us to organize our existence according to what the situation demands. Since in this area our knowledge is more often probable than certain, he calls this process "probability programming". Given the multiplicity of such contents, we need an organizer; this is the neopsyche or the Adult system and that is its function. Without it, we would not be able to find our bearings in the incessant and multiple flow of stimuli coming from the external situation; we could not sort out what is or is not important for us and for our objectives; we could not design relevant and suitable strategies.

> 2. Internal programming arises from indigenous biological forces. These may influence any of the organisers and hence the resultant phenomena. (…) Since instincts are phylogenetically archaic, it may be logically postulated that the archaeopsyche organizes internal programming.[13]

Berne calls "internal programming" the influence that internal factors of biological origin exert on our experience and behaviour. This should not be understood restrictively as Berne includes the person's drives, to which we can link his/her desires, fantasies and imagination. The organ we need to organize this incessant flow is the archaeopsyche, i.e., the Child system. Without it, we would not memorize the experiences which, from our subjective point of view, have been gratifying or not, disappointing or not, sources of satisfaction or suffering; and we would be deprived of reference points in this dimension.

In addition, since Berne includes the natural propensity to raise children along biological lines, he attributes it to internal programming.

It is interesting to note how the repetition perspective occurs in this passage where the systems' interaction is predominant: the archaeopsyche and the Child system are introduced in their "archaic" dimension and not as elements growing creatively throughout life.

> 3. External programming arises from incorporated external canons (…). And since the exteropsyche is the organ concerned with borrowed ego states, it may be allocated the task of organizing the external programming.[14]

The last factors are related to the internalized influences of others; their impact is what Berne calls "external programming". There is some ambiguity in the term, as these are in fact internal factors, though they are directly related to other people's actions and reactions. We need to find our way around this dimension and remember the experiences that relate to it: organizing this dimension is the function of the Parent system.

Influences

Berne does not stop there. Yes, each of Child, Adult and Parent systems has its own function in the proper sense; however, each system has a second function without which the first one could not perform: it can influence the other two systems. Without it, the three systems would be running wild without any coordination, and the organism's survival would be compromised.

> The next step is to postulate that each organizer has two functions, and the essential point is that these two functions are independent. One function is to organize determinants into effective influences, and the other function is to organize phenomena.[15]

This is when Berne starts introducing the interaction perspective.

Primary and secondary processes

In addition, the Child and the Adult systems perform their organizing roles via a particular process which is effective in the domain they are connected to:

> The characteristic of the archaeopsyche is what Freud calls primary process; that of the neopsyche, secondary process; and that of the exteropsyche something akin to identification.[16]

Freud introduced the term "primary process" in the context of dream analysis, and of symptoms (particularly hysterical). Laplanche and Pontalis,[17] summarizing Freud, give the term three interconnecting characteristics: free association, displacement and overdetermination.

- *Free association*, or association by proximity. For example, the event setting, or one of its elements, is associated with the experience this event has generated, as in the well-known case of "Proust's madeleine". In this, the taste of a madeleine reminds the hero first of the pastries he enjoyed during his adolescence, then of the context of this experience and, starting from that, of the whole atmosphere of his youth.
- *Displacement*: the experience linked to an event will be associated with other events, whether similar or different. "A representation that is often insignificant in appearance can be attributed all the psychic value, significance and intensity originally attributed to another one".[18]
- *Overdetermination* or *condensation*: the same content can carry different meanings, which often belongs to different contexts. One motivation can hide another, as in Ms White case, which Berne analysed in *Games people play*.[19]

Here is another example:

A man has been abandoned by his wife. He is full of hatred for his rival, "that bastard", and he does not hide the violence of his impulses: "If I held him, I would…". Yet, when questioned, he replies that he has no anger against his ex-wife. Part of his impulses against the other man are, in fact, the result of avoiding his deeper anger against her, which he will only feel at a much later stage of his therapy. This defence mechanism, in turn, allows him to maintain an acceptable image of his ex-wife: "She has allowed herself to be manipulated"; it protects his continuing love for her. At the level of his sense of self, it protects him from the hurt he would feel if he had to admit that his marriage was a mistake: "I couldn't have been so wrong"; moreover, it has a reassuring side for his image of men in general, as passed on to him by his father: "Men are the ones who run the game". At the same time, his divorce fulfils his mother's secret desire[20] and elicits real or imagined gratification from her at the unconscious level.

When we encounter such "tangles" in practice, dealing with one aspect frequently has a minor impact because the other aspects maintain the status quo. We often need to address two or three aspects before we can establish a new structure to enable another direction.

The primary process is opposed to the "secondary process". According to Laplanche and Pontalis, "Functions classically described as secondary processes in psychology – alert thought, attention, judgement, reasoning, controlled action – are described as such in opposition [to the primary process]. Thought identity is pursued in the secondary process".[21]

Berne relates the primary process to the Child system and the secondary process to the Adult system. Free association does relate well to the way the Child system connects different experiences based on a very subjective resemblance; the Child system is also familiar with displacement and overdetermination. The secondary process is closer to "logic", specifically to coherence or non-contradiction and shows many links with the Adult system. *However, this classification cannot be absolute.* The primary process is characteristic of the whole unconscious, not only of the Child system. It emphasizes the unconscious aspects and deepest strata of the whole personality. D. Stern conversely demonstrated the existence of an elementary secondary process very early in life: "From birth on, there appears to be a central tendency to form and test hypotheses about what is occurring in the world. Infants are also constantly 'evaluating', in the sense of asking: Is this different or the same as that? How discrepant is what I have just encountered from what I have previously encountered?"[22]

Since there is no tertiary process, Berne reverts to the origin perspective to characterize the Parent system as dominated by "something akin to identification". What he means presumably is that, by borrowing norms from another person and making them theirs, the person does something reminiscent of identification, although this belongs to the primary process.

How it relates to the rest of the ego state theory

It seems then Berne develops a second overall version of the ego state theory from the interaction perspective. He declares, "we are now in a position to review some of the ambiguities encountered in structural analysis".[23] Here is the list:

1. Contamination is reduced to influence[24]: more precisely, the Child and/or the Parent system exert an influence on the Adult system when they impose specific outlooks or contents, and inhibit the Adult system's functioning whenever an experience would be likely to call them into question.

2. With regard to the nurturing and "prohibitive"[25] attitudes in the Parent system, Berne gives us a choice between two theoretical explanations, one in terms of libido and mortido determinants, the other in terms of influences: the "nurturing" Parent could result from the Child influence, the "prohibitive" Parent from its absence. In this text, Berne does not consider the beneficial and structuring aspects of the Parent "normative" manifestations.
3. The "influential Parent" and the "active Parent" are none other than the two organizer's functions Berne mentioned earlier on, applied to the Parent-specific case.
4. Consequently, the Adapted Child and the Natural Child are distinct: the Adapted Child features the Child manifestations when under the Parent influence. Berne does not address the notion of a child (and therefore of a Child ego state) that would suddenly find itself deprived of any parental influence and therefore of any structuring.
5. On the next point, Berne simply says: "It is evident that this also has a bearing on the second-order structure of the Parent".
6. He then comes to the case of "rational" and "authoritarian"[26] authorities, which he explains by a play of influences between the Adult and the Parent systems, whereas the Child system is the one programming unpredictable autocratic authorities.
7. Berne emphasizes that the "integrated Adult" is entirely explained in terms of influences (see Chapters 7 and 11): "the ethical Adult" is an Adult under the Parent influence, "the sensitive Adult" is an Adult under the Child influence.

In short, Berne says that, in practical terms, all concepts from the ego state theory can be expressed within the interaction perspective, which is at times an even simpler way than the Transactional Analysis (TA) traditional mode Berne developed at the beginning of his book.

Personality systems and the id, the ego and the superego

The book ends with a comparison with the Freudian structure of the unconscious: the id, the ego and the superego.[27] Berne points out that they relate to the same three dimensions as the Child, Adult and Parent systems:

> What are here called determinants, generalized from the clinical material of transactional analysis, resemble another set of concepts derived much earlier from similar material. This correspondence is gratifying, since it tends to support the validity of both systems by independent sets of observations.[28]

Specifically:
- id activity resembles "internal programming";
- the ego "resembles the self-programming probability computer (…) which is the model for neopsychic programming";
- "the superego is a reservoir for exteropsychic influences".[29]

For Berne, there are two essential differences: the id, the ego and the superego are not organizers; the Freudian approach is not a phenomenology centred on experience with all its dimensions (thought, emotions, behaviour, bodily and imaginary experiences). In the chapter's last sentence, he reminds us that:

> Freud does not raise any question of systematic phenomenology and it is here that structural analysis can usefully fill a gap in psychological theory, just as transactional analysis fills a gap in social theory.[30]

In his later works, Berne is more concerned with avoiding confusion between the three personality systems and the three Freudian concepts; he also seems less and less comfortable with psychoanalysis. In *Principles of Group Treatment* (1966), he underlines that:

> The superego, ego and id as defined by Freud are regarded as determinants of special characteristics of each type of ego state, but neither the ego states themselves nor the organs that "give rise" to them correspond to the Freudian "agencies". Superego, ego and id are inferential concepts, while ego states are experiential and social realities.[31]

In this instance, I do not fully agree with Berne, as he gets carried away by the comparison between personality systems and persons, and by his preoccupation with distancing himself from psychoanalysis. From the repetition perspective, Berne is right: personality systems do draw their content from past concrete realities, from relationships experienced by real people. That is the basic principle of Erskine and Trautmann's integrative psychotherapy, "transactional psychoanalysis" and social TA. However, Berne is so fascinated by the degree to which repetitive ego states sometimes resemble their origins that he sometimes refers to personality systems as three persons in one individual.[32] But they are only structures, and any structure is a theoretical entity, hence abstract and constructed by inference; it accounts for concrete experience but is not itself concrete, any more than the visual system is a person.

Berne's text on the transactional psychic apparatus at the end of *Transactional Analysis in Psychotherapy* is his most precise and open text on the relationship between personality systems and Freudian concepts.

Another version of the three systems' function

In *Games people play*, Berne gives a less technical description of the systems' functions. The term "function" here no longer covers the specific role that defines them as structures, but has the vaguer meaning of "utility in certain contexts":

> Each type of ego state has its own vital value for the human organism. In the Child resides intuition, creativity and spontaneous drive and enjoyment. The Adult is necessary for survival. It processes data and computes

the probabilities that are essential for dealing effectively with the outside world. It also experiences its own kinds of setbacks and gratifications. (...). Another task of the Adult is to regulate the activities of the Parent and the Child, and to mediate objectively between them. The Parent has two main functions. First, it enables the individual to act effectively as the parent of actual children, thus promoting the survival of the human race. (...). Secondly, it makes many responses automatic, which conserves a great deal of time and energy. Many things are done because "That's the way it's done". This frees the Adult from the necessity of making innumerable trivial decisions, so that it can devote itself more important issues, leaving routine matters to the Parent.[33]

The three systems as resources for life and development

Berne clearly states that Child, Adult and Parent systems all belong to the healthy domain:

> All three aspects of the personality have a high survival and living value, and it is only when one or the other of them disturbs the healthy balance that analysis and reorganization are indicated. Otherwise each of them, Parent, Adult, and Child, is entitled to equal respect, and has its legitimate place in a full and productive life.[34]

In numerous texts, Berne forcefully denies that the Child system constitutes by itself a pathological personality system:

> The word "childish", since it has taken on a derogatory sense, must likewise be excluded. The Child may be confused or loaded with unconstructive feelings, but child-like qualities are potentially the most valuable aspects of the personality.[35]

This conceptualization is different from Erskine and Trautmann's ego state theory[36]. They view the integrated Adult system as the only evolving and truly useful system for the person in their present reality. Child and Parent ego states are only considered from the repetition perspective as receptacles for dynamics from the person's past (Child), or from others (Parent), or from the person's past relationship with parental figures. Child and Parent then are not systems strictly speaking, and certainly not organizers, but bundles of repetitive ego states "encapsulated" in the psyche and ready to generate repetitive reactions if reactivated.

Erskine and Trautmann, and all authors who embrace their ego state theory, react on a practical level against Berne's and especially classical TA's tendency not to be concerned with transference and counter-transference, unconscious communication, projective identification and other phenomena emanating from the deepest personality strata. However, it was by no means necessary to reduce the notions of Child and Parent systems to their most defensive and archaic form; one can just as easily, and this is what the present book attempts to do, explore how the notions of Child, Parent and Adult systems are to be expanded so that these dimensions are included while preserving their fundamentally positive character.

Notes

1. In the following chapter, the term "function" is to be understood in this primary sense, even though classical TA has come to give it the dubious meaning of "operation".
2. Unless it is a "witness organ" of an outdated function, as is the case with the appendix.
3. To infer is to lay down the existence of something which is not manifest (here: the structure) to account for what is manifest (the manifestations).
4. See VARELA, F., 1980; BATESON, G., 1972, 1979.
5. According to Berne himself, the notion of Parent ego state refers to the "psychic presence" of P. Federn's disciple E. Weiss. "This is 'the mental image of another ego', sometimes a parental one, which affects the emotions and behavior of the individual". WEISS, E., 1950, quoted by BERNE, E., 1961, p. 3. See another theoretical elaboration of this presence in Stern's "evoked companion" (STERN, D., 1985).
6. Also called a "meta position".
7. Heidegger uses the term "existential" to designate the great permanent dimensions of human existence, and notably "being-there", "being-in-the-world", and "being-with". See HEIDEGGER, M., 1927.
8. A diagram is never self-explanatory: it only has meaning through its commentary. Other diagrams are possible depending on the author's objectives. What is essential, however, is not to confine an idea within a diagram, nor to use diagrams in a mechanical or stereotyped way, to the detriment of theoretical creativity.
9. BERNE, E., 1961, pp. 188–193.
10. BERNE, E., 1961, p. 189.
11. See the note in Chapter 1, p. 28, on the meaning of this term in *Transactional Analysis and Psychotherapy*.
12. BERNE, E., 1961, p. 189.
13. BERNE, E., 1961, p. 189.
14. BERNE, E., 1961, p. 189.
15. BERNE, E., 1961, p. 189.
16. BERNE, E., 1961, p. 190.
17. LAPLANCHE, J., and PONTALIS, J., 1967, art. "Processus primaire, processus secondaire", pp. 341–343.
18. LAPLANCHE, and PONTALIS, 1967, art. "Processus primaire, processus secondaire", p. 342.
19. BERNE, E., 1964a, pp. 50–58.
20. The mother's desire, being of external origin, is an element of the Parent system.
21. LAPLANCHE, J., and PONTALIS, J., 1967, art. "Processus primaire, processus secondaire", p. 342.
22. STERN, D., 1985, pp. 41–42.
23. BERNE, E., 1961, p. 189.
24. BERNE has just said that one of the functions of the organizers is to influence the other two. BERNE, E., 1961, p. 189.
25. The term "normative" is an excellent interpretation, probably authored by R. Hostie. This side of the Parent is usually called "critical", "prejudiced", etc., in English.

26 On this subject, see RAMOND, C., 1992.
27 BERNE, E., 1961, pp. 191–193.
28 BERNE, E., 1961, p. 191.
29 BERNE, E., 1961, pp. 192–193.
30 BERNE, E., 1961, p. 193.
31 BERNE, E., 1966, p. 220.
32 E.g., BERNE, E., 1970, p. 93: "Each individual is three different persons, all pulling in different directions... so it is a wonder anything gets done".
33 BERNE, E., 1964a, p. 27.
34 BERNE, E., 1964a, pp. 27–28.
35 BERNE, E., 1961, p. 186.
36 ERSKINE, R.G., and others, 1988; ERSKINE, R.G., 1988; ERSKINE, R.G., 1991; ERSKINE, R.G., 1994.

4
GROWTH AND PERSONAL DEVELOPMENT

More than any other living being, humans evolve throughout their lives: physically from birth to death, socially from dependence to a more or less assumed independence and psychologically from the first relationships buried in the earliest memory to the capacity to speak, think and act in an autonomous and creative way. Child, Parent and Adult personality systems evolve throughout life and cannot be understood separately of growth.

Evolving combinations of ego states

The process of the person's evolution is based on the ego state combinations related to their experiences.

Associated ego state trios

The concept for ego state trios derived from the previous chapter. From the interaction perspective, the three systems react simultaneously to the person's experiences, and each one perceives them through its own function. Each system keeps a partial trace of these experiences. Consequently, *any relational episode gives rise to a trio of associated ego states*: the Child ego state keeps the personal experience's memory; the Parent ego state does the same, according to the person's perception, for her partner(s)' memory; and the Adult ego state records the scene, free of these subjective experiences.[1]

Here is an example: a father regularly takes his young son to a football match. He pays the entrance fee, carefully protects them from being pushed and shoved, and chooses a place where the boy will have a good view of the playing field. The boy simultaneously records a Child ego state that reflects his enjoyment of these matches, a Parent ego state that will allow him to be inspired by his father's conduct when he takes his own son to the stadium, and an Adult ego state that links the two perceptions and captures their coherence.

If we compare ego states to the different positions of a camera in a scene where two characters are talking, the Child "films" the person's life from their own point of view, as if the camera were in their own head. On the other hand, when the camera shows us the person as seen by someone else, it is similar to the Parent.

When the camera shows both characters at the same time "in field", we have an analogy of the Adult position.[2]

When considering social experiences during early childhood, both D. Stern's theory and the theory of object relations confirm, though from different approaches, that *the whole social experience is memorized with each character and each relationship*. At that time of life, Child, Parent and Adult ego states, grouped in trios, are still only aspects of social experiences memorized globally: the pole of the Self (Child ego state), the pole of the Other (Parent ego state) and their mutual relationship (Adult ego state). *This is the starting point of development.*

Whatever their time of origin, the contents of the three ego states forming a trio preserve a strong relation between them permanently. This is clearly visible when a person relives a past event in therapy[3]: usually, they start the story in a narrative mode, including the parental figure and themselves (Adult), but as soon as they "enter the scene" and start reliving more or less intensely (Child), the parental figure (Parent) is right there: they address the parental figure, fear their judgement or reactions and feel ashamed, demanding, submissive or even so terrified that they do not dare to look straight at them, etc. When the therapeutic work ends with a resolution, this person can integrate these three aspects into an overall vision.

Generalized representations of events

M. Gilbert[4] and J. Hine[5] introduced D. Stern's[6] concept of generalized representations of events into TA. J. Hine defines them as follows: "A generalized representation of an event is the knowledge and reactions to that knowledge, that are synthesized from perceptions of several different occurrences of similar events until it becomes the expected stereotype for *future occurrences of the same experience*. An 'event' should be thought of as the occurrence of an extremely wide variety of different types of mental or even physical experiences. It may be an affective experience, a cognitive experience, a somatic experience, an interaction, an internal reaction or a passive perceiving, to name only a few".[7]

From the very beginning, the child combines similar experiences in order to develop "generalized representations"[8]: these are necessary for the child not to have to devise new expectations and strategies for every minor variation. Take "bathing with Mommy" as an example. As long as the procedure remains the same, the child is not in the least disturbed or his participation altered, even if details like towel colour change. They develop a generalized representation of "bathing with Mommy" with essential features only, leaving out minor details like towel colours; actually, each new experience allows them to make it more and more effective. If, on the other hand, something happens that the child cannot integrate into the "bathing with Mommy" representation, they create a new representation,[9] for example, "bathing while camping" or "bathing when I swallowed water"; they then construct a new way of reacting and a new representation, in other words, a new set of ego states.

These combinations link not only experiences but also pre-existing generalized representations. In this way, the person synthesizes ever larger generalized representations throughout their life. The representation "bathing with Mommy", for example, will be included with many others into "being in a relationship with Mommy" and then into "being in a relationship with a woman" and finally into "being in a relationship" in general.[10] The same generalized initial representation can also be integrated into multiple new representations, so that "bathing with Mommy" will also be involved in the elaboration of "taking care of my body", "having fun (or being uncomfortable) in the water", "my body as others perceive it", etc.

Usually, when the person activates their most general representations, they are not aware of the multiple original situations, nor of their associated emotions, nor of the elements this process put aside. However, most aspects do not seem to disappear entirely, because they can be reconstructed in experiences such as regression; one could say that they are "switched off", but not destroyed.

The process of elaborating generalized representations has a direct consequence for transactional theory: it shows us that *it is impossible to analyse evolving ego states, particularly creative ones, with the classical TA definitions of Child and Parent ego states* (repetitions of the person's or their parental figure's experience). The underlying question, "what is *the* origin (singular!) of this ego state" is meaningful only for ego states within the repetition perspective. As a matter of fact, this is why it is so tempting to resort to descriptive terms, often without even realizing it, in an attempt to unravel whether an experience "is" Child, Parent or Adult (which shifts the question of past origin to the dominant features of today's manifestations). In most cases, however, people's strategies draw on multiple sources.

For example, if a man curbs his anger, it is usually the consequence of numerous past experiences: "Dad avoids conflict", "Mum seems sad when I am angry", "One day I hit my little brother because I was angry, he was bleeding and I got scared", plus experiences at school, with peers, at work, in the street, etc. The therapist cannot *assume* it will be enough to deal with a single early experience, even the most archaic. It is great if that is the case, but they should not be surprised to have to work with two or three early or recent experiences, which they will have to choose among the most representative or the most outstanding in order to achieve a good resolution.

This is even more so when one needs to understand creative ego states, as they result from combinations of multiple previous ego states. Here is an example about a "game". A three-year-old boy, who can barely walk, is playing ball with his brothers and friends. The ego state content is quite primitive. It amounts to a vague association between moving and catching the ball; the idea of passing it on to another player is not yet included, so that the little boy keeps the ball when he has caught it and does not understand why anyone wants to take it away from him. By age four, the ego state is enriched: it now includes the idea that the ball must move in a certain direction and pass from one player to another. By age six, the ego state includes a rough version of the rules, the prohibition of cheating and how to tell who has won. The ability to lose with fair play may come later. In adolescence, the ego state can be enormously enriched again; by this time, the boy may have synthesized experiences relating to official competitions, physical risks, relationships with coaches, teammates, opponents, etc. At each stage, creativity in the game can increase considerably. How could this process be accounted for with a single experience?

Reinforcements and inhibitions

As soon as the process of constituting generalized representations starts to combine experiences, ego states and pre-existing generalized representations, some aspects are reinforced and others are avoided or even repressed.

1. In *repetitive ego states* (Figure 4.1), the person develops no new generalized representations. Berne cites Ms Enatosky.[11] Although the original scene's ego state trio is represented in the figure, the sheer repetition perspective only considers one of the three ego states, here the Child ego state.
2. *Combinations of ego states leading to inhibition.*

When the generalization process reinforces avoiding contact with a particular experience, two cases arise, depending on whether it gives rise to "overgeneralisations".[12] This term means that the avoidance pattern "spills over", i.e., invades an increasingly wide area of the person's existence and eventually leads to significant limitations. Here is an example (Figure 4.2).

A man is unable to be firm with his five-year-old son: "I am afraid of traumatizing him". He realizes that this inhibition is linked to scenes from his childhood when his father beat him. His contact with the experience (Child ego state) with its accompanying terror was initially repressed, which is indicated by the square in the Child system. But the Child already knows from experience that if this contact is revived in any way, the repression will not hold. The inhibition extends to all that could provoke such a reawakening, particularly to the violence model internalized from the father; this Parent ego state is in its turn inhibited

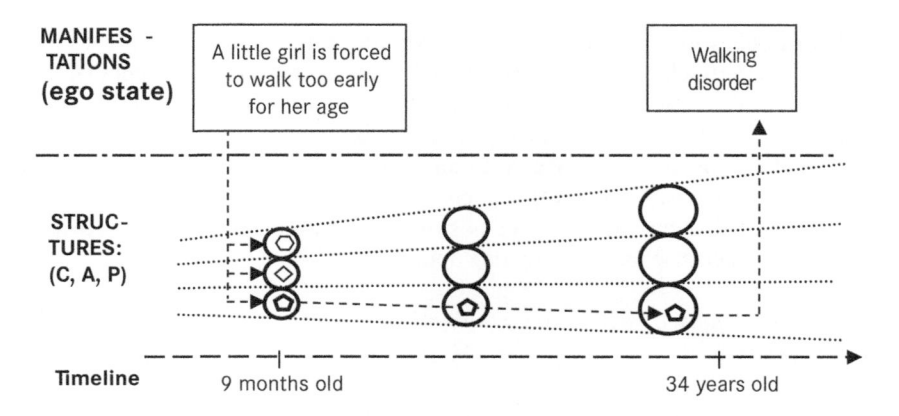

Figure 4.1 A repetitive ego state

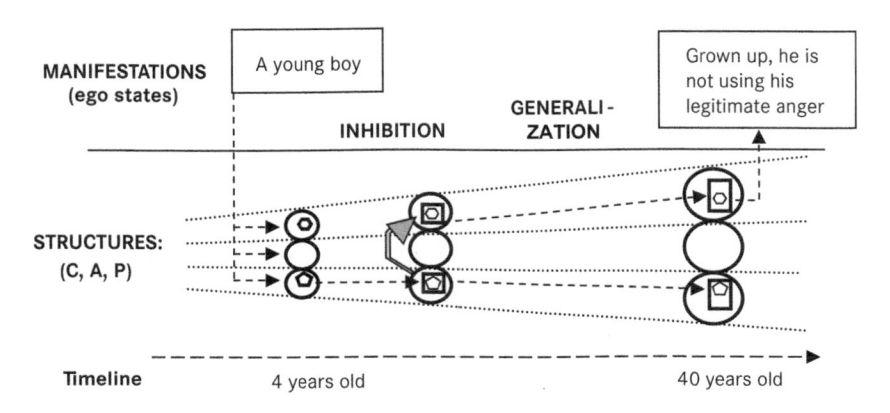

Figure 4.2 Generalization of an inhibition

(in terms of influences, the Child system influences the Parent system, which is indicated by the grey arrow). But as other situations could make this second repression unstable, the process continues and extends to increasingly broad conflict situations, independently of the objective risk of violence. Finally, through ever wider generalized representations, this man arrives at the level of his sense of Self: "This is my nature, I am incapable of asserting myself". Overgeneralization is like some medieval castles: first the keep is built, then a moat to protect it, then a second wall to protect it all, and so on. Traumas often cause the most extensive and, therefore, most damaging overgeneralizations.

If there is no overgeneralization, this type of ego state combinations can set up limits and supportive structures. This process does not go beyond its usefulness and enables avoiding destructive or harmful acts and reactions. These combinations are *structuring reinforcements*.

3. *Combinations of ego states leading to constant orientations.*

Instead of leading to avoidance, this type of combinations can increasingly reinforce a particular mode of reaction or action. If there is overgeneralization, one goes towards stereotypes, even compulsive reactions. In the example of the man above, such an overgeneralized representation could be: "In case of conflict, always please others", resulting from an accumulation of experiences such as: "By pleasing others, I have avoided conflict and fear of conflict". In the absence of overgeneralization, these may be positive qualities or traits; however, there is no creativity because there is only one option.

4. *Combinations of ego states resulting in flexible and potentially creative responses.*

These multiple combinations (Figure 4.3), which are usually constructed from ego states belonging to the three systems, evolve towards increasingly greater

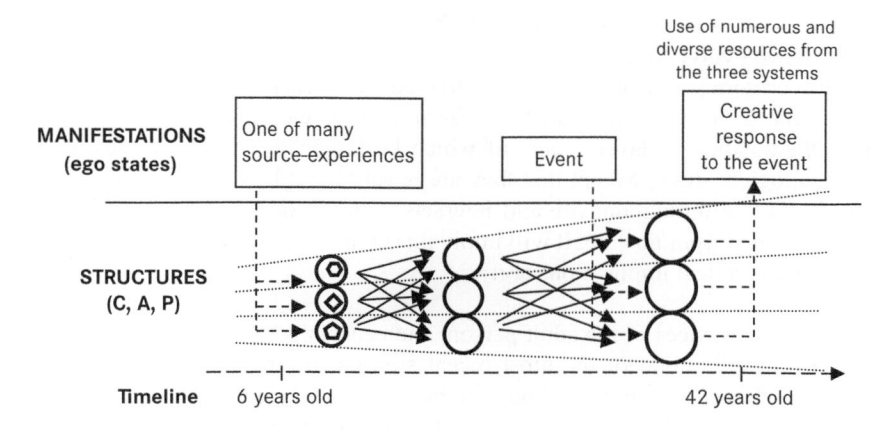

```
                                                    Use of numerous and
                                                    diverse resources from
                                                      the three systems
                                                    ┌─────────────┐
                                                    │  Creative   │
MANIFESTATIONS  ┌─────────────┐                     │  response   │
                │ One of many │    ┌───────┐        │ to the event│
 (ego states)   │source-experiences│    │ Event │        └─────────────┘
                └─────────────┘    └───────┘
```

Figure 4.3 A creative response

flexibility, which opens the possibility of creativity. The diagram above shows the multiplicity of influences that make creativity possible. An example is the game mentioned above.[13]

Note how this conceptualization highlights the intimate links between ego state theory and script theory when ego states are theorized in terms of "messages"[14]: injunctions and drivers result from overgeneralizations, the former when they lead to inhibitions, the latter when they generate never-changing orientations, whereas healthy limits (protections) and "permissions" are related to structuring reinforcements and creative responses. Other concepts can also be understood as the result of continuous elaboration of generalized representations, such as the existential life position, the group imago,[15] the frame of reference,[16] discounting,[17] redefining,[18] etc. In this light, TA theory appears not as a sprinkling of concepts with no real mutual links but as a unifying theory around the central concepts of ego states and script.[19]

Development and personality systems

D. Stern[20] is essential among recent contributions in this field. Several transactionalist authors have made his input the basis of their development conception, notably M. Thunnissen[21] and H. Hargaden and C. Sills.[22] What follows is Stern's findings about personality systems.

Overall perspective

Stern bases his work on live observation of children's *healthy development and relationships* from birth rather than on pathology, dreams and fantasies of a later age. He also draws on psychodynamic approaches to make sense[23] of them. Stern presents his findings as the evolution of a particular dimension of the psyche: the sense of Self, i.e., the child's subjective perception of themselves. This perception is intrinsically social, as this sense of Self is inseparable from the sense of Other, and the two evolve together.

Furthermore, development is not divided into "stages",[24] one stage ending before the next one starts.[25] Instead, Stern sees development as resulting from the superposition of layers, each of which builds on the previous ones, rather like geological strata, except that they are never "buried". On the contrary, each remains active throughout life and interacts with the others. Whenever "strata" are mentioned from now on, it will imply this conceptualization. Some of its very important practical implications are:

- The experiences of the adult person, and especially their social experiences, do not only concern the most recent stratum, but resonate simultaneously with the earliest strata without automatically implying pathology or regression. W. Cornell insists on the radical difference between "rooted in the earliest ages of life" and "fixed" or "archaic".[26]
- All strata, even the earliest, play a role in our most personal resources and creativity,[27] as well as in our most fragile vulnerabilities.
- When a current resource or problem appears to be linked to the psyche's earliest strata, this does not automatically imply that its origin is chronologically old. Suffering trauma in adulthood hurts the earliest strata without necessarily having antecedents in childhood.

The earliest strata

To start with, we unconsciously internalize entire social episodes "as they come" with their inseparable aspects of personal experience (Child ego state), perception of others' experience (Parent) and the link between the two, which implies a minimal perception of the whole (Adult). At this level, the three systems are only secondary differentiations within an overall memory that records the episodes in their entirety.

This internalization is what neurophysiologists call "implicit memory". This "is nonconscious. It involves emotions, sensations and behaviours, but there is no sense (…) of time, or that something is being recalled".[28] The memories recorded in it are overgeneralized and unprocessed; they are experienced as if they were happening now.[29] Stern describes this process from a different point of view and states it covers at least the two initial strata, the emergent Self and the core-Self.

In the emergent Self's stratum (Figure 4.4, left), the person's experiences, represented by the vertically connected ego states, only bring about an unstable and fleeting sense of Self (in grey), which needs the "Self-regulating Other's" active presence in order to come into existence and develop. The mother usually plays the central role in this; her action and social presence act on the child to provide a holding environment for the child's internal experiences and to channel them. She brings into play her integrated and coherent part (represented by the orb around most of their personality systems) and, inevitably also, her non-integrated, incoherent and sometimes destructive parts (symbolized by the small arrows emanating from her non-integrated parts).

The Self-regulating Other   The Other related to Self and distinct from Self

Integrated aspects   Non-integrated aspects

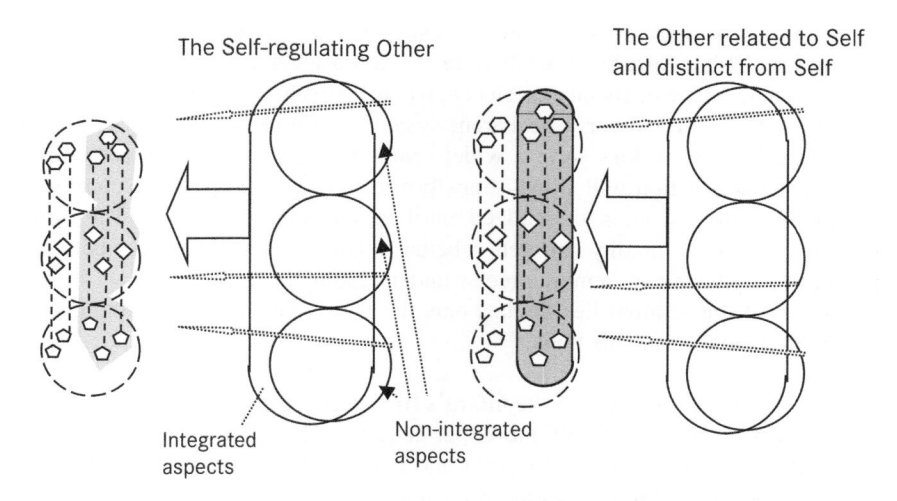

Figure 4.4 A transactional diagram for the emergent Self and the core Self phases

According to Stern, the core-Self layer (Figure 4.4, right) covers the emergent-Self layer at an early stage. At this point, the person already has a more coherent core at their disposal to elaborate their sense of Self. They already stand as related to and distinct from the Other[30]; this implies having the experience of agency, coherence, personal affectivity, continuity and permanence.

These early strata are the foundation of all that follows; the person's very first learnings and earliest resources are rooted there, together with what Berne calls the script "protocol",[31] its most primitive level.[32] If destructive contents buried in the earliest strata are reactivated without getting either a holding environment or some meaning, violent and unpredictable outbursts can occur. This holding environment can come from the person, who benefits from the interaction of these early strata with the more recent strata, or from a relationship between the person and an Other, provided that the Other remains lucid and sufficiently stable as to what is happening and as to her own reactions, which usually implies awareness and allowing for counter-transference reactions.

The more recent strata

The first two strata are then covered by another stratum, i.e., the subjective Self and the subjective Other: I find out I have a mind, so do others, others' minds are different, and my subjective experiences can be shared. This opens a new dimension, which is the intersubjective interpersonal bond. "When it does occur, the impersonal action has moved, in part, from overt actions and responses to the internal subjective states that lie behind the overt behaviors. This shift gives the infant a different 'presence' and social 'feel'",[33] so that "both separation/individuation and new forms of experiencing union (or being-with) emerge equally out of the same experience of intersubjectivity".[34]

According to Stern, this step precedes speech acquisition and must therefore deeply alter Child, Parent and Adult systems. At this level, the Child system gains access to a new type of social experience, where an exchange can take place from one subjectivity to another. The Parent system continues to internalize, which is its function, but it does so in a wider space. Interactions with other systems and speech acquisition will slowly transform this space into possible conscious positionings about what is internalized, until adolescence and beyond. The Adult system gains fresh lucidity and gets a better grasp of what differences between people mean; it achieves a more precise understanding of relationships.

On top of this stratum lies the last one, the verbal Self and the verbal Other, which Stern analyses in his book.[35]

> During the second year of the infant's life language emerges, and in the process the senses of Self and Other acquires new attributes. Now the Self and the Other have different and distinct personal world knowledge as well as a new medium of exchange with which to create shared meanings. A new organizing subjective perspective emerges and opens a new domain of relatedness. The possible ways of 'being with' another increase enormously. At first glance, language appears to be a straightforward advantage for the augmentation of interpersonal experience. It makes part of our known experience more shareable with others. In addition, it permits two people to create mutual experiences of meaning that had been unknown before and could never have existed until fashioned by words. It also finally permits the child to begin to construct a narrative of his own life. But in fact, language is a double-edged sword. It also makes some parts of our experience less shareable with ourselves and with others. It drives a wedge between two simultaneous forms of interpersonal experience: as it is lived and as it is verbally represented. Experience in the domains of emergent, core- and intersubjective relatedness, which continue irrespective of language, can be embraced only very partially in the domain of verbal relatedness. (…) Language, then, causes a split in the experience of the Self. It also moves relatedness onto the impersonal, abstract level intrinsic to language and away from the personal, immediate level intrinsic to the other domains of relatedness.[36]

Explicit memory predominates in these two last strata. It covers implicit memory but does not interrupt its functioning; it only channels it in a more nuanced and socially acceptable form, accompanied by emotions, which this time can be preconscious, conscious and even verbalized. However, implicit memory processes take over if severe stress occurs. "Explicit memory, in contrast, is conscious. There is an accompanying sense of self, time and that something is being recalled. (…) Implicit memory develops earlier that explicit memory. It is nonverbal and nonsymbolic, but it is not less rich or more primitive. It is not replaced by explicit knowledge".[37]

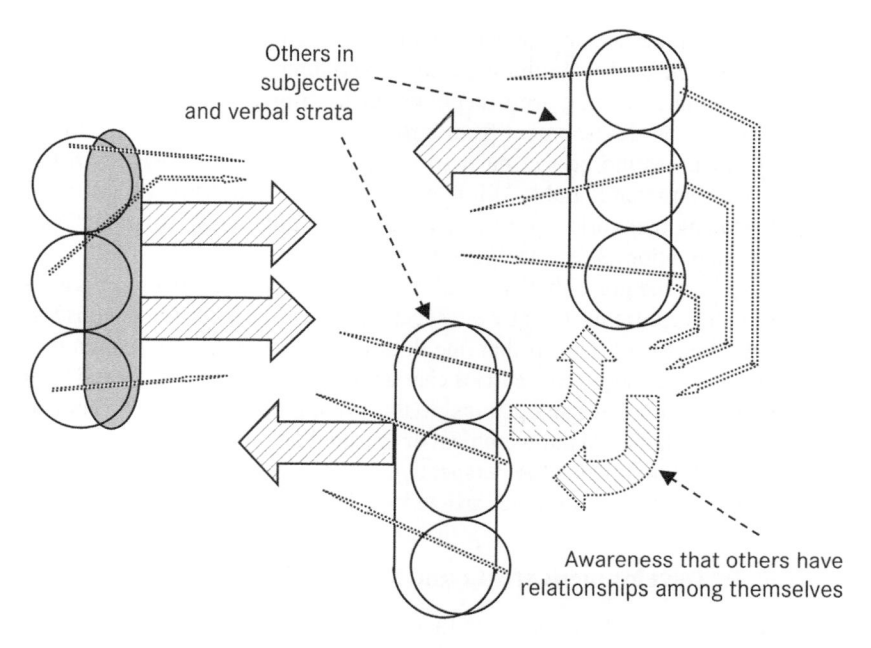

Figure 4.5 A transactional representation of subjective and verbal strata

Labels in figure: "Others in subjective and verbal strata"; "Awareness that others have relationships among themselves"

These two strata allow a type of relationship which expands its interpersonal side without putting an end to what precedes it. The person grows into their sense of Self in relation to others, who will be less and less restricted to parental figures.

Figure 4.5 represents "the others" (here reduced to two persons, on the right side). We are not talking about "the Other" only, as it is important to realize that the Other has a subjectivity of their own, being the subject of their own life with their own relationships. For the child, to be in relation means to be in relation with people who are themselves in relation with third parties whom the child knows (as is represented here) or not and who are present or "elsewhere": their parents' colleagues, for example.

Over the unconscious script "protocol", Berne sees the preconscious "palimpsest", which is a defensive attenuation of it, and the conscious script elaboration. Although these clinical concepts cannot be made to coincide exactly with Stern's, their preconscious or conscious quality makes it possible to attribute the palimpsest and the conscious script especially, to explicit memory and strata of subjective and verbal Self.

Development beyond childhood

The notion that the sense of Self and the psyche in general keep on evolving means that *development cannot be declared ended at a given moment*, whether it is the resolution of the Oedipus complex, the object independence or the appearance of Stern's verbal Self. Yet, few psychotherapists and psychoanalysts have been interested in the person's development beyond childhood, as if they did not have to concern themselves with the person's development today.

Eric Erikson and G. Jung are exceptions. Erikson listed "eight ages of man", which define human development from birth to death. He gave them the form of existential dilemmas the person must solve: 1) basic trust vs. basic distrust; 2) autonomy vs. shame and doubt; 3) initiative vs. guilt; 4) industry vs. inferiority; 5) identity (facing the world) vs. role confusion; 6) intimacy vs. isolation; 7) generativity vs. stagnation; 8) ego integrity vs. despair.[38]

Jung describes the great challenges along the human being's path in his archetypes theory: he represents them by the successive encounters of the unconscious, the Shadow (the part of oneself that one does not want to see), the Anima or the Animus (the part of oneself that carries characteristics of the other sex) and finally the Self (which symbolizes an openness to that which is beyond oneself, independently of one's beliefs and philosophical or spiritual commitments).[39]

In TA, Pam Levin opened the perspective of a continuous development represented in the form of a spiral in her article[40] on development.

Development strata and personality systems

The interaction perspective considers that since all three personality systems are necessary for survival, development and creativity, they are necessarily present in some form from the beginning of life. All three are rooted in the implicit unconscious memory and in the earliest, but still active, development strata. We cannot therefore restrict them either to the conscious, as classical TA tends to do,[41] or to the unconscious, as Erskine and Trautmann's theory of ego states does in Child and Parent systems' case.[42] This perspective, on the contrary, leads to a close articulation of these two dimensions.

D. Stern's findings enables us to improve our understanding of the personality systems' evolution. They are initially closely entwined within the ego states related to each experience. But it is logical to think that, as soon as the generalized representations' game comes into play, some of the innumerable possible combinations regularly bring together experiences similar to the person's experience. If this experience is subjectively perceived as positive, other similar experiences will be perceived as desirable. This generalized representation will then tend to reinforce this type of experience; it will diversify it while enriching itself and opening the possibility of greater and greater creativity. If perceived as negative, it will tend to inhibit them. In this way, the person gradually forms a general mechanism in which we can recognize the action of the Child system. It acts as an organizer which, as described in the previous chapter, classifies experiences according to the type of subjective experience they contain, and on this basis develops conclusions and strategies linked to affects in order to favour desirable experiences and avoid the others.

The same applies to the Parent system, though with the Other as the pole for the groupings that are essential to generalized representations. Usually, the sets of experiences where the Other's reaction is considered desirable will be favoured,

GROWTH AND PERSONAL DEVELOPMENT

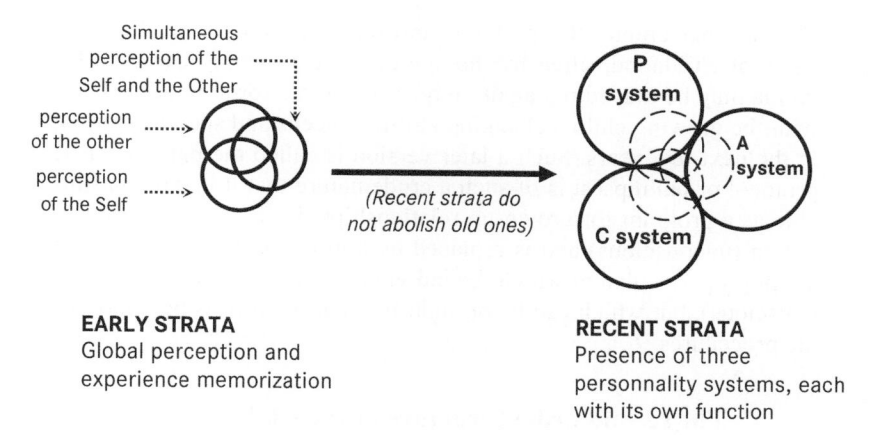

EARLY STRATA
Global perception and experience memorization

RECENT STRATA
Presence of three personnality systems, each with its own function

Figure 4.6 Genesis and evolution of personality systems

the others will be slowed down or inhibited. With increasingly general representations, we get to the level of "what arouses in everyone (or almost everyone) desirable or undesirable reactions" and then finally at values.

In a similar way, the Adult system is built from sets of experiences grouped by their "in-field" pole, i.e., independent of the protagonists' reactions.

We can go one step further and say that as the distinction is better perceived and represented between the Self and the Other, then between the Self and the various Others, the three personality systems will be less and less "stuck" to one another; they will evolve into systems, each with its own distinct function, though without ever being able to fulfil it without the others. The systems' function as organizers is increasingly clear, but their realization can only build on the previous strata.

This evolution can be represented by the diagram in Figure 4.6.

Berne rarely uses an evolution perspective, except in two important cases: the group imago (analysed in greater details in Chapter 13) and the script. We already discussed the script but here is Berne's own summary of its evolution. Then we address a problem linked to development representation in classical TA and TA in general, i.e., the convention of representing the person's evolution by second and third order structures of the Child system. This convention has become an implicit obligation and is linked to the repetition perspective.

TRANSACTIONAL TEXTS

Script evolution for Berne

The following text shows that, for Berne himself, the script's different dimensions constitute strata which do not cancel out previous ones. Practice shows that script protocol remains active and can manifest itself in a powerful and abrupt manner.[43]

The original drama, the protocol, is usually completed in the early years of childhood, often by the age of 5, occasionally earlier: This drama may be played out again in more elaborate form, in accordance with the growing child's changing abilities, needs and social situation, in the next few years. Such a later version is called the palimpsest. A protocol or palimpsest is of such a crude nature that it is quite unsuitable as a program for grown-up relationships. It becomes largely forgotten (unconscious) and is replaced by a more civilized version, the script proper: a plan of which the individual is not actively aware (preconscious), but which can be brought into consciousness by appropriate procedures.[44]

The second order structure of the Child system

It is common practice in TA to record the earlier evolutionary states of Child, Parent and Adult systems within the Child system as second and third order structures (Figure 4.7). A notable example is the diagram representing the three impasse types in K. Mellor's theory[45]: these substructures allow him to diagram three successive development strata and three intervention modes. Another example is Hargaden and Sills's clever but visually complicated translation of Stern's theory into transactional diagrams.[46] This graphic representation draws its meaning from the repetition perspective and is frequently used in TA in very different ways. True, this type of diagram emphasizes the fact that dynamics of the past are still active in the person today. But it can nevertheless lead to various confusions from the interaction perspective's point of view:

- It gives the impression that there are Adult and Parent ego states within the Child system, which is contradictory since the three systems have distinct functions that are non-reducible to one another.

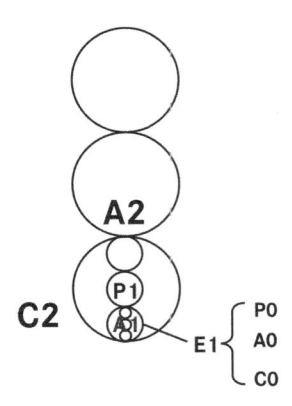

Figure 4.7 The parallel in Berne's theory to the theorizing of growth in terms of overlaid strata: the diagram of second and third order structures of ego states.

- It also suggests that the Child system (E2) is a composite aggregate although its unity is defined by its specific structural contribution.
- It blurs the close link between the Parent early strata (P0, P1) and the current Parent (P2), whereas these are different strata of the same system. The same applies to the Adult system; this is why this evolution has been deployed along the time axis in Figures 4.1–4.3.[47]
- It allows showing that early dynamics are still active, but it pulls back elements that belong to the past, into the present.

Therefore, from the interaction perspective, it is preferable to introduce a "timeline" into the diagrams; after all, it is logical when it comes to visualizing an evolutionary process. The aim here is not to replace traditional diagrams with new ones, but to open creativity in this field and to allow each practitioner, whatever their area of expertise, to create their own diagrams according to their objectives and the needs of those they are addressed to.

What led Berne to use the Child second order structure in this way? This is how he presents it:

> Mr Deuter (A), a twenty-three-year-old patient, reported the following dream: "I dreamed that I was a little boy (C) sucking my thumb, though I felt I was too old to do it, and worried about what my mother would say if she saw me. You know, I've always felt guilty (P) about deceiving her." It is evident that it is the Adult (A) who relates the dream, the Child (C) who appears in it, and the disapproving Parent (P) who makes him feel guilty (…). In order to represent this in a structural diagram, not only the thumb-sucking urge, but also the guilt feeling and the objective appraisal must be included as part of the Child. It was this Child who appeared in the dream. (…) Therefore, the Child reproduces (…) the complete personality structure of a regressive thumb-sucker while Mr. Deuter's current Adult and Parent may be represented in the usual way.[48]

The repetition (or regression) perspective introduces and justifies the idea of a Child ego state in this text. The fact that today Mr Deuter has a dream that reproduces a scene of his childhood[49] means one can rightly diagnose a repetitive or "regressive" Child ego state. Engrossed by the repetition perspective, Berne does not mention here the Adult and Parent ego states that the original scene aroused in Mr Deuter as a child. However, in a nearby passage, he reminds us that a child has three personality systems:

> When [visitors] went to greet the children in the playroom, they would usually find Aaron in one or other of these three states: sulking (C), playing with his sister [teaching her to build with blocks], (A) or rebuking her in loco parentis (P).[50]

It is clear that a child has three distinct personality systems: a Child system, a Parent system and an Adult system; *one cannot see there three Child ego states*. But *in the repetition*, together they are part of the content in the Child system which reproduces the little boy or girl's experience. This *experience* is the entity that *was* including three systems.[51] The Child system is like a layer of an old colour photographic plate: one does not conclude from a photograph of a child playing with his sister that these are substructures of a particular layer of the plate, but that they are elements of a past scene which has been "photographed"!

Today's Adult and Parent systems also have their perception of this past event.[52] Additionally, the early Parent (often referred to as P1) is a stratum of the Parent system, not a part of the Child system.[53]

The consequence of this perspective confusion is that, in some texts by Berne and others, P1, A1 and E1 have come to designate aspects of the Child system functioning instead of designating early strata in personality systems, without this change of meaning being explained. This is the case in Holtby's article[54] on script decisions: C1 means the internal perception of the Child system, A1 its elaboration of conclusions and strategies and P1 its memorization process. This changes nothing about the important insight the article provides on script decision.

Finally, when one diagrams development as a successive development of C1, A1, A2, P1 and P2,[55] one does not talk about ego states but about the states of the whole person, so that each of these acronyms represents nothing more than the totality of their three personality systems at different moments of their development. As for C2, it has no real place in this presentation and is, in fact, only there for theoretical terms symmetry.

Notes

1 LITTLE, R., 2001[ES], goes the same way with his notion of "social unity". Although he starts by stating: "the Parent, Adult and Child ego states are not separate ego states, but on the contrary, they are linked in social units" (p. 7), he then considers only the Child and Parent ego states. But without the Adult aspect, no representation of the link between the Child and Parent elements would be possible.
2 In neuro-linguistic programming, these three positions are called "perceptive positions"; see, for example, GRINDER, J., & DELOZIER, J., *Turtles All the Way Down*. Grinder & Associates, 1987.
3 Especially with techniques like two-chair work.
4 GILBERT, M., 1996.
5 HINE, J., 1997[ES].
6 STERN, D., 1985.
7 HINE, J., 1997[ES], p. 279.
8 STERN, D., 1985, pp. 95–98, and passim
9 See on this point the description of HINE, J., 1997. This process presents some analogies with what J. Piaget said about assimilation and accommodation: See DOLLE, J.M., 1999, pp. 50–56.
10 Nota bene: "being in relationship" is remarkably close to the notion of "existential life position" (BERNE, E., 1972, pp. 85–89), which Berne considers as a construction, not as an *a priori* quality of the child. See also ENGLISH, F., 1975.

11 BERNE, E., 1961, pp. 117–120, pp. 197–205. We have already met Ms "Enatosky" in Chapter 1, p. 27.
12 HINE, 1997[ES], p. 280.
13 See pp. 63–64.
14 Script theory also includes a narrative dimension: the "life plan" (BERNE, E., 1972, pp. 31–35, et passim), i.e., the account of the person's life as they imagine it. This aspect belongs to the building of the sense of Self, which we will discuss later.
15 BERNE, E., 1963, pp. 220–226.
16 SCHIFF, J.L., SCHIFF, A.W., and SCHIFF (SIGMUND), E., 1975.
17 MELLOR, K., and SCHIFF (SIGMUND), E., 1975.
18 SCHIFF (SIGMUND), E., 1975.
19 At the International Congress of Group Psychotherapy in 1968, Berne said: "Ego states are the key to transactional analysis. Anything that you cannot reduce to ego states is not transactional analysis, and this distinction is worth making" (BERNE, E., 1973, p. 71). It cannot be said, however, that he himself was always very careful about clarifying the link between various transactional concepts and ego states.
20 STERN, D., 1985.
21 THUNNISSEN, M., 1998[ES].
22 HARGADEN, H., and SILLS, C., 2002[ES].
23 See STERN, D., 1985, pp. 18–23.
24 In his reflection on psychoanalysis, J. Laplanche, among others, already reacted against "stagism": LAPLANCHE, J., 1987, p. 73.
25 As is the case in the conception of Freudian stages, elaborated by Alexander or developed by M. Mahler, of whom D. Stern was one of the assistants (MAHLER, M.S., PINE, F., and BERGMAN, A., 1975).
26 CORNELL, W., 2003[ES], p. 39.
27 Talented artists' works usually draw on the earliest, most unconscious and often most painful strata of their personality: Van Gogh, Vian or Ferré, to name but a few.
28 ALLEN, J., 2000, *TAJ* 30, 4, p. 262.
29 GILDEBRAND, K., 2003[ES], p. 6, p. 24 (n.10).
30 Stern distinguishes two successive strata: "Self versus Other" (Chapter 4) and then "Self with Other" (Chapter 5).
31 Berne regularly deviates from the "accessible" terms that he promotes in other circumstances! Here he compares the script to an ancient manuscript that has been used several times for different texts. In palaeography, the "proto-cole" (prôto-kollos, what was glued first) is the oldest layer, i.e., the support material obtained by gluing two or three layers of fibres in the case of a papyrus. If the text is roughly erased, wax or chalk is applied over it and the support is reused, it is a "palimpsest" (palim-psêstos, that which has been scraped off and [used] again), another term we will encounter later.
32 Berne says that the protocol is established at around five or six years of age, but much clinical evidence would lead us today to believe that it is much earlier. In any case, it must be remembered that the earliest strata can be reached and changed throughout life, so that the question of age is superseded by that of process: when the script protocol manifests itself in its raw state, the process of that manifestation indicates very early strata that have not had a container.
33 STERN, D., 1985, p. 125.
34 STERN, D., 1985, p. 127.
35 In his recent thinking (2007), Stern introduces a further stratum, that of the "narrative Self", characterized by the development of an awareness of being not only a different

subjectivity, but a person who has a unique story of their own; they represent and tell this story in an evolving and interactive mode. Stern, D., lecture, Geneva 2004. SMALL, L., private comment, 2007.
36 STERN, D., 1985, p. 162.
37 ALLEN, J., 2000, *TAJ* 30, 4, p. 263.
38 ERIKSON, E., 1950, pp. 247–274.
39 See von FRANZ, M.L., 1964, pp. 158–229.
40 LEVIN, P., 1982[ES].
41 See Steiner, C., in STEINER, C., and NOVELLINO, M., 2005.
42 GREGOIRE, J., 2007a, 2007b.
43 See CORNELL, W.F., and LANDAICHE, M.N., 2006.
44 BERNE, E., 1963, pp. 227–230. In *Transactional analysis in psychotherapy*, the three strata are called differently: protocol, adaptation and script proper. BERNE, E., 1961, p. 87. He illustrates these various levels and their complexity in the case of Mrs Catters, ibid, pp. 88–89.
45 MELLOR, K., 1980.
46 HARGADEN, H., and SILLS, C., 2002.
47 See pp. 68–70.
48 BERNE, E., 1961, pp. 149 and 150.
49 Berne relates the trauma at the origin of this repetitive ego state's fixation in pp. 149–151.
50 BERNE, E., 1961, p. 149.
51 See on this point COX, M., 1999[ES].
52 The same remarks apply to the second order structure of the Parent, of course.
53 Berne and other transactionalists very often speak of it in this way, as we shall see in the following chapters. See also BERNE, E., 1969.
54 HOLTBY, M., 1976[ES].
55 E.g., LEVIN, P., 1982.

5

THE CHILD

The system that experiences life

The Child is the system that puts us in touch with the subjective dimension of our experiences in both gratifying and frustrating aspects; it does so by incorporating our most primitive reactions of attraction or repulsion, our desires, our dreams and our imagination. This is its function in the primary sense of the word. At the earliest strata's level, raw experiences are stored in the unconscious implicit memory, in the form of latent experiences ready to be reproduced. In the resulting ego state trios, the Child represents the Self, i.e., the person's experiences. The multiform play of generalized representations of interactions extends to the three personality systems through every stratum and leads to reinforcing or inhibiting combinations.

The Child system is essential because it is crucial for our survival and well-being that we keep track of our subjective reactions, whether conscious or not, and the experiences that gave rise to them. As a result, if we encounter again a situation that brought us pain, we tend to avoid it; if, on the other hand, it was an experience that brought us satisfaction or pleasure, we tend to repeat it. Otherwise, we could live through the same painful situation dozens of times without being protected any more than the first time. This is, unfortunately, one of the things that can happen to us when our psychic equipment malfunctions.

This chapter examines in more detail the Child characteristic processes and its necessary link with the other two systems.

Perception and memorization

The Child system perceives existence in terms of what is *attractive* or *repulsive*, *pleasant* or *unpleasant*, *pleasurable* or *painful*, *gratifying* or *frustrating*, *rewarding or unrewarding* for the person. For any experience, it registers the way in which the person subjectively experiences it, while the Parent system deals with others' reactions, and the Adult system with what is not related to anybody's experience. It is therefore the *whole of the person's existence* that is perceived by the Child system from this perspective: their physical state, internal experiences, social life and activity, as well as the events that concern them or that they witness. It is also from this perspective that it influences the development of their sense of Self and their personal history. This system is focused on the rewarding or unrewarding aspects of existence and is alien to the limits of reality and morality. It cannot therefore be reproached for its unrealism or amorality; it is up to the other two systems to introduce the discernment it lacks.

What does "subjective experience" mean?

From the interaction perspective, it is impossible to draw up a restrictive list of experiences that are specific to this system since the Child "scans" the whole of existence within the dimension of subjective experience, and *any experience* has a subjective dimension to which this system is connected. To list the experiences recorded in the Child system would therefore be tantamount to listing the entirety of human experience.

However, it is useful to explain the angle from which the Child relates to each experience, and the different dimensions included in the term "subjective experience":

1. The first dimension is the experience of pleasure or pain, fulfilment or non-fulfilment of one's body, or one's drives; within the earliest and still active personality strata, the experience is written in the bodily dimension of the script[1] and of our most fundamental learnings.
2. The second dimension takes this experience through *affect* and *emotion*, both inside and outside aspects, through which the person seeks, consciously or not, to make them known, understood and accepted by others.
3. Then comes the *relational* dimension: the person feels approved, appreciated, loved, admired or the opposite. This is where the stroke theory comes into play; it teaches us that, when unfulfilled, the Child system can push the person to seek out experiences such as disapproval, devaluation or hatred,[2] in order to avoid relational void, which they perceive as even worse.

Many approaches emphasize the vital importance of this dimension. Berne conceives the script, i.e., the whole of a person's life, as a social drama. The object relations theory and the recent transactional trends it inspired[3] see relationships as the primary engine of human development, the source of its blocks and the place where it can be resolved.

But being in a relationship is not only about receiving strokes: it is also about *giving* them. The Child often seeks the subjective experience of giving or being useful; conversely, the Child generates frustration if it is deprived of it. R. Erskine and R. Trautmann have highlighted this in their list of "relational needs".[4] This is also a list of subjective experience aspects through which the Child perceives and organizes experience:
1) to be safe;
2) to be validated and accepted, and to feel important in a relationship;
3) to be accepted by someone on whom one can allow oneself to depend;
4) to receive confirmation of one's own experience;
5) to define oneself;
6) to have an impact on the other;
7) for the other to take the initiative;
8) to express love.

Since the Child perceives the other not in terms of what he or she is, but in terms of its own gratifications or frustrations, it is not wrong to say that it is "self-centred".[5] This does not, however, condemn the Child to selfishness, for its desire may very well be to see or make the other person happy[6] or to give pleasure or joy. It may even "take upon itself" others' joy or suffering, because it does not have, like the Adult in its most recent strata, a clear perception of otherness and separation between people, which would enable opposite processes like projection or identification.

4. However important the relationship, it does not constitute the whole subjective dimension to which the Child system is connected. There are also satisfactions or frustrations connected to *activity*, such as the feeling of being active in the world and having an impact, or of being incompetent and failing. The activity referred to here is not limited to material activity, but also includes playful, intellectual or aesthetic activity.
5. Another dimension of gratification or frustration is *existential*. This concerns the meaning of the Self and of existence. Along with the other two systems, the Child system takes part in the search for meaning. But just as it may aim for positive strokes, it may also be more interested in confirming a well-established[7] sense of Self, even if it is pejorative, limiting or destructive, rather than risking "existential void" or uncertainty about itself.
6. Finally, there are the *aesthetic* dimension of experience in art, contact with nature, and "*peak-experiences*"[8].

Imagination and fantasy

Gratification or frustration implies *desire*, *imagination* and *fantasy*. When these are the person's own,[9] they connect closely to the Child system, for several reasons:

- because the Child system is neither intended nor equipped to distinguish between real and imaginary (this is the Adult's role);
- because desire can create a compensatory satisfaction by imagining or fantasizing its object, as Freud[10] has already pointed out;
- and because the Child system can react to imaginary experiences as well as to real ones. This is why R. Erskine and M. Zalcman[11] included this dimension in their description of the parasite system. Therapeutic interventions in which the person addresses someone else in an imaginary mode, usually a parent figure, benefit from this characteristic. The dialogue that takes place is a fiction, as it never existed in reality, yet it has a very real impact on the Child system.

Intuition

Berne places great emphasis on intuitive perception, which he attributes entirely to the Child system. But he focuses on the first phase of the intuitive process, i.e., perception, while forgetting the other necessary phase, i.e., the passage through the Adult system.

The Adult does not replace the Child: it ratifies its plausibility and assesses its possible risks. We will discuss this in Chapter 11 on integrated activities.

The Child's language perception

At a verbal level, the Child's ability to *identify with...* makes it especially sensitive to *metaphors* and *stories* such as myths and fairy tales or animal stories. But it perceives language subtleties in an often unpredictable way. It may leave out "maybe, I think, probably, somehow, etc.", confuse modal[12] auxiliaries or fail to grasp the difference between "so-and-so said that..." and "that is the way it is". Even negation does not always make sense[13]; double negation may well be bewildering, at least for a moment. Sometimes, the Child notices words more than sentences and changes the meaning by focusing on a word, rather than on the concept. It does not always grasp innuendo or "second degree" humour, unless an internal or external signal alerts the Child that there is some kind of game or riddle to be solved, which it then enjoys enormously. Berne gives an example of the multiple meanings the Child can attribute (I would add simultaneously) to a sentence, such as "You're too small to drink whisky!".[14] The Child system can also understand sentences literally, for its own happiness or misfortune. For example, the little girl who was told by her mother, "You'll end up in an asylum", fulfils the prophecy... by becoming a psychiatrist. All this has practical importance: the practitioner must consider the three systems' perception modes to phrase their interventions.[15]

Memorization

The Child system records and connects experiences according to the subjective experiences they contain, in the different dimensions specified above. At the implicit memory level, it preserves the traces of what we lived in our very first relational experiences, whether they were our first structuring skills or relational failures that constitute our script protocol. Stern[16] highlights the positive aspect of these processes as a basis for development from life beginning; this means that these processes are not reduced to pathogenic "fixations", as Erskine and Trautmann describe in their ego state theory. These structuring and limiting elements remain as an unconscious foundation of our most intense relationships and experiences, especially our intimate[17] relationships.

As development strata span all three personality systems, the Child system holds conscious and unconscious contents and mechanisms simultaneously. These can be interpreted in two ways: via implicit memory and via psychodynamic concepts, such as repression. *The two conceptualizations do not overlap or exclude each other:*

- implicit memory does not presuppose any prior awareness,
- whereas repression evokes psychodynamic processes, where contents become inaccessible or pushed out of consciousness.

These contents are not erased, as they can be recovered, at least in some cases, by appropriate methods: it is as if a library book listing had been destroyed or rendered illegible, so that the book itself, although existing and occupying space, has become untraceable. Another image, due to R. Erskine,[18] is that these contents recorded in the Child system are "encapsulated", which rather evokes the defence mechanism of isolation, close to repression.

The Child's organizer role: combining and developing experiences

Association modes for memorized experiences

1. According to Berne, as we saw in Chapter 3, the specific process by which the Child system classifies and connects internal and external events is the "primary process", which, for Freud, characterizes the unconscious. This process is broader than the Child system and defines a whole stratum of the person's evolution. However, in order to accomplish its function, which is dominated by gratifications and frustrations' subjective dynamics, this system does not establish strict coherence, so that even in its most elaborate strata, the secondary process does not really impose itself.

   This does not mean that the Child system is pure chaos, like the id in Freudian concepts. Yes, it can lead the person towards objects that are contradictory ("wanting to have your cake and eat it too"), unattainable and impossible ("wanting the moon") or even amoral ("I want to kill him!"), but it also clings to conclusions and strategies that introduce an element of coherence into its associations.

2. The Child associations are not limited by *temporal distance*, which it perceives vaguely… or only when convenient. Since it does not distinguish clearly between the *past, present* and *future*, it can "live in the past" or "live in the future". In Child perception mode, a childhood experience can appear as close as a recent one; it sees time as a sprinkling of separate moments, each of which can be brought closer to any other, as long as the experiences concerned have something in common.[19] It builds a web between experiences, which it connects together in ways that cannot be predicted from the outside. This is one of the reasons why "respectful inquiry"[20] (inquiring without presupposing that one knows) is essential for the practitioner. The practitioner's skill, whatever their field, implies getting to know the person's or the group's "web" and putting it to good use.[21]

3. It would be a mistake to view in a pejorative light this relative freedom from constraints among associations. It plays an important role in phenomena such as entertainment,[22] intuition and creativity, and whenever it is important for the person to be free from their own frame of reference in its aspects, both Adult (the world as I know it) and Parent (the world as it should be), in order to invent something of which the person can say neither "This I already know", nor "This is how it 'must' be".[23] For example, while playing, children imagine themselves in a situation they have not experienced

(playing Mommy, aeroplane pilot, etc.) and draw conclusions from it; this saves them from experimenting in reality with its risks and energy consumption. Creativity is like playing, in that one can consider different possibilities, even far-fetched ones, without judgement, "just to try it out" and for the pleasure of creating things. As for intuition, it frees access to what the Adult and Parent systems find difficult to consider, as it is not what they aim for. Without our Child system, all this would be impossible.

Drawing conclusions associated with affects

The Child system develops *conclusions* or *beliefs* from remembered experiences, usually multiple or, more rarely, single and intense. These are part of this system's contribution to the person's *sense of Self, the Other and existence*.[24] The distinction between these three domains is not clear-cut: for example, "I am not capable", "Others are more competent than I am" and "My life is a succession of lost rivalries" are just three different formulations of the same experience and are mostly associated with the same emotional tone. The fact remains that in the Child system, the sense of Self has a special place, because its function directs it towards the experience of the person.

Since the Child system has no limiting principle other than its own experiences, its conclusions easily go to extremes. This manifests itself in many ways:

- illusion of "omnipotence" or "impotence";
- illusion of being responsible for everything, being in charge of solving everything or illusion of "absolute incompetence" in case of "failure";
- idealization or demonization of the Self and/or the Other;
- enthusiasm, even euphoria or despair;
- blind trust or general distrust...

Strategies and impact on action

1. One might think that, under these conditions, the Child cannot produce very effective *strategies*. Yet Berne emphasizes how creative the "Little Lawyer"[25] is in finding strategies that meet several needs or desires simultaneously (condensation); in Berne's script theory, the Child's role is above all to find a compromise as rewarding as possible between its creative expression of Self and its search for others' acceptance or love.

   If the Child motivates the person to achieve something at all costs, it can give them an almost indomitable energy; were it not for the other two systems' influence, they would not shy away from any stratagem or sacrifice. If, for example, the Adult system assesses a goal as unreachable, the Child system does not automatically give up; it may continue its impossible quest "behind the backs" of the other systems for years or even for a lifetime. But if the "rubber band snaps", it causes a deep crisis that the person can only overcome through a process of "letting go" or in other words, "mourning".

One example is how love can survive even after an atrocious experience. Another example is as following: a woman is systematically belittled by her widowed father, who prefers her sister. Yet she is the one who goes to his house every weekend to do the cleaning, cooking and gardening. In her Adult system, she knows that "he won't change", but in her Child system she continues to hold out hope and expect a gesture of gratitude or love, even a simple "thank you". For fear of losing this hope, she cannot even dare to face her rage towards her sister, or even her secret desire: "I would like to be in her place and she in mine". It took her years to "stop waiting" and to decide to mourn the affection she was fully entitled to, but would never have or too late.[26]

2. Actions dominated by the Child system can also be violently impulsive, especially if its earliest strata are aroused without a holding environment. The Child plays a part in many criminal behaviours, in terrorism or in outbursts spurred by combat or war situations; alcohol or drug addicts consume impulsively without even having the time to realize with their Adult system what they are doing.

However, this happens only when there is no relationship to another person providing a holding environment[27] and when the Adult and Parent systems' influence is deficient, because either these systems have not evolved in a healthy way, or they are disconnected, or because they conspire with the Child system (for example, by providing it with Parent-like approval, e.g., "Any harm you do to an enemy is heroic").

3. Strategies coming from the Child system are known for their propensity to "magic". This comes from the Child relationship with what it can imagine and from its inability to distinguish between what is effective and what is illusory. "Magic" comes in many forms, some of which are listed below:

- an action from the inside to the outside through thought, wish or emotion. For example, the Child perceives "I would like to hit him" as the same as having actually hit him; experiencing guilt about thoughts or wishes often obeys this mechanism;
- a "superstitious" action: crossing fingers, touch wood, etc.;
- an action that is not connected to its goal by a recognizable cause-and-effect link: "I'm going to be very good so that Mommy will get well"; often this type of action leads to panic in the Child system, which starts to "do more of the same" in the absence of any result;
- an action crossing the boundaries between people: trying to relieve someone's suffering by suffering in their place…

TRANSACTIONAL TEXTS ON THE CHILD SYSTEM

Berne

1. *The repetition perspective.*
The repetition perspective is the one, Berne and his successors usually adopt when they talk about the Child system on its own. Berne describes it as if the

child that the person once was bursts into the present. Among many texts, several of which have already been quoted, is this excerpt from Chapter 19 on "regression analysis":

> The position is just the same as if there were two people in the room with the therapist: an observing adult and a pathological child, except they are physically inseparable. The problem is how to separate them psychologically so that the child can speak for himself (…). When a previously buried archaic ego state is revived in its full vividness in the waking state, it is then permanently at the disposal of the patient and the therapist for detailed examination. Not only do "abreaction" and "working through" take place, but the ego state can be treated like an actual child. It can be nurtured carefully, even tenderly until it unfolds like a flower, revealing all the complexities of its internal structure (…). Such an active ego state is not regarded as a memory (…) but as an experience in its own right.[28]

2. Berne uses the sequential or descriptive perspective to identify ego states in the repetition perspective. The text on the three systems' function in *Game people play* restates the metaphor "the Child system is like a child": "In the Child resides intuition, creativity and spontaneous drive and enjoyment".[29] Mr Quint, on the other hand, from whom the Child is excluded, "was devoid of the charm, spontaneity and fun which are characteristic of the healthy child".[30]
3. For the interaction perspective, we examined in Chapter 3 Berne's texts on the *function of* the Child system as an organizer of biological programming.

Furthermore, in his use of descriptive terms, Berne distinguishes between two main types of the Child system's manifestations: the "adapted" style, where it complies with the demands or desires of an external or internal Parent, and the "free" style, where it acts according to its own[31] tendencies. However, this distinction is not only descriptive: it leads to the interaction perspective through the concept of *influence*. These two forms of manifestation, in fact, allow us to hypothesize the presence or absence[32] of influence from the Parent system:

> The adapted Child is manifested by behavior which is inferentially under the dominance of the Parental influence, such as compliance or withdrawal. The natural Child is manifested by autonomous[33] forms of behavior such as rebelliousness or self-indulgence.[34]

Note that in *What do you say after you say Hello?*, Berne separates the rebellious attitude from the free[35] attitude. Both the rebellious and the adapted attitudes indicate a Parent's influence.

In addition, Berne regularly shows the Child seeking *gratifications*. In psychological games, and especially in rackets, he shows the Child acts "behind the back" of the Adult and the Parent[36] looking around for suspicious "advantages".[37]

While Berne sometimes describes these gratifications in Freudian drive terms, he usually emphasizes the craving for strokes, either harbingering or joining many psychoanalytic[38] currents in their view on social importance.

4. Finally, Berne does not doubt that the Child system is a *positive resource* for the person. From his first two articles on ego states,[39] to *Transactional Analysis and Psychotherapy*,[40] to his last book, he adheres to the idea that the Child system cannot be called "infantile" in a pejorative way. He even states that it contains "the most valuable part of his personality".[41]

At the time, the prevailing concept was to consider all manifestations of the psyche's earliest strata as regressive or pathological. Even today, psychodynamic approaches think along these lines, although data provided by D. Stern[42] and others on child development show the opposite. Berne, however, not only veers from this point of view, but he also overturns it: childhood becomes a "lost paradise" that, ideally, one would like to reach; "we are born princes and the process of education makes us frogs".[43]

We can certainly join Berne in his wonder at children's capacities. However, let us not forget that these capacities cause them much suffering and make them more vulnerable when in contact with an adult's early strata, especially the script protocol.

Early transactionalists

- According to the reparenting school,

The Child is the most clever ego state. Its primary concern is how to maximize gratification or comfort and minimize discomfort.[44]

- Another text about the Child system from the redecision school shows how its founders (R. and M. Goulding) are in line with the evolutionary perspective:

Some TA transactionalists believe that the Child ego state stops developing at an early age. We see the Child as ever growing and ever developing, as the sum total of the experiences he has had and is having in the present. [...] A woman of 50 may drive with comfort in a large heavy car, but when she is driving in a small, light subcontact, she behaves as she is about to be struck by an approaching truck, as she relives again the time when she was hit by a truck at age 40. Her Adult knows it is the same, but nonetheless she *feels* as if she were back in that other just before the accident. The Child develops. We have stressed that the *Child* does the work. The Child both experiences and copies, and then incorporates. [...] Therefore, if he takes in originally, and if he continues to take in as he grows, mature, and ages, he can change, re-experience, and realign — from his own decisions and redecisions. This is tremendously important from a practical, therapeutic position.[45]

Debates

Around 1990, many transactionalists from a psychoanalytic background became increasingly sceptical about the idea of a Child system as a resource for the person: "Personally", said one, "I no longer treat the Child as a healthy, appropriate and necessary ego state".[46]

The repetition perspective becomes exclusive to Erskine and Trautmann's ego states theory and to the authors who take it up. The Child system is considered only under its repetitive aspect, whereas its function (in the literal sense) and all its positive usefulness are transferred to the integrated Adult, which collects all the positive functions of the personality systems:

> This neopsychic state of the ego was contrasted by Berne with an archaic ego state which consists of fixations at earlier developmental stages. (...) This Child ego state perceives the external world and internal needs and sensations as the person did in an earlier developmental stage. Although the person may appear to be relating to current reality, he or she is actually experiencing what is happening with the intellectual, social and emotional capacities of a child at the developmental age of unresolved trauma or confusion, i.e., fixation. (...) The Child or archaic states of the ego are the *entire personality* of a person *as he was in a previous developmental period of time*. This includes the needs, desires, urges and sensations; the defence mechanisms; and the thought processes, perceptions, feelings, and behaviors of the developmental phase where fixation occurred. The archaic state of the ego is the result of developmental arrest which occurred when critical early childhood needs for contact were not met. The child's defences against the discomfort of the unmet needs became egotized-fixated; the experience cannot be fully integrated into the Adult ego states until these defence mechanisms are dissolved.[47]

This repetition in the Child system leads to a postulate: when a Child ego state is free, it becomes *ipso facto* an element of the integrated Adult. In the interaction perspective discussed here, one does not see how a Child ego state could become an Adult ego state, since the two systems have different functions, each one essential to existence. Not only a Child ego state that ceases to be fixed remain a Child ego state, but it (re)becomes a Child ego state with all its diversity, i.e., capable of evolution and likely to serve as material for the person's creativity and development. This perspective agrees with Erskine and Trautmann on the key point that the Child is always likely to be integrated or included in evolutionary combinations of ego states. That is what this theory expresses with the concept of an integrated Adult at the origin of all evolution. But the evolution perspective does not involve any unification of the integrated elements in a single ego state; on the contrary, it implies that they keep their own function, but are now connected through a higher-level coordination.

Peg Blackstone, in her paper integrating TA, object relations theory and Self psychology,[48] shows that it is not necessary to devalue the Child and make it an exclusively pathological system in order to integrate these approaches. She convincingly supports the plausibility of the following conclusions:

1. the Child (C2) develops throughout life;
2. the pathology in C2 reflects that which marred the child's original relationship with those who cared for them;
3. C2 does not only contain pathological fixations;
4. using an E2 metaphor such as the "Inner Child" in the therapeutic context can facilitate change.[49]

Blackstone quotes Erskine's passage above and comments:

> Here Erskine seemed to equate the terms "archaic," "arrested," and "defensive." By implication, then, C2, as the archaic ego state, must be pathological and definitely in need of work. Replying to Goulding and others on the panel (Erskine et al., 1988), Erskine said, "I hope your Child is not growing, and that it's also shrinking to the point where it's integrated within the Adult" (p. 9). I believe this is a limited way to think about the Child ego state. I agree with Clarkson in understanding archaic states to be historic states, not just fixated ones, that is, the view that C2 is dynamic and healthy.[50]

This is not just a theoretical controversy: it implies a difference in our conception of the human person and our relationship to the earliest, still active strata of our development. Blackstone's position, like mine, does not turn away from what is most archaic and crude, even brutal, in us. On the contrary, both are based on the idea that part of our task is to provide a holding environment for these aspects, to understand them and even to make them our allies as far as possible.[51] This implies being aware that we cannot do without them to develop ourselves, and that it is illusory to pretend to draw a rigid boundary within ourselves that would separate development and creativity from our archaic aspects.

Notes

1 See WALDEKRANZ-PISELLI, C.K., 1999.
2 See among others BERNE, E., 1961, pp. 60–61. BERNE, E., 1964a, p.14–15., etc. STEINER, C., 1971.
3 Especially Erskine and Trautmann's integrative psychotherapy, "transactional psychoanalysis", relational TA and co-creative TA. See GRÉGOIRE, J., 2007c[ES].
4 ERSKINE, R.G., and TRAUTMANN, R., 1996, *TAJ* 26, 4.
5 In its earliest strata, the Other can be perceived as an instrument at the service of the Self, what H. Kohut and the psychology of the Self call a "Self-object" (OPPENHEIMER, A., 1996). BLACKSTONE, P., 1993, reminds us that the persistence of such relationships in adulthood is not pathological.

6   We must beware here of the tendency, favoured by the classification of the descriptive (so-called "functional") model, to attribute exclusively to the Parent any *behaviour* or *attitude* of the type "taking care of" or "wanting the good of", or simply "showing benevolence". From an interaction perspective, these behaviours, like all others, have a Child component which is discussed here.
7   STEINER, C., 1974, speaks of a "position hunger".
8   Maslow, A.H., 1968.
9   Others' desires, imaginations and fantasies are the Parent responsibility.
10 See LAPLANCHE, J., and PONTALIS, J., 1967, art. "Désir", pp. 120–122, and "Fantasme", pp. 152–157.
11 ERSKINE, G., and ZALCMAN, M., 1979.
12 These are verbs such as "can, may, must…".
13 Telling some children "Don't overturn the vase!" is like suggesting that they do. People who are addicted to alcohol or drugs are familiar with these mechanisms: repeatedly saying or hearing "Don't go for a beer" reinforces their inner image of it and increases their desire.
14 BERNE, E., 1972, pp.100–101.
15 Training in natural language processing verbal aspects and Ericksonian hypnosis is largely aimed at talking to the person in the context of their Child system.
16 STERN, D., 1985.
17 See CORNELL, W.F., and LANDAICHE, M.N., 2006.
18 ERSKINE, R.G., 1988.
19 ERSKINE, 1974, named "rubberband" the present situation's aspect which can "recall" the early situation.
20 ERSKINE, R.G., and TRAUTMANN, R., 1990.
21 The group is not a person, but interactions between participants end up weaving a network of common associations.
22 See WINNICOTT, D.W., 1971.
23 The Adult and Parent systems are not excluded: they will take part, but on the basis of what the Child system has "invented".
24 R. Erskine and M. Zalcman have also distinguished beliefs about the Self, about Others and about quality of life. ERSKINE, R.G., and ZALCMAN, M., 1979.
25 BERNE, E., 1972, pp. 104–106.
26 R. and M. Goulding repeatedly asked the question "How much longer are you going to wait for him/her to change?"
27 See the concept of "holding environment" again in Chapter 13 on relationships.
28 BERNE, E., 1961, pp. 177–178.
29 BERNE, E., 1964a, p. 27.
30 BERNE, E., 1961, p. 25.
31 For example, BERNE, E., 1961, p. 14.
32 From the interaction perspective, the idea of a system completely removed from the influence of another can only be an approximation.
33 See the note on the meaning of "autonomous" in *Transactional Analysis and Psychotherapy*, p. 35.
34 BERNE, E., 1961, p. 53. See ibid, p. 191.
35 BERNE, E., 1972, p. 13.
36 BERNE, E., 1966, pp. 307–309.
37 BERNE, E, 1964a, pp. 50–51.
38 NOVELLINO, M., 2005.

39 BERNE, E., 1957b, p. 142.
40 BERNE, E., 1961, p. 186–187.
41 BERNE, E., 1972, p. 12.
42 STERN, D., 1985.
43 BERNE, E., 1972, p. 203.
44 SCHIFF, J., a.o., p. 24.
45 GOULDING, R., and GOULDING, M., 1979, p. 20.
46 CORSOVER, H., quoted in BLACKSTONE, P., *TAJ* 23, 4, 1993, p. 216.
47 ERSKINE, R.G., 1988, *TAJ* 18, 1, 1988, pp. 15–19.
48 BLACKSTONE, P., *TAJ* 23, 4, 1993, pp. 216–234.
49 BLACKSTONE, P., *TAJ* 23, 4, 1993, p. 233.
50 BLACKSTONE, P., 1993^{ES}, *TAJ* 23, 4, 1993, p. 219.
51 In his conception of the encounter with archetypes, G. Jung presents them as potentially destructive insofar as they are not integrated, but as unexpectedly rich resources when they are. See von FRANZ, M.L., 1964.

6

THE PARENT

The system that internalizes

In some ways, the Parent system is symmetrical to the Child system. The Child's function is to organize the person's experiences according to its subjective dimension, which gives an essential place to their experience. The opposite is true for the Parent, which is focused first and foremost on the Other(s) and on their reactions, as they are perceived by the person.

In any relational experience, the Other's reactions are an essential complement to the person's reactions: they are like the opposite sides of the same coin. If a relational experience is memorized, then both poles of the relationship, the Self and the Other, must be memorized at the same time. Without this, the memory is useless. Like a telephone conversation in which only one speaker can be heard, it only makes sense if we know what the Other may have done or said. A memory from the Child system, focused on the person's reactions, usually has no meaning or usefulness without the associated memory in the Parent system, nor without the Adult memory allowing the whole to be combined into an intelligible narrative. In other words, the experience's aspect recorded in each system necessarily refers to the corresponding ego state trio, especially in relational experiences, whether they are recorded at the level of implicit memory alone or simultaneously at the level of implicit and explicit memory.

The Other's experience is crucial to us for a second reason: as we are part of a relational and social world we did not invent, we need others to introduce us to it and to do as they do, at least initially.

We cannot do without the Other's experience. Its organizer is the Parent system. Berne gives it the role of organizing "external programming", which means that its *function* is to be in touch with what we assimilate from others. The important points assimilated in this way are usually elaborated on by the individual, but this usually only happens later.

Parent system, autonomy and creativity

The Parent system is like a gateway, an antechamber or a vestibule, through which others' reactions are assimilated by the person. Is this a permanent threat to our autonomy and creativity?

In the 1960s, Berne and many of his colleagues believed it. As a result, the Parent system usually got a bad press with them[1]: it was the system that turned the Prince or Princess into a frog. Some texts even implied that the best way to reach autonomy would be to put the Parent system out of action[2] altogether. The music roll image Berne[3] uses implies two possibilities only: either the piano plays in our stead, or we improvise from scratch. But there is *no creativity without a pre-existing base*. In music, for example, there is no improvisation, especially when collective, that is not based on a theme or at least on a chord sequence. With his study on geniuses' creative strategies in very different fields, like Mozart or Einstein, Dilts[4] showed that human creativity always operates on something already existing, even if it is in opposition to it. Great creators were not 'feral children', but people who had integrated their predecessors' work well enough to own its resources... and to perceive its limits. Quantum mechanics is not conceivable without classical physics, the Renaissance would not have been possible without Ancient History and Middle Ages, nor literary Realism without Romanticism against which it reacted, and so on.

This is how it is in our personal existence: to create, we have to position ourselves in front of something that others have created. This means the Parent role is neither demonized nor overestimated. From the repetition perspective, it does lead to a limitation of our autonomy, but from the interaction and evolution perspectives, it provides us with material for our creativity. Sometimes this creativity expands what we have been taught; sometimes it goes in the opposite direction; sometimes it transposes into a completely different framework or gives a completely different meaning; but it never starts from nothing.[5]

Perception

The material on which the Parent works, complementary to the Child and Adult, is above all the relational experience in all its dimensions. In this domain, *all reactions and interactions can be internalized*. The Child system memorizes the person's experience, the Parent system memorizes the Other's experience, the Adult memorizes the overall vision connecting the two. Of course, the Other's experience is internalized as the person has perceived it and represented it to themselves at the time of internalizing; while this perception often includes very perceptive intuitions, it is not immune to imaginary or projective distortions. We will begin by exploring how the human being perceives someone else's experience.

Our perception of others' experiences

Berne highlights how insightful our perception of others[6] is. From the repetition perspective, his examples show to what extent and with what precision someone else's experience can be reproduced years later if this experience has been internalized in the Parent system. This demonstrates how acute our intuitive perception of someone else is and how inclusive of all dimensions in their experience: body, emotion, imagination, thought and behaviour. Of course, we do not perceive everything that others experience, and this knowledge is by no means infallible; furthermore, we can only express a small part of it in words. However, it is much more accurate and deeper than we believe; in addition, it would be a mistake to reduce this perception to external behaviour and words. Internalized experiences often turn out to be much richer and more precise than the person imagines. The parent interview[7] is a good example: often the person "discovers" aspects of the parent figure's experience that they had internalized without being aware of them.

We often have a very powerful intuition of what others' Child system contains, especially if we have a close connection with them. This remains the case even if these others do not know about this content or disavow it. Children know a lot about their parents' desires and fears for them, even if they have not been expressed openly. They know that Daddy's dream is that they will be engineers, musicians, doctors, teachers, priests, union activists…, or that Mummy's never-expressed fear is that she will be alone and that her secret desire is for one of her children to be with her in her old age. These parental desires can also be negative: do not become a politician, a nurse, a craftsman, there has never been a divorce in the family, women in our family have never been good at maths, etc.

Internalizing both relationship and communication

In any given situation, *both relationship and communication can be registered in Child, Parent and Adult ego states*. Internalizing includes verbal, para-verbal and non-verbal. It may also include processes such as permission, protection and potency, or conversely, manipulation, intimidation, psychological games and power plays. In their article on script elaboration, Conway and Clarkson[8] listed nine processes: positive or negative use of shock or extreme emotional states, pain, febrile delirium, intimate physical contact, confrontation with an impossible task, insufficient stimulation, excessive stimulation, cross-transactions (or redefinition), systematic disregard for the person's autonomy or abuse of personal power. All these processes can be internalized together with the transaction content. Another process is Martorell's "mystification": "Mystification involves giving a plausible but false explanation of some aspect of reality, whether it is something that is happening, something that someone does, or something that a person feels, notices, or is. Mystification hides or rejects an aspect of reality, and it always assumes a predetermined outcome. It forces reality in a certain direction, and consequently, mystification can be linked to maintaining power and to power itself".[9]

Internalizing from an observer position

What the Parent system sees is not restricted to direct interactions between the person and another person. It also includes other reactions the person *witnesses*: for example, the way the father treats siblings, and the relationship between the parents themselves.

The Parent system may also internalize *stories* told by others, whether they are about the person's own history, family, race, nation, etc., or in the form of myths or tales. This may happen, especially if these stories are of interest to the Child system (influence), because they can be seen as conveying information about "What happens to someone like me?", "Who am I in the eyes of others?".

Internalizing sources

"*To whom* does the Parent look for information?"

Anyone's experiences can be internalized. Of course, this will happen more often if the Other "matters" in the person's life, hence the importance of parents. To "matter" comes in various ways: a grandmother, a nanny, an older brother or sister, a childhood friend, a "master" who was a model and a guide, a teacher with whom the relationship was particularly close or hostile, a neighbourhood bully, a stranger who uttered insults in the metro, a persecutor or a rapist...

The Parent does not look for information exclusively from individuals. It can be from *groups* of varying sizes, from school friends to larger cultural groups: men or women, age groups, groups of various professional, social, religious or philosophical, national or international backgrounds.

Here is an example: a teenage girl, whose parents are both teachers and whose intellectual potential is high, has recorded in her parent system their message, "Do well in class". But what she hears from her peer group is: "As long as you pass, what's the point of trying harder?" And in her case, the latter message prevails: she manages brilliantly... to just about pass, much to the annoyance of her parents, but in a way that makes her acceptable to the group.[10]

The social Parent is very close to "habitus", a concept introduced by the French sociologist Pierre Bourdieu. Habitus is what makes individuals capable, within a given social context, of adapting to the possibilities and constraints of that context. It is not restrictive, as it also has a creative aspect that allows the individual "regulated improvisations"[11] within the socially accepted frame of reference. Although past experiences often have a decisive weight in it, habitus is enriched by experience and can inspire new actions: it is "capable of inventing, in the presence of new situations, new ways of fulfilling old functions".[12] It is essentially evolutionary: "Habitus is never done once and for all, it evolves through adjustment to the conditions of action, which themselves evolve".[13]

Bernard Lahire, who was Bourdieu's student, reacted on one particular point: Bourdieu generally speaks of a single habitus linked to social class, whereas Lahire describes a social process in which belonging and habitus are manifold. Habitus is manifold, because it is always linked to a context: one of the things that education teaches the child is precisely to behave differently in different environments, the firsts being family and school. Although these different contexts generate "multiple opportunities for misalignment and crisis",[14] they also constitute an invitation for the individual to implement personal decisions and creativity.

Memorization: its conscious and unconscious aspects

The Parent memorizes its perceptions, then uses them as material for its elaboration phase. The following terms are distinctive and should not be considered as interchangeable:

- "*Internalizing*" refers to the fact that the person absorbs an external content, they then consider as belonging to themselves to the point of saying "I", when they put it into action. In this book, we will use "internalizing" in this sense (although many authors, influenced by the object relations theory, use the term with the same meaning as "introjection").
- Some experiences are "*introjections*", which is the name of an unconscious defence mechanism where the Other is internalized to alleviate separation anxiety or to compensate for social[15] failure.
- In psychoanalysis, the term "*identification*" covers many different mechanisms, which J. Laplanche and J. Pontalis group together in this overall definition: "a psychological process by which a person assimilates an aspect, a property, an attribute from the other person and, totally or partially, transforms themselves, on the model of the latter; a personality is comprized of and differentiated by a series of identifications".[16]
- Finally, the term "*imitation*" implies the reproduction of a behaviour that the person does or did observe. It implies an Adult intervention: it can examine the "model" and check if the imitation matches.

Evolution

The Parent and Stern's theory

Stern[17] develops two concepts about the Parent system and its function:

- the *self-regulating*[18] *Other*, which we have already encountered in Chapter 4: initially, the child is dependent on this "Other" (usually the mother) to meet its physical needs and internal reactions. The child will then have to perform this task themselves more and more, so that they will gradually have to internalize it.
- the *evoked*[19] *companion*, which begins with the appearance of the core Self (around two- or three-month-old). The first forms of what can be called a positive archaic Parent are found there. The evoked companion is the experience of an imaginary presence elaborated from real encounters, in other words a true Parent ego state: "The evoked companion is an experience of being with, or in the presence of, a Self-regulating Other, which may occur in or out of awareness".[20]

This phenomenon is essentially beneficial. The evoked companion is a *point of reference* to first "compare the current interactive experience (…) with the simultaneously occurring experience with the evoked companion",[21] then either to integrate it into an already existing generalized representation or to create a new one. Furthermore, the evoked companion allows the child to relive a past situation *when alone*, with an intensity almost as strong as in the presence of the real Other. In this case, "It is partly a social response, but (…) it occurs in a non-social situation. (…) So that even if actually alone, the infant is 'being with' a Self-regulating Other in the form of prototypic lived events".[22] This is what we call an internalized Parent ego state based on social experiences.

Interestingly, according to Stern, the experience of the evoked companion is not fusional; on the contrary, "the integrity of core sense of Self and Other is never breached in the presence of an evoked companion".[23] The child does not absorb themselves into the Other and does not absorb the Other: it is a true relational situation. In transactional terms, we would say that, very early, the archaic Parent (Stern's core Other) is distinct from the archaic Child (Stern's core Self), even if it belongs to the same ego state trio. The evoked companion's experience differs entirely from repetitions of the parental figures' reactions, during destructive enactments emanating from the script protocol, where it seems that the person's internal Parent has momentarily attributed to itself both the executive power and the "real Self" without any counterpart.

Stern adds that "The evoked companions never disappear. They lie dormant throughout life, and while they are always retrievable, their degree of activation is variable".[24] They become latent ego states, waiting to be reactivated.

This system also evolves so that, from a certain point in development, this evocation is no longer necessary: the child can draw on its own experience and use more cognitive, less emotional and less absorbing representations, freeing up its attention and energy for other tasks. This step is just as necessary for personal development as the evoked companion is; systems must be allowed to evolve; initial workings must give way to richer and more complex processes as development strata are laid one on another.

From internalizing to rules and values

1. The Parent system begins by internalizing others' reactions "as they are" and, according to Berne, ends by being a holder for rules and values. Berne moves from one to the other with surprising casualness. Two pages apart, he can state that "the Parent is the guide to ethical aspirations and empyrean esuriences", then refer to it as the origin of "voices" in schizophrenia,[25] without explaining how this shift is possible. The distance between this starting point and this ending point, however, implies a very long evolution. According to J. Piaget[26] and R. Kegan,[27] values such as collective ideals only come into play at the stage of formal thought during adolescence. This requires an organizing system that manages both the transformation of what we have taken from others (i.e., the Parent system) and its interaction with an evolved Adult system. From the interaction perspective, I would add that the Child system must also benefit from this evolution in order not to destroy its effects.

2. Shea Schiff[28] has described the Parent developmental phase in his "parental systems" theory.[29] His perspective is based on the following idea: initially, the Parent system assimilates others' reactions as ready-made patterns. A *model* simply states that "this thing is done this way": Dad kisses Mom, Mom puts oil in the pan before using it, the neighbour yells, my older brother slams the door, my uncle gets drunk and so on. These patterns gradually generate *rules*. From "Every time I hit my little brother, Mom gets mad" or "Dad won't let me put my elbows on the table", the Parent system elaborates elementary rules: "I can't hit my little brother", "I can't put my elbows on the table". Shea Schiff does not mention generalized representations, but their mechanism is clearly what he describes.

According to Shea Schiff, this jumble of rules[30] initially lacks structure.

- There is *no hierarchy* between rules: "Do not hit your little brother" is no more important than "Do not put your elbows on the table". They are both forbidden, full stop!
- Rules are absolute, i.e., there are *no exceptions*. "Do not steal fruit from a shop" stands always and everywhere, even for a starving person.
- There is *no method for resolving conflicts between rules:* if Mom and Dad give opposite orders, the Parent gets stuck (and leaves the decision to the other systems).

The Parent System's[31] development, if left undisturbed, ultimately leads to a set of rules that:

- are hierarchical (it is more important not to hit someone than not to put your elbows on the table);
- may have exceptions based on particular circumstances;
- give procedures for resolving possible conflicts between them.

In this progressive association mode, models are gradually related to one other, prioritized and made more flexible. This process culminates in the development of a personal value system: refining their models, the child will increasingly be able to orientate themselves according to personal values. At least, this is what happens if the Parent system's evolution is not interrupted; that happens especially when the person's models and rules are inconsistent or non-existent,[32] which makes this process impossible.

3. What R. Kegan said about moral sense's development clarifies the evolution process of the Parent verbal strata. Based on Kohlberg's[33] studies on the child's and adolescent's "moral sense", Kegan describes their successive motivations, comparing them with Piaget's "stages":

- Two to five years old: submission to authority or fear of punishment.
- Six to ten: respect for the benefit of others, which makes it possible to demand that others do the same for you.
- From 11: the desire to be a "good person" in one's own eyes and in the eyes of others.

- Up to 18: the group's benefit comes over the individual's.
- Their ethical motivation takes into account the value of the Other.
- Finally, their universal values: at this stage, the young adult understands, for example, that respect for the individual takes precedence over the group's racial prejudices.[34]

Whether one accepts this elaboration's details or not, it confirms two points about the Parent system and ego state theory:

- The repetition perspective alone is not enough to understand the link between internalizing others' behaviours and developing coherent moral values. Like any living system, the Parent system is essentially an evolving system, and this evolution does not stop with the verbal stratum's appearance, nor with childhood; indeed, it goes on throughout the life.
- The evolution of one personality system is not possible without the influence of the other two systems, which are evolving themselves. This is particularly true for the Adult system: for example, universal value implies that the person can make generalizations beyond their immediate[35] experience.

"Sorting out the legacy"

Life would undoubtedly be better if the Parent was equipped from the outset with a sorting system sophisticated enough to retain only others' positive patterns and judgements. However, "sorting out the legacy" is a complex process which can only be achieved after a long evolution and which requires other systems' influence. At first, the Parent registers all others' reactions in a jumble, whatever they may be, without considering their mutual contradictions. Later, it develops a sorting system capable of rejecting what does not suit.

The Parent development of rules and values does not produce consistent results. It very often includes different rules depending on circumstances: ways differ between work and home, language tolerance is not the same for men and women, reactions change from one cultural environment to another, etc.

Inevitably, a person's internalized experiences involve contradictions:

- Contradictions within people: the people from whom the person draw their models may have internal contradictions. They may act in ignorance of their desire (which is nevertheless usually internalized), or they may act in a "Do as I say, not as I do" mode; they may be ambivalent themselves or they may go back and forth between contradictory models.
- Contradictions between people: for example, Dad gives the model of abusive alcohol use, while Mom says that alcohol has ruined his life.
- Contradictions in groups' messages and cultural messages: for example, our society continues to be tolerant of alcohol while berating addicts.

All these contradictions can be internalized and become established within the Parent system.

Impact on the action

As far as implicit memory is concerned, the Parent system can lead us to impulsive reactions where we do to ourselves or to others what was once done to us, and where we react as others reacted to us. This is not necessarily a problem: for example, we can act in this way as a "self-regulating Other" for our children, at least as long as they do not need a different education from ours, or a more lively contact with our Child system. But it can be harmful: it is through the same process that a trauma victim may later become an abuser.

As for explicit memory, the verbal and symbolic dimension of family rules, social and cultural rules and ethical values comes as another layer over these internalized models.

For both types of memory, the Parent system acts first on the person; this is what Berne calls the "internal Parent" or the Parental influence. It acts mainly on the Child system, but also on the Adult system, because it can either encourage Adult investigations or label certain subjects as "taboo" (death, sexuality, "family secrets"; groups' or institutions' unspoken issues). The Parent turns into a control centre for the person's internal and external life: it can allow or forbid not only behaviours, but also various thoughts and experiences for the person's imagination, fantasies or body. If its prohibitions fail, it can still manifest its disapproval via the intrapsychic, for example, in guilt. Script theory is built on the idea that most script limitations, originally internalized from parental figures, emanate from this internal Parent. The interaction perspective also considers permissions and prohibitions from the Child system; to be more precise, it assumes all three systems have their role in setting up script elements.

The Parent system acts towards other people: this is the "external Parent", where the person, under the influence of their own Parent system's contents, encourages others to act in accordance with them. This external Parent can be permissive, limiting or forbidding, fanatical or tolerant. The other two systems also tend to "rally others to their cause", the Adult system to convince them of its vision of "what is real", the Child system to benefit from them in its search for gratification or protection from frustration.

The internal and external Parent are sometimes concordant (the person treats others as they treat themselves), sometimes divergent (many people, for example, are very tolerant of others, but ruthless with their own weaknesses, or vice versa).

The Parent system also acts in transference. Drawing on its usually implicit memory of others' reactions in its past, it expects the Other to act in the same way. The Child system wants and/or fears this repetition. Both systems push the person to behave accordingly in a relationship.

SOME TRANSACTIONAL TEXTS ABOUT THE PARENT SYSTEM

The specific function of the Parent system for Berne

In the seminal text about the transactional psychic apparatus in *Transactional Analysis and Psychotherapy*, Berne defines the Parent system through its function, as an external programming's organizer (see Chapter 3).

The Parent according to the redecision school

As with the Child system, most transactional texts dealing with the Parent on its own are about the sequential or repetition perspective. Consequently, there are few texts concerning the Parent system's evolution.

R. and M. Goulding, however, take for granted that Parent contents are constantly changing. They state that every element of our mental equipment has a positive aspect, including P1, which they understand here as an early state of the Parent system:

> The young child also develops a rudimentary Parent ego state, labelled P1. [...] The early Parent is the incorporation of the real parents by the nonverbal child and is compried of the child's early *perception* of his parents' behavior and feelings, prior to the recognition of language. [...] It is this irrational, destructive element in the early Parent that some TA therapists consider to be the totality of P1. They may call this early ego state the Witch mother, the Ogre father and the Pig parent. *We object to this nomenclature.* It is pejorative, and we object to pejorative terms in scientific literature. Also, such labelling ignores the part of that is nurturing, as well as the part that is the incorporation of joyful, excited messages from the Child ego state of father and mother.[36]

This early Parent is covered by the conscious verbal Parent, labelled "P2":

> We view the Parent as the sum total of beliefs, emotions and behaviors that a person *chooses* to incorporate on a remembered, verbal level, plus the Parent he or she creates for self and continues to create throughout live.[37]

Clearly, the authors who developed the parent interviewing procedures and the Parent system therapy, have a connection with the redecision school. These methods consist of getting the person to identify with their own Parent system, or rather with a part of it (usually the Parent from the mother or the Parent from the father) with a two-chair work; this is an imaginary process in which one works with the person in their Parent system as if they "were" the parental[38] figure. These methods from the redecision school are also often used in Erskine and Trautmann's integrative therapy.[39]

The reparenting school

This school describes the Parent system as follows:

> The Parent ego state contains definitions of the world, the Child, and the Child's relationship to the world. (*Example:* "You're going to be the best card player in the world.") It gives prescriptions and advice.

(*Example:* "Scared money never wins"). It demands action or enjoins actions. (*Example:* "Don't just stand there! *Do* something!") It also contains rules and programs for accomplishing certain tasks. (*Example:* "In order to solve a problem you first have to define it.").[40]

This is a content-focused approach, which therefore belongs to the sequential or descriptive perspective.

Erskine and Trautmann's theory of ego states

In this theory, the Parent system is conceptualized as the Child system is:

> Since the child's perception of the caretaker's reactions, emotions and thought processes will differ at various stages of development, so also will the actual content and intrapsychic function of the Parent ego state vary in relation to the developmental age when the introjection occurred. Introjection is a defence mechanism frequently used when there is a lack of full psychological contact between the child and the significant adult; the resulting conflict is internalized so that the conflict can seemingly be more easily managed (…). Introjected elements may remain as a kind of foreign body within the personality, often unaffected by later learning or development but continuing to influence behavior and perception. They constitute an alien chunk of personality, embedded within the ego and experienced phenomenologically as if they were one's own, but in reality, they form a borrowed personality.[41]

I will not repeat this position's critical examination here as my points are the same as for the Child[42] system.

Notes

1. See HOSTIE, R., 1987.
2. See Berne's texts on autonomy in Chapter 11.
3. BERNE, E., 1972, p. 277.
4. DILTS, R., 1995.
5. R. Dilts has shown the diversity of "geniuses'" strategies such as Mozart or Einstein: they all have their starting point in a given prior. See DILTS, R., 1995.
6. The neurobiological support for this capacity could be related to the "mirror neurons", also called "empathic neurons". These are active "when an individual (human or animal) performs an action, when he observes another individual (especially of his own species) performing the same action, or even when he *imagines* such an action". en.wikipedia.org/wiki/Mirror_neuron. See RIZZOLATTI, G., FOLGASSI, I., and GALLESE, V., 2007.
7. McNEEL, J., 1976[ES].
8. CONWAY, A., and CLARKSON, P., 1987.
9. MARTORELL, J.L., 1994, p. 242.

10 Of course, there is *simultaneously* a reaction of the rebellious Child towards the parents and of the adapted Child in relation to the group of friends. Let us not forget that a submissive or rebellious attitude allows us to infer the influence of the Parent; it is the latter that we are talking about here.
11 BOURDIEU, P., 1980, p. 95.
12 BOURDIEU, P., 1980, p. 91.
13 MOUNIER, P., 2001, pp. 43–44.
14 LAHIRE, B., 2001, pp. 56–59.
15 See FOWLIE, H., 2005[ES].
16 LAPLANCHE, J., and PONTALIS, J., 1967, p. 187; "identification", "identification avec l'agresseur", "identification primaire" entries, pp. 187–192. The last sentence refers to the Freudian conception of the Oedipus and its resolution.
17 STERN, D., 1985.
18 See p. 72. STERN, D., 1985, pp. 102–105 and passim.
19 STERN, D., 1985, pp. 111–119.
20 STERN, D., 1985, p. 112.
21 STERN, D., 1985, p. 113.
22 STERN, D., 1985, p. 113.
23 STERN, D., 1985, pp. 115.
24 STERN, D., 1985, p. 115.
25 BERNE, E., 1961, pp. 38 and 40.
26 PIAGET, J., 1932. XYPAS, C., 2001.
27 KEGAN, R., 1982.
28 Shea Schiff's theory was never written down. Kouwenhoven gave an excellent summary of it in KOUWENHOVEN, M., 1982a, 1982b.
29 The term "parental system" here refers to different elaboration degrees of the Parent system's contents; they range from the hyper-structured "neurotic parental system" to the "deficient and absent parental systems" where structuring is minimal or non-existent. SCHIFF, S., quoted in KOUWENHOVEN, M., 1983[ES].
30 Shea Schiff uses the acronym "P1" for this relatively primitive mode of the Parent system. This acronym is ambiguous, as I mentioned in relation to the Child second-order structures (Chapter 4, pp. 81–83). In Shea Schiff's theory, "P1" unambiguously designates an early state of the Parent system.
31 Shea Schiff refers to the elaborate state of the Parent system as "P2".
32 See KOUWENHOVEN, M., 1983 [ES].
33 KOHLBERG, L., 1984.
34 In philosophy, J. Habermas' theory on "discourse ethics" opens the Parent evolution, in interaction with the other two systems, to the critical examination of its own culture's values. HABERMAS, J., 1983, pp. 43–115.
35 For Piaget, this implies an advanced form of the formal operations' "stage". PIAGET, J., 1936. DOLLE, J.M., 1999.
36 GOULDING, M., and GOULDING, R., 1979, p. 16.
37 GOULDING, M., and GOULDING, R., 1979, p. 21.
38 E.g., McNEEL, J., 1976. DASHIELL, S., 1978. MELLOR, K., and ANDREWARTHA, G., 1980.
39 See ERSKINE, R.G., and TRAUTMAN, R., 1996.
40 SCHIFF, J. and others, 1975, p. 23.
41 ERSKINE, R.G., 1988[ES].
42 See pp. 106–108.

7

THE ADULT

The system that integrates reality

The reality system, known as the Adult system, is sensitive to the way reality functions independently from our subjective experiences or desires, and from others' reactions and judgements. This is its function, and it is a necessary complement to the other two systems. Usually speaking, reality (whether ours, others' or the world's) obeys neither our desires nor others' models, for it has its own rules and laws. I want good weather, but it is raining; my family thinks I should be happy and cheerful, but I am not; I would like to be full of energy, but I am tired.

Therefore, we must consider another dimension, away from subjective experiences (ours or others') and away from what we have internalized. In order not to face an endless series of mishaps, we need to keep in mind usual reality rules: "In winter, there probably will not be much sunshine here"; "If I say unpleasant things to another person, they are likely to show irritation"; "If I work too hard, I will be tired and probably will not be able to keep going for very long", etc. When we want, desire or fear one thing, we need to assess how much of it is possible and, if so, what we need to do in order to get what we want. When we feel bound by parental decree to act in a certain way, the mere fact this decree exists does not guarantee that it will be feasible[1] nor that it will lead to positive consequences.

The "constructivist" philosophical perspective holds we can never access reality free from our personal and social constructions; this does not mean the Adult system is any less valuable. This perspective seeks to put right an over-assessment of concepts that would "reify" them, i.e., that would lead to consider them as absolutes. True, the human mind, both collective and individual, can reach a "truth" that is both always "partial as incomplete and partial as biased". In other words, it is neither exhaustive nor free from the points of view and structuring processes that have led to it. It is always the result of an interpretation, which may or may not be well founded. Nevertheless, in real life, we cannot do without a system that allows us to establish and assess how our mind and life articulate logically.[2] This is how the term "reality" is used below: the outcome at a given moment of a never-ending dialogue between conceptual mind and experience.[3] To be able to tell the difference between the "reality" world, the imaginary world and the principles' world is essential to our survival, even though no "genuine" truth is ever reachable. Acquiring this skill is particularly important for people whose reality system has not developed under normal conditions, or has been disrupted by "mystification",[4] ideology, psychosis or neurosis, splitting or trauma.

The Adult system is sometimes devalued because, for most, it seems to lack emotion and creativity. When it is misunderstood, it might seem basic, academic or, as one transactional analyst put it, "hopelessly sane and boring". Berne contributed to this reputation by comparing it to a computer and labelling it as "rational" a little too often. However, Berne insisted on the phenomenological approach, which considers *each* ego state comprises all dimensions of existence: emotion, thought, behaviour, body and imagination. Better use the term "lucidity" than "rationality" to acknowledge the Adult system's rich contribution.

The reality system's function, in the strong sense of the term, implies multiple links to *emotional, even imaginary* experiences:

- on one hand, because searching for or discovering something give rise to emotional experiences such as curiosity, joy or disappointment;
- on the other hand, because *relating to reality is based on emotion.* Authors such as A. Damasio[5] have shown that a person can neither make correct decisions nor act according to their objective if their relationship to emotional experiences is seriously disrupted.

The Adult system aims at reality but that does not make it infallible. It may contain errors, and, quite frequently, its processes lead to only probable conclusions. Moreover, its functioning can be distorted by influences from the other two systems,[6] by external[7] relationships or by an inappropriate attachment to pre-existing conceptions and frames of reference, when it would be time to open to something new.

Perception and memorization

The Adult system perceives what in our life and in the world is *independent of our subjective experience and desire,* as well as others' experience and desire. In everything that happens to us, the Adult system selects "reality", material or social "facts": what is possible or not, what means to use to achieve what goal, etc. Therefore, *any experience* can in principle be perceived and stored in its reality within the Adult system. However, the Adult system can disconnect if the person is experiencing trauma, because what the victim is being subjected to cannot be accommodated in any accessible frame of reference. As a result, they experience the event as literally "unthinkable", unabsorbable by the more recent strata of their personality: only a raw untranslatable memory is stored in the person's implicit memory.

Apart from these tragic cases, the Adult perception complements Child and Parent perceptions. Memorizing its contents is necessary for survival. Here is an example: a young child is in front of an open fire. For the child and its Child system, it is fascinating: there is light, colour, noise and, above all, constant movement. It is essential the child learns without any danger that "it's lovely to look at, but it can burn". Some people take the child's hand gently closer to the fire; the child feels the heat and draws back. At that moment, they *know* "fire can burn". The Child keeps being fascinated by the display and enjoying it, while the Adult has assimilated the necessary information: "It hurts when you touch it".

What happens when the person is in a social situation with one person or more? Their Child is primarily interested in its own experience, while their Parent, on the contrary, is primarily concerned with the others' experiences. The Adult's specific role is to be able to consider interactions *from a viewpoint which can enclose everybody in a single glance*. This "panoramic" position allows interactions and relationships to be understood as such. This does not imply that the person changes position, but that they are able to perceive *both* their own position and the others', without being overwhelmed by either. The expression "distancing oneself" is inadequate here, as it gives the impression of breaking contact: it would be better to use *"wider contact"*. In technical terms, the Adult is capable of figuring out similarities and differences while seeing several frames of reference.

For example: a couple has a joint decision to make. He wants to go to the seaside; she wants to go to the mountains. To start with, each is convinced not only that there are "objective" reasons for their choice, but that it is the only "rational" choice possible. For him, sea means rest that they both need, and deep down he blames her for not understanding him and not agreeing with him. For her, mountains mean a change of scenery they "undeniably" both need, and she is baffled he does not accept this obvious solution. Eventually they both listen, explain and, at some point, absorb the other's point of view: he realizes she needs a change of scenery, and she understands he needs rest. They get to a position where it is possible for them to consider both needs.

The Adult system makes it possible to be lucid about oneself; this is called *self-awareness*. Like the other systems, its perception is not limited to external events and relationships; it includes *the intrapsychic content of the other systems*. If someone is regularly irritated by interruptions, either the Child system, the Parent system or both may tend to ignore this tendency; the Reality system will accept it as a fact, not as an object of desire or fear. This does not mean there is no "judgement" in lucidity, but this judgement primarily deals with triggers and internal/external consequences: it does not lead to being unaware of this fact or its significance, nor accepting it blindly, nor feeling guilt or self-aggressiveness.

The Adult system tends towards a "lucid" and reformable perception, which is *not immersed in experience but in contact with it*. Lucidity is the ability to look reality in the face. For example: the past happened as it did; the other person's intentions are not what we thought they were; some of our reactions do not match our self-image; some of our desires, even our most cherished and secret ones, are unattainable… But also: others love and appreciate us; we are successful; we have resources. All this is not without emotions, some of them quite strong…

Conscious and unconscious aspects

"Adult" in TA usually implies consciousness. Berne built his ego state theory in connection with decontamination practice; in this context, the Adult is the gateway to careful reflection (which enables change) and lucid consciousness (which allows autonomy). Like Freud, Berne states the Ego has both conscious and unconscious aspects, though minimizing the latter[8]; in any case, he never spoke about the Adult's unconscious aspects, and neither did his successors, at least until recently.

1. According to Novellino, however, analysing unconscious[9] communication leads to considering such aspects: "(…) my own affirmation of unconscious communication theory, in which I describe the Adult ego state as directly involved in the social and psychological levels of bilogical[10] transactions, in which the psychological level remains unconscious and in fact derives from the Adult ego state".[11] As the psychological message testifies to a lucid perception of the situation, one rightly detects in it the mark of the Adult[12] system; if it does not reach the conscious level, it is because the person cannot for some reason express this content openly, either to themselves or to others.

    The example Novellino gives is the decision to end therapy. Both therapist and client have an obscure feeling that this is not a good idea but, as they can find no rational basis for doubt, they deter themselves from realizing and expressing it. Then, without any apparent connection to the context, the client mentions how sad her daughter is about her art teacher transferred to another school. The therapist, reacting to his own disproportionate discomfort, asks: "Why are you telling me this now?". This allows them to interpret and verbally elucidate the unconscious transaction.

    Note that the Child system also plays its part in this communication by providing the unconscious association, which allows the patient to "say without saying what cannot be said".
2. Unconscious communication is not the only reason to consider unconscious aspects in the Adult system. Object relations theory tells us that, in relational failure, repression includes the memory of the situation itself, together with its associated ego state trio. In some cases, however, the Adult memory remains, while the Child memory and the Parent memory are repressed: this is what happens when the person relates what happened to them in a "neutral" way, as if it had happened to someone else. In other cases, the Adult memory itself disappeared into the unconscious, so that the person cannot even disclose it. In any case, if the person reconnects with the repressed memory, their insight intensity, emotional reactions and subsequent psychic upheaval demonstrate how strong the earlier repression had been. As we have seen, Berne highlighted such processes in his description of phenomenological[13] experience.
3. Last, but very much not least, the idea that the Adult system carries unconscious aspects follows from the concept of development, as elaborated in Chapter 4. If all three personality systems are necessary to exist, each of

them must exist in some form from the beginning of life; consequently, each has early strata characterized by implicit memory. This is also true for the Adult system, since, according to Stern, this memory contains knowledge and skill about how reality functions independently of any subjective state and internalization.

Stern says: "What was not recognized at the time of the formulations (of Spitz, Werner and others) was the extent of the infant's formidable capacities to distill and organize the abstract, global qualities of experience. Infants are not lost at sea in a wash of abstractable qualities of experience. They are gradually and systematically ordering these elements of experience to identify Self-invariant and Other-invariant constellations. (…) This global subjective world of emerging organization is and remains the fundamental domain of human subjectivity. It operates out of awareness as the experiential matrix form which thoughts and perceived forms and identifiable acts and verbalized feelings will later arise. It also acts as the source for ongoing affective appraisals of events. Finally, it is the ultimate reservoir that can be dipped into for all creative experiences. All learning and creative acts begin in the domain of emergent relatedness"[14] (i.e., psyche's earliest strata).

Combining experiences (or ego states) of "generalized representations of interactions" appears to include an Adult dimension, as these representations are independent from the here-and-now experience of both child and the "Other" who looks after them. They are useful to ensure anchoring and to give stable reference points that are progressively independent of the protagonists, open to an evolution towards increasingly vast generalizations.

Forming conclusions and strategies related to affects

Berne states the secondary process is the Adult innate process. It is linked to the psyche's most recent strata (as seen in Chapter 3); it does not concern implicit memory where conclusions are built with generalized representations, as in the other systems.

At conscious and verbal level, in order to explore how reality works independently of our Child and Parent systems' contents, we can implement and combine different approaches: 1) seeing and learning for ourselves; 2) using and testing others' testimony; and 3) checking how coherent an element is with what we already know.

Admitting something simply because someone else says so does not belong to the Adult system but to the Parent system: "Two plus two equals four because the teacher said so". The Adult system checks, often intuitively, whether what is said is believable and probably true: "Two plus two equals four because I have checked it often (at least, I have never experienced it was not true); besides, everyone agrees, and it is unlikely everyone is lying or wrong". The same applies to other types of knowledge: "The Andromeda galaxy exists because people who can test this statement (astronomers) all agree on this point, I think they are competent in their field, and I have no valid reason to doubt their assertion".

To check how consistent an element is with what we already know, "logic" is useful, however usually not in the hypothetical-deductive modality with which mathematical and physical sciences formulate their results[15]: it is, very often, just an intuitive check for non-contradiction.[16]

Impact on the action

Like the other two systems, the Adult is also about action. It develops strategies or skills that answer questions such as: if I set this goal, how can I achieve it? It is the system we use to assess whether a particular strategy will be effective, whether it concerns the physical world, relationships or intrapsychic life, including managing our emotions.

In order to do this, the Adult system must always be able to consider new conclusions, new strategies and inhibit those that are no longer useful.[17] As it records and enters results into its "data bank", this system allows us to learn from our successes and failures, as Berne[18] states.

TRANSACTIONAL TEXTS ABOUT THE ADULT SYSTEM

The Adult specific structural contribution

In *Transactional Analysis and Psychotherapy*'s main theoretical text, Berne states the Adult system organizes probability programming and is connected with the secondary[19] process (as previously said).

In addition, he often describes the Adult system as "adapted to the current reality"[20] or in contact with the here and now.[21] These texts contrast the Adult with the Child and Parent from the repetition perspective. This is particularly useful in his decontamination practice, since it is the Adult who becomes aware of where the Child or Parent comes from; the Adult enables the person to position themself in relation to the Child and the Parent in a new and freer way.

But from the interaction perspective, *being in contact with the here and now cannot be considered to be the Adult exclusive prerogative*, because all three systems have a positive contribution to the person's life, which implies a minimum of contact with the here and now. For the Adult to have that privilege would be in contradiction with texts where Berne states the three systems each have their specific positive contribution to existence.[22] The Adult specificity is that, when it turns to the here and now, it considers it from the reality angle, independently of people's subjective experience and internalized elements.

In *Games people play*, Berne defines the Adult ego states as the "ego states which are autonomously directed towards objective appraisal of reality".[23] While describing the Adult role, Berne mentions the emotions it arouses:

> The Adult is necessary for survival. It processes data and computes the probabilities which are essential for dealing effectively with the outside world. It also experiences its own kinds of setbacks and gratifications.

Crossing a busy highway, for example, requires the processing of a complex series of velocity data; action is suspended until the computations indicate a high degree of probability for reaching the other side safely. The gratifications offered by successful computations of this type afford some of the joys of skiing, flying, sailing, and other mobile sports. Another task of the Adult is to regulate the activities of the Parent and Child, and to mediate objectively between them.[24]

Berne never considers the Adult from the origin perspective, although obviously Adult ego states also have their origin in learning or awareness experiences.

Intuition and the Adult early strata

Before he first published his ego state theory, Berne had been working on the difficult question of intuition for several years and had published articles[25] on this subject. These are of great interest to understand how he came to formulate his ego state theory; they also contain many illuminating elements on unconscious communication and on the Adult early strata.

The first article defines intuition as follows: "The intuitive function is part of a series of perceptive processes which work above and below the level of consciousness in an apparently integrated fashion".[26]

The following articles explore its crucial role in psychological and psychiatric[27] diagnosis and communication.[28] They describe unconscious processes related to early relationships which can without any doubt be attributed to the Child early strata:

> A primal image is the image of an infantile object relationship [...]. (It) is the understanding (correct or incorrect) of the potentialities of the object relationship represented by the image. In the normal adult, under ordinary conditions, neither the primal image nor the primal judgment comes into awareness. Instead, a more or less remote derivative, which is called here an intuition, may become conscious.[29]

> Primal judgment give rise to part of the emotional substance of everyday life. This is most apparent in the encounters with strangers. [...] The significant thing is that all these social judgments are made through social communications. [...] An individual of either sex may merely observe a strange man walking down the street and be impelled to remark: "I'd sure hate to meet him in a dark alley!"[30]

Berne added to this the "ego image"[31] which derives from primal judgements and can become conscious. Berne published both this article on ego image and his first article on ego states the same year:

> The 'ego image' complements the ultimate orientation given by the primal image. It offers a much more useful guide in the preliminary phases of treatment and undiluted forms of treatment, particularly in helping

avoid unnecessary hostile responses whose significance may be clouded by labelling them 'unexpected transferential reactions' [...] The primal image, then, refers to an instinctual orientation, the ego image to an ego state. It is difficult to apply usefully the first piece of information, 'This man is concerned about buggery'. [...] The second message is more useful: 'He is writhing inwardly with almost unbearable embarrassment'. From the moment this message is perceived, it can profitably be applied in the immediate situation. Doubts about the proper technique can be resolved by asking oneself: 'What would I say or do if a three-year-old who was writhing with embarrassment behaved the way this patient is doing?'. This is a much easier question to answer than 'What do you do if a passive anal homosexual behaved the way the patient is doing?'.[32]

Berne, as we can see, shows us how to use intuition and its unconscious sources to get an idea of what the person's Child is experiencing. This is a form of counter-transference analysis, which, in Berne's case, is more specifically oriented towards erogenous zones: "Think sphincter". But what is of interest here is how intuition goes deep into its unconscious sources to get us to know the person as they are with us and not as we dream them to be. This process is the result of an interaction between two systems' early strata: the Child system, which brings its instinctive reaction, and the Adult system, which uses it to grasp the other's experience as it is.

All of Eric Berne's thought, even his epistemology, is centred on intuition. For him, intuition was the main key to understand others, to heal (via decontamination) and to build theory. Hence his repulsion and distrust for intellectualization, both in patients and in therapists: in both cases, he unmasks it as a source of psychological games or power plays. But, unlike many of his contemporaries, he never spoke ill of theory as such.

His studies on intuition led Berne to a firm conclusion. In his very first article, he wrote:

> Intuitive faculties may be more important than is often admitted in influencing judgments about reality in everyday life. The intuitive function is useful and worth cultivating.[33]

All these articles confirm that we have effective ways of acquiring knowledge that cannot be reduced to secondary process, let alone deductive logic. These phenomena are not oddities to therapists, for they are at the heart of how humans communicate and how therapists make an intuitive "diagnosis" at first contact. For Berne, even and perhaps especially when it comes to professional[34] diagnosis, the difference between a beginner and an experienced professional is precisely that the latter can use information that comes to them through unconscious and subconscious channels, notably through counter-transference.

Better than his later works, Berne's articles on intuition foretell how vital the unconscious, transference and counter-transference are; Erskine and Trautmann's integrative psychotherapy, "Transactional Psychoanalysis", relational TA and W. Cornell, today all insist on it.[35]

The "Little Professor"

From *Transactional Analysis and Psychotherapy* onwards, Berne thinks more in terms of repetition perspective than evolution perspective; he uses terms like "second order structure of the Child system". He attributes intuition to the "Adult in the Child", also known as A1, "Little Professor" or "Little Lawyer".[36] Berne is so fascinated by the latter's ability to perceive someone else's personality at first contact that he forgets this type of perception can be seriously flawed when on its own:

> Thus, the Adult in the Child is a keen and perceptive student of human nature, and is therefore called the Professor: In fact, he knows more practical psychology and psychiatry than any grown-up professor does, although after many years of training and experience, a grown-up professor may know as much as thirty-three percent of what he knew when he was four years old.[37]

It should be noted that, for Berne too, this Adult in the Child is unquestionably an early state of the Adult system:

> This kind of shrewdness in appraising and manipulating personal relationships is an important aspect of the growing child's personality and is part of his neopsychic functioning, since it requires sensitive and objective data-processing based on experience.[38]

Is the Adult a computer?

Berne's computer metaphor has often been understood as if he regarded the Adult as emotionless. However, it is clearly not so in his writings. The following passage is complex, but it speaks explicitly of the emotions generated by the Adult in its search for truth:

> The neopsyche is a partially self-programming probability computer designed to control the effectors in dealing with the external environment. It has the special characteristic that its energy state at each epoch is determined by how closely the computed probabilities correspond with the actual results. This energy state is signalled as discharge or overload (e.g., a green light, experienced as pleasure, satisfaction, or admiration; or a red light, experienced as "frustration", disappointment, or indignation.) This characteristic (…) accounts descriptively (…) for the admiration of the striving toward such qualities as responsibility, reliability, sincerity, and courage. Interestingly enough, each of these four qualities can be reduced to a simple probability statement.[39]

In other words, the pleasure or frustration generated by the Adult activity is related to the outcomes "I planned right" or "I was wrong". This is an emotional dimension directly related to the Adult activity. But Berne does not stop there: he goes on to list human qualities in which the Adult plays an essential role:

- responsibility, because it is based on a clear appreciation of one's own role in what has happened;
- honesty and sincerity, because it involves a clear recognition of truth;
- courage, because it involves a correct assessment of risks.

This view of an Adult system not reduced to the cognitive dimension alone makes it possible to understand this:

> Reality-testing is a function of discrete ego states, and not an isolated "capacity" (neopsychic functioning).[40]

In other words, Adult ego states are real ego states involving all dimensions of human experience: body, emotions, imagination, thought and behaviour. They are not reduced to the "faculty" of thought.

Another famous passage on the integrated Adult, or rather on the integrated person,[41] shows how open the Adult system is to ethical and sensitive dimensions.

> Turning now to the Adult, it appears that in many cases certain child-like qualities become integrated into the Adult ego state in a manner different from the contamination process. The mechanism of this "integration" remains to be elucidated, but it can be observed that certain people when functioning qua Adult have a charm and openness of nature which is reminiscent of that exhibited by children. Alongside with these go certain responsible feelings towards the rest of humanity which may be subsumed under the classical term "pathos". On the other hand, there are moral qualities that are universally expected to people who undertake grown-up responsibilities, such attributes as courage, sincerity, loyalty, and reliability, and which meet not mere local prejudices, but a world-wide ethos. In this sense, the Adult can be said to have child-like and ethical aspects, but this remains the most obscure area in structural analysis, so that it is not possible at present to clarify it clinically.[42]

Historically, this text raised many questions of a completely different type, so we discuss it again in Chapter 8 about interactions between ego states.

After Berne

1. The *redecision school* is characterized by the importance of the evolution perspective, although the key role of the repetition perspective in Berne's

theory is never explicitly challenged. R. and M. Goulding start with the early strata, which they call "early Adult":

> The infant begins to make observations about his environment and himself and begins to develop the early Adult (which Berne labelled 'Little Professor' because of its intuitiveness). This developing Adult is labelled A_1. The infant learns, for instance, that the breast or bottle is not part of self but comes and goes: he learns that his fingers and toes are part of himself, and under his control. He is now developing his little storehouse of information. He processes that information and makes decisions based upon it. This information is preverbal and consists of experiential, possibly pictorial, processes.[43]

The proper Adult comes over the early Adult to which R. and M. Goulding, surprisingly, deny any emotional quality:

> The Adult "is an observable state of being, without feelings, in which we store data retrieve data, and act upon data, The difference between the Little Professor, or A_1 and the Adulte, or A_2, is that the Adult has the ability in words to test out the data, to prove it, to discern what is reality in terms of both his own and other's experience and tested information".[44]

2. After Berne, and perhaps already during his lifetime, the idea that an Adult system is richer than its cognitive dimension alone recedes. As early as 1971, transactionalists such as M. James and D. Jongeward wondered whether the Adult "had" emotions or feelings. Their answer is astonishing: it is not the Adult, as such, who has feelings, but rather the "integrated Adult".[45]

    Of course, a system that is deprived of the other two's influences cannot generate either development or creativity. On a theoretical level, however, this formulation diverges from Berne; in his text on the integrated Adult, Berne did not mean a different ego state from the Adult, but the full Adult in all its diversity. Later, Gillespie[46] and Steiner[47] took a stand against R. and M. Goulding's position and for emotions in the Adult system.

3. The *reparenting school* does not grant much autonomy to the Adult, which it seems to reduce to thought:

> The Adult ego state is a data processor and a data bank. It uses the Parent's structure for solving problems. It is not self-cathecting. Only when the Parent or Child requests that the Adult think about something does it so. Most people keep their Adult functioning to some extent all of the time. This is because thinking is a primary survival adaptation.[48]

As a result, these authors consider the Adult to be dependent on the Child influence:

> Fantasy is crucial to effective thinking. For example, memory is a fantasy which has been defined as having been real. Anticipation of events to come and easy preparation (structuring) for those events comes out of fantasies. Perception involves much fantasizing. For example, in looking at a table from an angle where all four legs are not visible, most of us do not have difficulty identifying the object as a table. We utilize fantasy to define that part of the object that cannot be seen. Much of our conceptualizing, that part of our thinking which comes from Little Professor, is a fantasy structure. The Parent ego state is incorporated as a fantasy.[49]

4. In contrast, *Erskine and Trautmann's ego state theory* considerably extends the scope of the integrated Adult text: it makes the Adult the *only* system open to present reality and it denies the Child and Parent any use for development, except in its early phases:

> The Adult ego state consists of current, age-consistent emotional, cognitive, and moral development; the ability to be creative; and the capacity for full, contactful engagement in meaningful relationships. The Adult ego state accounts for and integrates what is occurring moment-by-moment internally and externally, past experiences and their resulting effects, and the psychological influences and identifications with other significant people in one's life.[50]

Erskine and Trautmann's ego state theory is often referred to as the "integrated Adult theory". Actually, "their" integrated Adult has become identical with the person's development and creativity functions, in short with their Self, considered only in its development-promoting aspects. The Adult is no longer a system that interacts with the other two systems, equally essential to existence: it comprises all the person's positive possible selves. It is a bit like deciding to call all the healthy organs of the body "head", so that the terms "lung" and "leg" only refer to their diseased aspects.

5. Novellino defines unconscious communication from the Adult system in these terms:

> Unconscious communication consists of the patient sending the therapist a psychological message, described as follows:
>
> 1. The psychological level is unconscious, that is, inaccessible to consciousness through an act of will.
> 2. The message is sent in a narration centred on facts, events, and people that are extraneous to the therapeutic relationship.

3. The psychological level of the message is not expressed through nonverbal channels (as with psychological games) but by unconsciously constructing associative links.
4. The goal of the message sent on the psychological level is not a payoff but an effort to communicate to the therapist consciously unacceptable emotional content.[51]

This does not, of course, preclude the existence of unconscious communication from the Child or Parent systems, or of synergy between two or three systems.

Notes

1. "Be perfect" is a good example of an unachievable directive, but there are more pernicious and paradoxical ones. LOOMIS, M.E., and LANDSMAN, S.G., 1980, for example, mention in the case of manic-depressive dynamics "You can achieve anything you want... but you will never satisfy me", which implies the paradoxical message "Satisfy me by not satisfying me".
2. See on this issue GREGOIRE, J. 2015d. GRÉGOIRE, J., 2015a,b.
3. See GREGOIRE, J. 2015d. GRÉGOIRE, J., 2015b.
4. See p. 107. MARTORELL, J., 1994.
5. DAMASIO, A., 1994. D. Goleman, on the other hand, developed the concept of emotional intelligence. GOLESAN, D., 1995.
6. Among other things, through what Berne calls contamination. BERNE, E., 1961, pp. 27–29.
7. This can go so far as to cause a person to ignore the reality of their own findings or emotions.
8. See BERNE, E., 1972, p. 404. See on this point GRÉGOIRE, J., 2007.
9. NOVELLINO, M., 1990, 2005.
10. Bilogical: "*Bilogical* transactions are characterised by the coexistence of a level guided by the secondary process and a level guided by the primary process". NOVELLINO, M., 2005.
11. NOVELLINO, M., 2005, p. 166. See his text at the end of this chapter.
12. The fact that Novellino follows Erskine and Trautmann's ego state theory, in which the Adult has a much broader meaning, does not make this statement wrong.
13. See p. 22 and the description of Ms Enatosky's case, p. 27. Certain "contaminations" involve repression in the unconscious, but not all; many only reach the level of the preconscious. See also GREGOIRE, J., 2007a.
14. STERN, D., 1985, p. 67.
15. Their mechanisms of invention and evolution, on the other hand, rely heavily on intuition or sociological influences. See KUHN, T., 1970.
16. GREGOIRE, J. 2015d. GRÉGOIRE, J., 2015a,b.
17. HOUDÉ, O., 2004.
18. BERNE, E., 1964a, p. 27.
19. BERNE, E., 1961, pp. 189–190.
20. BERNE, E., 1961, p. 52.
21. BERNE, E., 1964a, p. 27.
22. See Chapter 3.

23 BERNE, E., 1964a, p. 23.
24 BERNE, E., 1964a, p. 27.
25 BERNE, E., 1949, 1952, 1953, 1955, 1957a, 1962. These articles are included in BERNE, E., 1977.
26 BERNE, E., 1949, In BERNE, E., 1977, p. 30.
27 BERNE, E., 1952.
28 BERNE, E., 1953.
29 BERNE, E., 1955, 1977, p. 67.
30 BERNE, E., 1955, 1977, pp. 81–82.
31 BERNE, E., 1957a.
32 BERNE, E., 1957a, 1977, pp. 102–103.
33 BERNE, E., 1949, 1977, p. 31.
34 See especially BERNE, E., 1952.
35 See CORNELL, W.F., and LANDAICHE, N.M., 2006, pp. 209–210.
36 BERNE, E., 1972, pp. 104–106.
37 BERNE, E., 1972, p. 104.
38 BERNE, E., 1961, p. 162.
39 BERNE, E., 1961, pp. 52–53.
40 BERNE, E., 1961, p. 16.
41 BERNE, E., 1961, p. 152.
42 BERNE, E., 1961, p. 152.
43 GOULDING, M., and GOULDING, R., 1979, pp. 13–15.
44 GOULDING, M., and GOULDING, R., 1979, p. 23.
45 JAMES, M., and JONGEWARD, D., 1971[ES], pp. 269–271.
46 GILLESPIE, J., 1976[ES].
47 STEINER, C., 2002[ES].
48 SCHIFF, J., and others, p. 24.
49 SCHIFF, J., and others, p. 21.
50 ERSKINE, R.G., 1994[ES], p. 91.
51 NOVELLINO, M., 2005, p. 167.

8
FROM DISJUNCTION TO INTEGRATION

Life would not be possible without coordination between sensory and motor systems, as discussed in Chapter 2; similarly, the Child, Adult and Parent systems would not make sense unless they interacted with one another. If they did not, Berne's provocative comment would literally be true: "It is most fruitful to think of the human personality as being divided into three parts, [...] all pulling in different directions... so that it is a wonder anything ever gets done!"[1]

Interaction modes

The most basic interaction between ego states is the ego state trio resulting from the same experience (as seen in Chapter 4). This trio remains strongly connected. Whatever the complexity of ego state combinations in recent strata, one will always find in earlier strata experiences that are memorized unaltered, together with their ego state trio.

Within more recent strata, interaction modes between personality systems or ego state groups are more diversified. Why speak of "ego state groups" instead of Child, Parent and Adult systems, as classical TA does? Classical TA usually presents each personality system as containing only one ego state, i.e., the dominant one in the situation under consideration; that means one can speak of influences as if they were always exerted by one system upon another. The notion of "representations of interactions' that have been generalized"[2] opens another perspective though. There is no reason to believe these representations only gather experiences belonging to the same system; they can just as well gather ego states from different strata or belonging to different systems.

Here is an example. A woman wonders if she is going to divorce. The "yes" decision brings together a group of mutually reinforcing Child, Parent and Adult ego states from various strata which blocks the "no" ego state group.

On the pro-divorce side,

- Child reactions: "I am fed up"; and, from an earlier stratum, repressed terror.
- Parent message: "What he is doing to you is wrong".
- Adult data: "It has got worse in the last two years".

On the anti-divorce side:

- Parent message: "Divorce is a failure"; and, from an earlier stratum, the model of her mother who never divorced.
- Adult data: "If I leave him, I will have to find a job and it will not be easy".
- Child reactions: "I still love him"; and an archaic fear of being abandoned; and fear of what the other might feel and do if he is "abandoned".

There are five interaction modes:

1. *Disjunction*: the ego state systems or groups appear uncoordinated, each acting on its own account. The situation is chaotic and probably pathological; in any case, development and creativity are impossible. As this is how repetitive ego states usually act, it is very often seen in the repetition perspective. See Ms. Primus,[3] whose case is related in Chapter 1.
2. *Inhibition*: one ego state system or group neutralizes another (*exclusion*), or two neutralize each other (*impasse*).

    Berne mentions Mr. Quint's case, whose "real Self" was fixed in the Adult. "Thus, in nearly all situations, he managed to keep his Child and Parent under the iron grip of intellectualization. Unfortunately, the exclusion failed in his sexual activities".[4]

    An example of an impasse is the woman who is reluctant to divorce, mentioned above.

    A system is never one hundred percent inhibited. Berne warns that symptoms can be manifestations of an excluded[5] ego state or that the temporarily excluded and immobilized Parent continues to observe everything.[6] Berne regards repression as "a special selective form of exclusion"[7]; however, the term "selective" implies that the repressed ego state is not completely inactive.

    Splitting[8] and *dissociation*[9] are specific modes of exclusion. In these situations, the mechanism of producing generalized representations has separated two or more sets of mutually exclusive ego states; consequently, more comprehensive generalized representations cannot be formed. As a result, the person is torn between "sub-personalities" that cannot be synthesized.

    In the *splitting* situation (Fig. 8.1), two "sub-personalities" are formed by gathering all "good" relational experiences on one side, all "bad" experiences on the other. Each sub-personality gathers ego state trios belonging mainly to the psyche's early strata. As said in Chapter 4,[10] I prefer using such a diagram rather than a representation limited to the second-order structure of the Child system alone.
3. *Collusion* is a two-tiered process: one ego state system or group seems to inhibit another by dominating it or preventing it from acting. On closer inspection, one can see that the latter is "complicit" in what is happening and finds hidden "benefits". A collusion example is provided by some forms of guilt after death or separation: the person spends a lot of time and energy

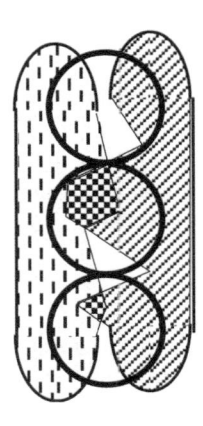

Figure 8.1 A particular example of exclusion: splitting, here diagrammed in terms of two antagonistic trios of personality systems, one gathering the "good" experiences, the other the "bad" ones.

on an internal dialogue about what happened, what could have happened, what they should have done or said, etc., in an emotional depressive tone. The Child feels all this as painful reproaches; *at the same time though*, talking about the past over and over again enables the Child to stay in it on an imaginary level, and to avoid the more archaic pain from abandonment and powerlessness.

4. *Conjunction:* each ego state system or group can perform its function. It is a "peaceful coexistence" without major conflict, but without much creativity. Berne mentions the case of a "young doctor": "His father was a physician, respected by his mother, so that his Parent, without internal conflict, approved of his career. His Adult was satisfied because he was interested and competent in his speciality and liked to do a good job. His Child's sexual curiosity was well-sublimated and well gratified in his practice. Hence Parent, Adult and Child all respected each other and each received appropriate satisfaction in his profession. But [...] he was at times quite unhappy when he was away from the office".[11]

5. *Integration* goes further than conjunction thanks to the multiplicity and importance of mutually reinforcing influences between systems and to the number of combinations they allow, so that high-level creativity becomes possible.[12] The three systems are so interrelated that it is impossible to separate them in a sequential fashion; their synergy[13] enables creativity, which is characteristic of integrated activities. Note that for these, the theatre analogy used in Chapter 1 is not enough: an opera trio would be more relevant. Since integrated activities represent a peak of human development and action, albeit an impermanent one, here are several examples.

Integrated activities

When we are creative, flexible and efficient, our three personality systems work in synergy. Integration seems to be a sign of health and creativity. It is not necessarily joyful, but it is accompanied by a positive sense of Self and a sense of competence and creativity.

- A pianist is playing her instrument. She is not necessarily a professional, but she loves playing. She is playing the first movement of Beethoven's *Moonlight Sonata* from memory. Her experience is the result of many pleasurable experiences playing this piece (Child), many training sessions to memorize the score (Adult) and many performance models by inspiring teachers or well-known artists (Parent). Her attention may be slightly more focused on one of these aspects at any given time, but it is impossible to say that any system disappears for even a second: this would result in the performance's interruption, like a false note.
- A teacher, or trainer, is now at his most powerful and creative. He intuitively senses and enjoys the group atmosphere while not ignoring any possible signal of slight deterioration; he uses humour and empathy when appropriate. He is in touch with contents, process and people at the same time, and can answer questions in a way that respects all three. He makes sure he stays within the guidelines of the institution he works for. His Child, Adult and Parent systems work together in creative synergy, without trespassing. His activity is integrated.
- A mother is changing her fourth child. It is impossible to distinguish between the pleasure she feels, the skills she has learned from experience and the models other women have given her, in the way she changes her baby and communicates with him or her. There might be sometimes no pleasure in it because she is worried, or something goes wrong. But she takes care of herself as well as her child, which is an integration of a different tone. Both experiences, as Winnicott[14] has shown, are helpful to the child: the one where their relationship with their mother is pleasurable, and the one where they feel that the mother is taking care of them adequately even when things are not going well. Without this, the slightest grain of sand in the relationship would seem like a catastrophe: how can the child feel confidence if their needs can only be considered when everything is for the best in the best of all possible worlds?
- A therapist uses all his resources in a session: he is aware of counter-transference and can express what he feels if he considers it useful, he is attentive to reactions from the person/group, he opens or channels process according to this unfolding situation. Are we going to say that:
  - at one point, he is in his Adult system so he can detect a psychological game beginning
  - at another point, he is in his Parent system to give an instruction?
  - then, he is in his Child system to rejoice together in the work done?

No, quite the contrary: if he is truly effective:

- his Adult system is constantly active and vigilant, because at no time should his lucidity be interrupted;
- his Child system does not withdraw, because this would mean losing the most fundamental aspect of empathy and contact with the person/group;

- and his Parent system remains constantly attentive to the frame of reference in order to restore it, maintain it or make it change.

Note that these high value[15] moments are not permanent and should not be. They come to an end, and they are vulnerable to internal or external interruptions: physical or social pain, injury in a vulnerable spot, a "crisis" starting. However, they have enough value in themselves to illuminate existence and nurture the person's sense of Self.

The notion of integration

The term "integration" is much used in recent TA trends, particularly in Erskine and Trautmann's ego state theory, and has multiple meanings. It is usually opposed to incoherence, fragmentation, chaos, but it remains vague until four questions are answered in detail:

- *What is integrated?* When Berne mentions integration, he usually means integrated activities in which the person's *skills* and *resources* work in synergy towards a specific activity such as artistic creation. In recent TA trends, however, integration is more about sense of Self integration, in the wake of D. Stern and Self psychology.
- *Which integration process are we talking about?* Basically, what degree of independent functioning do integrated elements retain once integration has taken place? As J. Piaget says: "A structure can enter as a substructure into a larger system. This modification of the system's boundaries does not abolish the structure's boundaries: there is no annexation, but confederation; the substructure laws are not altered but preserved; as a result, this change is enriching".[16] This notion best suits the interaction perspective. It means that each personality system, *while retaining its own function and a wide autonomy of* perception and reaction, is interconnected with the others in such a way as to *increase the interdependence of the whole* and the resources that flow from it. In Erskine and Trautmann's ego state theory, technically speaking, integration has a very different meaning: a Child or Parent element that becomes integrated loses its original system to become an element of the "integrated Adult".

Here is an analogy: I am walking towards someone who is calling me, but whom I cannot see; I need my visual system to see where I am walking, my auditory system to identify where the call is coming from, and my motor system to move. The fact that the visual system is integrated with the auditory system does not imply that it becomes part of it; on the contrary, it is because it functions according to its own characteristics that it can be usefully integrated into an action.
- *Is integration conceived as a linear and accumulative process, or as an ever-evolving task?* The way we outlined evolution before clearly suggests an ever-evolving task, which is confirmed if we consider what development really is. Development depends on crises during which previous integrations and collusions are dismantled and after which if all goes well, broader

integrations emerge, that are more open to creativity, even if often leading to more intense tensions. It is *impossible to imagine development as a continuous and accumulative integration without any backtracking.*[17]

To take a simple example, the adolescence "crisis" is not just adding new possibilities to what childhood's three systems offered. The Child system is enriched by the onset of genital sexuality, the Adult system by abstract thinking, and the Parent system by the perception of universal values and social pressure (Social Parent) to enter the adult world. However, these new possibilities deeply disrupt the previous balance and integration: the teenager has to "let go" of their former childhood. Any crisis, even a "development crisis", involves "letting go" of a previous state, whether as a child, adolescent, adult or older person.

Ego competence and sense of Self

The integration concept is now frequently used in the context of split resolution. However, this is only one specific case of sense of Self integration, i.e., the *person's perception of themself and their relationships.* A coherent sense of Self allows the person to recognize themself in all reactions and actions, instead of having experiences that they do not recognize as their own: "I did this, I had this emotion or this fantasy, but 'this is not me', I am not like that". This issue is a major point in Self psychology and for authors such as H. Hargaden and C. Sills.[18]

Integration can also focus, as mentioned above, on the *person's resources and skills* for dealing with internal and external conflicts. This enables the idea of three personality systems, each with a specific function in dealing with internal and external life events. Along the same lines, we find Ego psychology, with Berne's two psychoanalysts, P. Federn and Eric Erikson, and in many ways Berne himself. As Daniel Wildlöcher says, this trend "is based on Freud's distinction in the early 1920s which opposes the Id, an unconscious system of impulsive demands, and the Superego, a system of equally unconscious normative demands, to the Ego, a system of choices and rejections by which the person recognises themself as a coherent and autonomous individuality, with the dual task of adapting to the demands of external reality and mastering internal conflicts. Ego psychology tends to generalise this distinction. It integrates within the Ego the psychological functions of intelligence, language and, more generally, all functions that traditional general psychology classifies as cognitive and adaptive activities".[19] Note though that sense of Self is not a stranger to Ego psychology: P. Federn mentions it, and so does Berne, as we will see in his writings below.

Even though Ego competence and sense of Self are the major subjects of two different and often divergent psychoanalysis trends,[20] let us not pit them against one another. *The person's internal and external competence cannot be separated from their sense of Self and subjective perception of themself and their actions.* In healthy development, the two aspects reinforce each other: it is precisely by acting in one's relationships and in the world and by controlling one's internal conflicts that one builds a coherent, stable and flexible sense of Self. Stern[21] clearly shows that, from the beginning of life, in order to grow, sense of Self strata are nurtured by relationship, but also by the child's action within the relationship frame of reference: the two aspects go hand in hand.

It would be wrong to view as mutually exclusive the sense of Self (Self psychology's guiding principle) and the person's competence (central to Ego psychology and Berne's starting point). A perspective that includes both dimensions should find its place wherever the person's development is important: not only in non-therapeutic areas but also in psychotherapy. Indeed, psychotherapy cannot be limited to pathology resolution: it should accompany the person towards autonomy and creativity.

INFLUENCE, INTERACTION, INTEGRATION IN TRANSACTIONAL TEXTS

Berne's interaction modes

In *What do you say after you say hello?*, Berne explains how the three personality systems interact.

He starts with a patient's behaviour, "Bridy",[22] whose three personality systems are expressed through different body parts.

> Bridy is asked: "How is your marriage?", and replies pompously: "My ma-ridge; is perf-ict". As she says this, she takes hold of her wedding ring with the thumb and forefinger of her right hand and simultaneously crosses her legs and begins to swing her right foot. Someone then asks: "That's what you say, but what is your foot saying?" upon which Bridy looks down at her foot with surprise. Another member of the group then inquires: "And what was your right hand saying to your wedding ring?" whereupon Bridy begins to weep and ends up telling them that her husband drinks and beats her. When Bridy becomes more sophisticated in transactional analysis, she is able to tell them the origin of her three replies to the question. The sentence "My marriage is perfect" was said or dictated by a pompous, unyielding Mother Parent, who took over Bridy's talking apparatus as a final common pathway. Her right hand was taken over by her Adult to verify that she was really and possibly married to a scoundrel. Her legs were crossed by her Child, to keep him out, and then she offered him a few tentative kicks. The use of the passive voice in this paragraph signifies that the various parts of her body were merely instruments at the service of her ego states for final common pathway. There are three principal ways in which the final common pathway is selected: by dissociation, by exclusion, or by integration.[23,24]

- In Bridy's case, Child, Parent or Adult, each functions on its own: this is *disjunction*.

> If the ego states are dissociated from each other and do not 'communicate,' then each will find its own pathway for expression, independently of the others, so that each one is 'unconscious' of what the others are doing. Thus, Bridy's Parent was not aware of her fingering Adult or her kicking Child, nor were the other two aware of each other. This reflects the situation as it was in real life.[25]

Better call this first mode "disjunction" rather than "dissociation", which usually refers to other dynamics. This is interaction at its most basic. Berne often compares personality systems to people: in this case, he says that systems in disjunction "do not 'communicate'" and that "each one is 'unconscious' of what the others are doing".[26] This minimal interaction can also look like a fight: each system looks for the opportunity to manifest itself, does so whenever it can, and switches to "underhand" action as soon as another system pushes it to the background. Sometimes systems in disjunction find a way to manifest themselves simultaneously, as in Bridy's case.

- Berne's second interaction mode is *inhibition*, which he calls "exclusion", using a term from his ego state theory in *Transactional Analysis and Psychotherapy*.[27]

> Exclusion means that one ego state is much more highly 'cathected' than the others, and takes over at will regardless of their strivings, […] This again reflects the actual childhood situation.[28]

When in exclusion, one system prevents another from expressing itself. As personality systems naturally tend to manifest themselves, this requires a constant use of energy, and the pressure from the excluded system can generate anxiety. Berne mentions this in Mr Troy's case:

> His object, in group jargon, seemed to be "to keep his own Child from ever sticking his head out of the closet". This is a common attitude in patients who have had electric shock treatment. They seem to blame the Child (perhaps rightly) for the 'beating' they have taken; the Parent is highly cathected and, often with the assistance of the Adult, severely suppresses most Child-like manifestations.[29]

Note here Berne emphasizes the three systems' participation in this dynamic.

Within inhibition mechanisms, other defence mechanisms are repression, isolation, and impasse[30] in which the Parent and Child systems' tendencies are opposed and block each other, at a particular stratum of development.[31]

- Then comes *conjunction* between systems, where mutual inhibition barely happens; even if one system occupies the internal or external centre stage, its manifestations are not incompatible with the others' function, allowing them to remain momentarily in the background. Berne coined the paradoxical expression "normal exclusion" for this purpose.

> A 'normal' type of exclusion occurs in well-organized personalities, where one ego state takes over with the consent of others. The Child and the Parent, for example, let the Adult take over during working hours. In return for this cooperation, the Child is allowed to take over at parties, and the Parent at other appropriate times, as at PTA meetings.[32]

This description is part of Berne's metaphor about internal dialogue. It is as if personality systems were deliberating with each other to decide by mutual agreement which one will take centre stage. Reality is probably simpler: a system only opposes another if the latter is an obstacle to the accomplishment of its own function. If this is not the case, each one finds enough room to manifest itself in turn.

- *Integration* is dealt with very briefly:

> Integration means that all three ego states express themselves at once, as in artistic productions and professional dealing with people.[33]

Here, the systems work together to achieve a combined result which would be unattainable should any one system be missing. Berne mentions artistic creation and professional communications as examples. There are many other integrated activities, including several mentioned in this chapter. However, as they occur in health and creativity, Berne does not often mention them.

The integrated person for Berne

In the previous chapter, we discussed Berne's famous passage on the "integrated Adult"[34]: our aim then was to understand how Berne viewed the diversity of the Adult system. Here, the aim is to study how this text clarifies Berne's notion of integration. Berne wrote this in the final section of *Transactional Analysis and Psychotherapy*, entitled "Frontiers of Transactional Analysis"[35]; there he addresses more complex, abstract or hypothetical theoretical aspects than in the previous sections. Chapter 16, "Finer Structure of the Personality", introduces the ego state second-order structure.[36] He just explained the Child second-order structure and is about to explain the Parent's. Hence the question: are there also Adult subsystems?

There are several indications that this passage about the hypothetical second-order structure of the Adult was introduced at a later stage within an earlier version that dealt only with the Child and the Parent and that, more importantly, was not exactly in the same vein:

- perhaps uniquely for Berne, the text refers to a subsequent chapter, Chapter 20;
- the next chapter, entitled "Advanced Structural Analysis",[37] which discusses the same themes and is much clearer, deals only with the second-order structure of the Child and Parent;

- contrary to his usual style, Berne presents in this text a concept which is supported by some facts, but is not, or not yet, fully embedded in his theory. He is aware of that and separates clearly both dimensions, but it would be understandable if he would have been somehow reluctant, or even hesitated, to insert it in his first book on TA:

According to Berne himself:

> This remains the most obscure area in structural analysis, so that it is not possible at present to clarify it clinically. For academic purposes and in order to explain certain clinical phenomena, however, it would be defensible to subdivide the Adult into three areas. Transactionally, this means that anyone functioning as an Adult should ideally exhibit three kinds of tendencies: personal attractiveness and responsiveness, objective data-processing, and ethical responsibility; representing respectively archaeopsychic, neopsychic and exteropsychic elements 'integrated' into the neopsychic ego state, perhaps as 'influences' in the manner described in Chapter 20.[38]

Berne refers to his subsequent text on the transactional psychic apparatus discussed here in Chapter 3[39]: he announces a clarification connected to the interaction perspective and the concept of programming, i.e., of influence.

> The inference or concept of programming is particularly necessary in attempting to clarify the difficulties encountered in many instances concerning Adult ego states (...). The ethical Adult, "Ethos", may be regarded (...) as the Parent-programed Adult, the denotation being that good mothers behave ethically towards their infants. The feeling Adult, "Pathos", may be understood as a Child-programed Adult, referring to the fact that at a certain age little brother cries when bigger brother is in pain.[40]

In other words, Berne states that programming, or influence between systems, may allow us to understand how the person who functions from a sufficiently evolved Adult, can possess qualities from the three dimensions of human existence to which the three personality systems correspond.

But, on further examination, *neither the descriptive concepts nor the concept of influence supports the idea of substructures internal to the Adult system.* First, an object's descriptive qualities are not substructures, no more that colour and warmth are "zones" on the skin, but apply to the whole skin. The same applies to influence: the lung is related to the blood system and the bone system and depends on their influences, but this does not divide it into two parts, one irrigated by the blood vessels and another supported by the rib cage.

And here is a surprise when we re-read the passage known as "the text on the integrated Adult": the phrase "integrated Adult" is nowhere to be found, and hence cannot be taken as a literal quotation from Berne. If we look at "what is integrated", the text only mentions the "integrated person"[41] (in inverted commas). It is therefore questionable whether it would not apply more accurately to the integration of the three personality systems within the *person*, rather than to the integration of hypothetical subsystems in the Adult. This gives the word "integration" a very rich meaning.

Finally, Berne does not explicitly address our third question: to what extent are these integrated qualities stable, or do they only occur at specific moments?

The integrated Adult after Berne

Though taken out of context and despite the author's perceptible unease, this passage has experienced in TA what can be called a starring fate. As mentioned before,[42] it was first linked to the question "Does the Adult have feelings?" in *Born to Win*[43] where it seems to appear for the first time. However, the term "Integrated Adult" becomes central with Erskine and Trautmann's ego state theory.

What is integrated in this approach is primarily the Self. The integration process is the system switch: if a Child or Parent ego state is integrated, it loses its characteristic and becomes an Adult ego state.

However, this theory cannot be attributed to Berne. The text on the integrated Adult is too much on its own and contains too many reservations to support it. Berne does not assert the Child or Parent ego states "pass" into the Adult in any way. Instead, he speaks of positive, i.e., non-contaminating, *influences*, which implies the interaction perspective. He thinks the Child's and Parent's contribution represents for the Adult, and for the whole person, an enrichment and opening beyond what is simply "rational". Of course, this does not make any less valuable the theoretical and practical contribution of Erskine and Trautmann's theory, particularly about transference and relational needs. Simply, their conceptualization of the integrated Adult's role makes their theory fundamentally different from Berne's.

Collusion and ego state trios

Berne does not mention collusion in his list of interactions between ego states. Some transactionalist authors analysed it relatively early, but they were few in a time dominated by classical TA. As early as 1975, R. Phillips[44] had already proposed diagrams describing intrapsychic collusions, inspired by second-order[45] symbiosis. More recently, V. Joines' conception of transference is at the heart of the interaction perspective, because his theory of intrapsychic structures meets both ego state trios and interactions between ego state groups. About ego state trios:

> For every Parent message that is introjected there is a way of thinking about it (Adult -on whatever level- A0, A1, A2, or A3 (within P2) and feelings, fantasies, and decisions related to it (Child). These structures are the same as object-relations units, that is, self-object (Child-Parent)

representations along with the affect that binds them together and whatever Adult is available (usually contaminated).[46]

Here, Joines' terms A0, A1 and A2 represent the Adult various strata. He adds the Adult in the Parent, which is an element of the Parent system.

He then moves on to the connections between ego states. "Closed structures" are collusions, "open structures" are conjunctions, or integrations when they allow creativity:

> Joines writes; "In this view, ego states always function as structures, never as separate entities. What appears at the social level as a particular ego state is only part of the picture: behind the scenes there are always two other ego states that act as parts of the invested structure. Such a structure can be closed as in transference or open as in spontaneity".[47]

Notes

1. BERNE, E., 1970, p. 93.
2. STERN, D., 1985, pp. 97–99.
3. BERNE, E., 1961, pp. 11–14.
4. BERNE, E., 1961, p. 26.
5. BERNE, E., 1961, p. 39.
6. BERNE, E., 1961, p. 43.
7. BERNE, E., 1961, p. 43.
8. See HAYKIN, M.D., 1980[ES]. WOODS, M., and WOODS, K., 1981[ES].
9. See also HYAMS, H., 2002.
10. See Chapter 4, pp. 84–88.
11. BERNE, E., 1961, p. 35.
12. See Chapter 4, Diagram 3, p. 72.
13. This term means that their joint action is more complex and creative than the sum of what they could do separately. For example, an organ's cells are said to work in synergy: this means that what they produce together (e.g., a visual image) is of a different level than the sum of their individual productions (neuronal connections).
14. For example, WINNICOTT, D.W., 1971.
15. To this list of integrated experiences, one could add Maslow's "peak experiences": MASLOW, A.H., 1968.
16. PIAGET, J., 1968, p. 14.
17. In TA narrative approach, this fact is linked to the "post-modern" philosophical and literary perspective: we have never finished developing who we are and keeping within us imperfectly integrated "sub-personalities". See ALLEN, J., and ALLEN, B., 1997. PARRY, A., 1997.
18. HARGADEN, H., and SILLS, C., 2002.
19. WILDLÖCHER, D., 1997.
20. F. Pine distinguished four types of human motivation, which he compared with different psychoanalytical trends: the drive (the core of Freudian theory), the Ego (Ego psychology), the object (with object relations theory) and the Self (Self psychology). PINE, F., 1990, cited SILLS, C., 2004.

21 STERN, D., 1985.
22 This invented name evokes a young bride.
23 In *What do you say after you say hello?*, Eric Berne uses the same terminology for ego states and for personality systems, so that "ego state" here means "personality system".
24 BERNE, E., 1972, pp. 365–366.
25 BERNE, E., 1972, p. 366.
26 BERNE, E., 1972, p. 366.
27 BERNE, E., 1961, pp. 25–27.
28 BERNE, E., 1972, p. 366.
29 BERNE, E., 1961, p. 15.
30 GOULDING, R., and GOULDING, M., 1976. MELLOR, K., 1980.
31 According to K. Mellor, each impasse type corresponds to a particular stratum. MELLOR, K., 1980.
32 BERNE, E., 1972, p. 366.
33 BERNE, E., 1972, pp. 366–367.
34 BERNE, E., 1961, pp. 211–212.
35 BERNE, E., 1961, p. 147.
36 See pp. 85–87.
37 BERNE, E., 1961, pp. 156–164.
38 BERNE, E., 1961, p. 152.
39 See pp. 48–59.
40 BERNE, E., 1961, p. 191.
41 See SCHLEGEL, L., 2001.
42 See p. 148.
43 JAMES, M., and JONGEWARD, D., 1971.
44 PHILLIPS, R.D., 1975[ES]. The diagrams proposed by Phillips were essentially taken up in V. Joines' diagrams (see below).
45 SCHIFF, J.L., and others, 1975, p. 9.
46 JOINES, V., 1991[ES], p. 170.
47 JOINES, V., 1991[ES], pp. 141–142.

9
EMOTIONS

How do the interaction perspective concepts contribute to our understanding of intrapsychic[1] and relational[2] dynamics?

First, emotion. Its importance is both practical and theoretical. Practical, because a practitioner, whatever their field,[3] can neither ignore nor bypass emotional forces in people, in groups and in institutions. Theoretical, because emotion enables us to have a better understanding of what is meant by "three interacting personality systems". We know that:

1. they *simultaneously* steer the person's perception and their life, each system according to its own function;
2. according to Berne's fundamental definitions, *each* system includes *all* human experience's dimensions: internal experiences (emotion, thought, imaginary life, body) and behaviour.

The main question about the interaction perspective[4] is: "How does *each* system, Child, Adult and Parent, contribute to the person's internal and external reactions?" Or, more precisely: "How does *each system* contribute to the person's *emotional* reactions?" Of course, these reactions are not separable from the person's ego states; they are part of them and have played a major role in their evolution. They are the result of complex interactions between systems. With the exceptions of disjunction and inhibition, usually they cannot be attributed to only one of them. The interaction perspective is in line with common experience: it is the whole *person* who feels, thinks, fantasizes and lives in their body rather than just a part of themselves.

Emotion, the central element of ego states[5]

Recent research locates emotion at the very heart of ego states: it is the crossroads where body, imagination and thought meet and merge into the person's behaviour. According to the neurophysiologist R. Levenson, "emotion appears as a master choreographer, the ultimate organizing authority of disparate reaction systems.[6] It orchestrates the action of many systems in such a way that they act in a unified way in the service of problem solving. This view of emotion as an organising instance stands in marked contrast to the common perspective that sees it as disorganising or disruptive, the enemy of goal-directed behaviour and rational thought".[7]

Books like A. Damasio's *Descartes' Error: Emotion, Reason, and the Human Brain*[8] and D. Goleman's *Emotional Intelligence*[9] have widely spread the idea that *thinking* can only function when in close contact with emotion. The same is true of *relational abilities* across growth strata: "As emotions are remarkably early in terms of brain evolution, there is every reason to believe that underlying brain systems served as the foundation for the emergence of fundamental social and cognitive capacities. The brain's basic emotional systems imbue events with 'values' (i.e., it labels them with positive or negative valences) (…). It is likely that young children project their emotions onto the world, so that they initially assimilate cognitive structures only through intensely affective processes".[10]

Berne intuitively[11] said that the union between feeling, thinking and behaviour forms the very definition of ego states.

Emotion is just the core of a complex *process*, which starts from the body, includes cognitive elements and leads to behaviour:

1. this process begins with *affect*, which is a biological change, a kind of "amplifier to internal states, propelling them into the interpersonal sphere for attention and modulation"[12]; it manifests with physical signs such as tears for sadness (physiological phase). Affects can inhibit, in which case the process stagnates at this level, or, on the contrary, they can "enrich one's thinking and motivate action".[13]
2. M. Basch, a psychoanalytical theorist, said that "Emotion is the coassembly of an affect with our association to previous experience of that affect. Affect is biology, whereas emotion is biography".[14] In TA, we would add that these associations are not limited to situations where we have already experienced the emotion personally (Child), but that they also include situations where we have perceived it in others (Parent), and situations where we have been able to have a more "panoramic" perception (Adult), each situation with its corresponding ego state trios.
3. If we become aware of affect or emotion, this becomes a *"feeling"*[15]: we can then *name* the emotion (cognitive phase) and try to develop strategies. This is a transition to the more recent strata of the psyche.
4. The cycle ends with a decision and action phase.[16]

Not surprisingly, emotion is an essential factor in change: "Emotional processes promote change inherent in development on a daily basis and are linked to cognitive processes, and this is not only true in times of transition"[17] (which the individual goes through during development).

Emotional process includes both implicit and explicit memory and plays an important role in their articulation. From implicit memory, present throughout life, come "primary emotions" which number six, according to Damasio[18]: happiness, sadness, fear, anger, surprise and disgust[19]; when these primary emotions, especially fear, are not held nor oriented in explicit memory, they bring about poorly developed reactions, such as "fight or flight". Explicit memory, where thought is more important, allows to give *meaning* to stimuli; that meaning, in turn, breeds emotions.[20] For example, in a couple, one partner is particularly kind, which brings about pleasant emotions in the other partner; if the latter gives this behaviour the meaning of a proof of deep love, these initial emotions will be joined by probably even more powerful emotions.

The practitioner can expect complexity, due to elements from different psyche strata coming together: "At the physiological level, complexity results from the fact that in the emotional system we find some earliest elements of the person's construction, but also some most recent. The combination of the old and the new makes for an extremely complex system, which often serves us best in navigating the stresses, challenges, and opportunities of life, but which at other times is a diabolical burden, which can even undermine our health".[21]

Emotion and the three personality systems

What does each system contribute to the person's emotional life? As we said before, emotional processes make up all strata both recent and early though still active.

Whether we are dealing with very raw manifestations, such as rage or terror, or with more evolved manifestations, *each personality system keeps its function, its specific contribution.*

The Child reaction is in contact with the person's internal experience and is developed according to what they desire, fear or imagine. It tends to combine present and past experiences according to subjective criteria, so that current emotions can awaken past – even archaic – emotions. In the absence of adequate holding, these can engender violent, dramatic and poorly elaborated reactions that are more in touch with the past situation and its modes of expression than with the present situation.

The same is true of the Parent system: in its early but still active strata, it assimilates others' reaction or judgement as its own. But if it fulfils its organizing role and if other systems can influence it, it can provide the person with more elaborate and flexible strategies and models: expressing emotion, accepting it, "managing" it, rather than resorting to raw reactions such as repressing, discounting, replacing with substitute feeling (racket feeling), displacing, accumulating, etc.

The Adult system views the person's existence from an angle that seeks to perceive early or recent situations with lucidity. It roots emotions in reality, if influences from the other two systems do not interfere with its ability to do so. In its perception, each feeling is adequate:

- joy when the situation is realistically favourable to the person or someone else;
- anger, when it involves injustice, disregard of rights or lack of respect towards the person or someone else;
- sadness, when it involves what is lost or gone, including hopes, expectations or time;

- fear, when it involves a real, external or internal danger;
- surprise, when the person is faced with a really new or unexpected situation;
- disgust, when the person is faced with a material object of disgust[22], as opposed to an imaginary one.

Emotions relate to reality as feelings do, according to G. Thomson.[23]

The key fact is that emotion depends on what component comes from the Child, Parent and Adult systems, each with its own strata. Each component is not enough on its own:

- the Child would direct the person's emotions solely on the basis of its associations with past events and the gratifications it can obtain from them;
- the Parent would tend to elicit stereotyped reactions, sometimes effective, but lacking in creativity;
- the Adult would lack the energy and fervour needed to truly influence the person.

In short, *all three components are essential*. They can of course be in disjunction, inhibition, conjunction, collusion or integration, as we can see with substitute feelings.

The dynamics of substitute feelings

"Substitute feeling", also called "racket feeling"[24] or "parasite feeling", is a particularly interesting and original TA concept; it invites the practitioner not to let themself be taken in by the repetitive emotional manifestations that are stroke-seeking. Instead, the practitioner should take into account "repressed" ego states which appear neither internally nor externally as they are monopolized by the substitute feeling.

First, a vocabulary issue: it would be more precise to say that a repressed *emotion* (not a repressed *feeling*) is defensively masked by a substitute *feeling*, as the emotion is not named as such in the person's consciousness, whereas the feeling is, and as we know, naming is an essential part of this mechanism. "Racket" theory[25] shows that, at the internal level, experiences, feelings and emotions, memories, fantasies and body sensations[26] can serve as defensive screens for one another; this defence mechanism, which belongs to the script,[27] is reinforced at the external level by the fact it makes it easier or more frequent to get strokes.

Consider an unfairly treated person who represses anger and expresses sadness. What belongs to each personality system in this reaction? The Parent probably contains in a relatively early stratum an automatic and well-established pattern that leads the person to express sadness and determines their external behaviour (executive power) and very often also their sense of Self. It exerts a dominant inhibiting influence on the Child, but *it rarely annihilates the anger emotion in the Child*; usually it simply prevents it from becoming an anger feeling, i.e., from being consciously named ("I am angry"). As for the Adult, it is usually blocked by these conflicting internal influences.

There is an intermediate point between where the anger emotion becomes an anger feeling expressed as such, and where it is completely pushed back into the systems' unconscious strata. There, the person is *simultaneously* experiencing an *emotion* of anger and a *feeling of* sadness which gives anger an indirect hidden channel of expression. In many cases, this "camouflage" is only effective in the person's eyes, because the anger emotion is easily perceptible even by non-professionals in non-verbal communication and general body tension.[28] This is disjunction between personality systems or groups of ego states.

Note that the situation sometimes provides roots in reality for two emotions: the repressed emotion and the emotion from the substitute feeling; in this case, the practitioner cannot neglect either of them. For example, being abandoned can be experienced as loss, which is objectively rooted in sadness, or as injustice, which is objectively rooted in anger. Ideally, a person in this situation would feel both emotions and, recognizing both for what they are, would express both feelings. But if they are inclined to cover anger with sadness, the Adult system, under the Parent system's influence, will probably favour the "loss" side and ignore the "injustice" side. This is even more likely to happen if, in the Child system, anger is buried in unconscious strata because it is associated with catastrophic experiences or fear of abandonment, violence (either from others or from the person themself) or other such intense suffering.

"Mourning" or letting go

At some point in their lives, if they can, all human beings face grief or the need to let go. This does not only happen when losing a loved one or a relationship, but in any situation when the person feels that major parts of what they have built in the course of their development are collapsing. Whether this perception is about internal and external competence or about a sense of Self, or both, the person enters a "crisis". Such "crises"[29] with a strong emotional component can be triggered by painful circumstances, which can occur suddenly or gradually, unexpectedly or predictably (at least in others' eyes). The person can only emerge, rarely unscathed, through a process of deconstruction and reconstruction of a significant part of their personality systems and their interactions. The same is true of groups and institutions, so that practitioners in all fields encounter such crises.

The usual reference for "mourning" or letting go is E. Kübler-Ross' theory and practice[30] developed for accompanying someone dying. Kübler-Ross breaks down the process into four phases, some of which may not be experienced: 1) denial; 2) bargaining; 3) deep emotions: anger, sadness, and fear[31]; 4) "acceptance". The paragraphs below elaborate a more specifically transactional view of the letting go process, in the light of the emotion theory seen above. There are three phases, each building on the previous one:

1. *From denial to recognition that what happened is irreversible.* The person or group uses multiple defence mechanisms that aim at repressing or delaying

full realization of the situation/event viewed as catastrophic, and the rise of deep *emotions* linked to it. These mechanisms also allow the person to *cling to the past,* if only in a phantasmatic form: these two motivations are reinforced by *collusion.*

In *denial*, the Adult is obsessed by the other two systems' influences; its participation in the collusion comes from the fact that the event seems irreconcilable with its previous representations and convictions: "It is impossible, she can't ask for a divorce, she is opposed to divorce!" Consequently, the Adult tends, for a while at least, to ignore the reality of the event.

In *guilt*, the Parent system encourages the person/group to blame themselves. The Child system may perceive it as painful but is often "complicit" underneath. As long as the story of the past and of the catastrophe is played again, the Child can relive them in memory, which prevents it from letting go; and as long as the person questions over and over again what they could or should have done, the Child avoids feeling powerless. As for the Adult under the other two systems' influence, it can obsess exclusively on what could justify these reproaches, ending up inhibiting its lucidity.

Other defence mechanisms in this phase include substitute feelings, blaming others, psychological games, substance dependency, flight into activity ("life goes on"), etc.

Although all three personality systems participate in this defensive phase prior to "letting go", which the person/group usually needs temporarily, the Child system can be said to predominate, as it is mainly subjective experiences that drive these reactions. This phase does not end once denial is over, when the Adult system cognitively recognizes the reality of what has happened, while the other two systems resist taking it into account (disjunction). The block hidden spring is often located at the sense of Self level: what needs to be worked through are often pre-conscious or unconscious convictions like "This cannot happen to me"; "They could not do this to me"; "In our company, this does not happen"; "I am not powerless in the face of this kind of event: I could have acted in such a way and nothing would have happened", etc. It is often very hard for the Child system to admit that there was nothing to be done, or that there was something to be done then, but not anymore. The Parent system usually feeds this dynamic through others' models and expectations whether current, recent or past. The Adult system is so challenged by the crisis effect on its view of reality that it needs time to insert the "catastrophic" event into it, especially if it was unprepared by previous experiences.

2. *Emotional acknowledgement of reality.* Once the person or the group can face the fact that what happened is an irreversible fact, they need to go through the deep emotions this inevitably arouses: anger for injustice, sadness for loss, fear for the future. These emotions are anchored in reality; they do not have the "parasitic" or forced character of those encountered in the first phase.

They gradually bring the person or group back into more and more contact with present reality. In this phase, the Adult system holds a preponderant place, which, in the interaction perspective as we know, is in no way contradictory to the experience's strong emotional aspect.

3. *Reconstruction of the personality systems' conjunction, the person's or group's competence and their sense of Self.* This work, which brings into play the three personality systems' interactions, allows the person or group to resume growth and to recover creativity. Nothing is "forgotten", the memory of the crisis may still arouse emotions, but nothing is dwelled upon, and life goes on, with no doubt some additional lessons learned from what one has been through.

EMOTIONS AND FEELINGS: TWO TRANSACTIONAL TEXTS

Many texts on emotions have already been mentioned in this chapter. Here are two specifically transactional discussions concerning emotions and feelings: F. English's racket feeling and C. Steiner's emotional awareness scale.

Repressed emotion and substitute feeling

Fanita English describes the genesis of substitute feeling (racket feeling) and its relationship to "repressed" emotion as follows:

> A child who has had to suppress awareness of certain "forbidden" feelings makes up for it by expressing with extra emphasis whatever he *may* express. Thereby, at least he vents emotion; not the genuine one, to be sure, but some emotion; however, because it is not the real feeling, he is dissatisfied and remains with a continuing need to present the phony emotion. It is as though repetition would clarify what's unexpressed. Hence the "broken phonograph" effect of a racket.

> In the family his racket may gain him some strokes, but as he goes out into the world the strokes diminish or become ritualized as acquaintances become irritated with his stereotyped repetitiveness. To allay the increased feelings of dissatisfaction, and in a frantic effort to gain more strokes he enlarges the racket. Now the individual is embarked on a self-defeating cycle, seeking trading stamps to justify the enlarged racket, and then, in turn, increasing the racket as he finds more stamps.[32]

We can see how the so-called repressed emotion continues to remain active "under the table", to the point it is ultimately what determines the person's emotional dynamics.

The emotional awareness scale according to C. Steiner

C. Steiner presents an emotional awareness scale with seven levels, split halfway by the "verbal barrier" from which the psyche's most recent strata are clearly visible:

1. Numbness: People in this state are not aware of anything they call feelings. This is true even if they are under the influence of strong emotions which empathic observers can detect from facial expression or physical attitude (…).
2. Physical sensations: At this level of emotional awareness, the physical sensations that accompany emotions are experienced but not the emotions themselves (…).
3. Emotional Chaos: In this stage, people are conscious of emotions, but they are experienced as a heightened level of energy that is not understood and cannot be put into words (…) they are responsive to emotions but not necessarily able to comprehend or control them.

    The Verbal Barrier: beyond this, the impact of language and the ability to exchange information with others opens the possibility of developing emotional awareness (…).
4. Differentiation is a step towards both recognizing various emotions, their intensity, and causes, and learning to communicate about them. We are now able to extract from the emotional chaos the anger, love, shame or hate that were its constituents (…).
5. Causality: As we begin to understand the exact nature of our feelings, we also begin to understand the causes of those feelings (…).
6. Empathy: As we learn the different emotions that we have, the various intensities with which we feel them, and the reasons for them, and as our awareness of our own emotions becomes textured and subtle, we begin to perceive and intuit similar texture and subtlety in the emotions of those around us (…).
7. Interactivity: emotions are not static phenomena (…). Therefore, awareness of how they interact with each other, both within and between different people, further increases our degree of emotional finesse.[33]

Notes

1   Chapters 9–11.
2   Chapters 12 and 13
3   See CORNELL, W.F., and HINE, J., 1999.
4   See pp. 23–25.
5   The quotations from neurophysiologists below are mainly taken from articles by CORNELL, W.F., 2003, and GILDEBRAND, K., 2003.
6   Levenson considers them as neurophysiological systems.
7   LEVENSON, R.W., 1999, p. 495. Quoted in CORNELL, W., 2003[ES].
8   DAMASIO, A., 1994.
9   GOLESAN, D., 1995.
10 PANKSEPP, p. 141. Quoted in CORNELL, W., 2003.
11 But not necessarily Berne's personal practice, which tended to distrust emotional approaches: see, for example, BERNE, E., 1964a, pp. 142–143. BERNE, E., 1973.

12 CORNELL, W.F. 1994, p. 140, after Tomkins and Nathanson.
13 CORNELL, W.F. 1994, p. 140. W. Cornell lists four binding affects: guilt, anxiety, depression and shame.
14 BASCH, M., 1976. Quoted in NATHANSON, D.L., 1994, p. 125.
15 NATHANSON, D.L., 1994, p. 125.
16 This cycle is similar to that described by STEINER, C.M. 1984. See page 187 at the end of this chapter.
17 EMDE, 1999, p. 323. Quoted in CORNELL, W., 2003[ES].
18 DAMASIO, A., 1999.
19 GILDEBRAND, K., 2003, pp. 6–7. Authors differ as to the number and list of primary emotions, but all agree on their link with implicit memory. See, for example, NATHANSON, D.L., 1994, who recalls Tomkins' pioneering theory.
20 GILDEBRAND, K., 2003[ES], p. 12. (French ed.)
21 LEVENSON, R.W., 1999, p. 482. Quoted in CORNELL, W., 2003.
22 Disgust concerns mainly what is rotten or what comes out of a human or animal body. A feeling like "I disgust myself" is not a simple emotion and has many different levels.
23 THOMSON, G., 1983.
24 ENGLISH, F., 1971. See her quotation page 187 at the end of this chapter.
25 Its development can be traced back to four authors: Berne developed the concept of an external defensive phenomenon aimed at obtaining strokes (BERNE, E., 1962, 1966 and 1972, pp. 137–139). ENGLISH, F., 1971 and 1972, analysed the emotional aspect of racketeering. The other aspects have been listed and summed up by ERSKINE, R.G., and ZALCMAN, M., 1979.
26 ERSKINE, R.G., and ZALCMAN, M., 1979.
27 BERNE, E., 1972, pp. 137–139.
28 Anger tends to mobilize the sympathetic nervous system and put the body in a state of alertness and readiness for action, whereas sadness mobilizes the parasympathetic nervous system and decreases readiness for action.
29 A list of these "crises" can be found in SHEEHY, G., 1976.
30 KÜBLER-ROSS, E., 1969.
31 REUSS, H., 2003, rightly adds fear to anger and sadness.
32 ENGLISH, F., 1971, p. 29.
33 Summary from STEINER, C.M., 1984. See also STEINER, C.M., and PERRY, P., 1996.

10

THE SENSE OF SELF

Sense of Self covers everything the person experiences, feels and thinks about themself. The expression "self-image" implies visual perception, somewhat at a distance, as if the person could look at themself from the outside. A much better description would be a "background" filled with conscious and unconscious elements: it is an integral part of the person's experiences to which it gives direction and by which it is influenced. This background comes with an emotional tone of its own: self-confidence or self-distrust, self-satisfaction or self-dissatisfaction, self-love or self-shame,[1] etc. Whether the person deals with internal feelings, relationships or action, sense of Self influences them and is influenced by them. Both its successes and failures concerning internal and external competence usually contribute to its construction, whereas "crises" mean deconstruction. We saw in Chapter 4 how Stern[2] describes the sense of Self development during growth: four superimposed strata including the emergent Self, the core Self, the subjective Self and the verbal Self. Note that its evolution does not stop there: it goes on throughout life.

The Self is not an object whose characteristics can be described outside of its relationships and history, so the "sense of Self" is not separable from the "sense of Other", i.e., from the person's general perception of others. In Stern's description, each sense of Self's stratum goes hand in hand with a corresponding sense of Other's stratum: the emergent Other, the core Other, the subjective Other, the verbal Other. In general, any change in the meaning of Self leads to a corresponding change in the meaning of Other and vice versa. The latter has its own emotional tone, of which trust/distrust of Other is one aspect.

The more abstract sense of existence is the conscious and unconscious background representation of:

- the space in which the person's actions and relationship to others are situated (the "world");
- the time frame in which they are situated (from birth to death, with the perception that others have existed and will exist outside these boundaries);
- its connection, favourable or unfavourable, to the Self and its relationships.

The distinction between the sense of Self, the sense of Other and the sense of existence is only a means to describe a single complex reality, which could be synthetically called the *sense of Self in relation to others in existence*.

For Eric Erikson, Berne's psychoanalyst, "basic trust or distrust" in oneself, in others, in life, is human development's foundation stone.[3] Its keystone, which he names "integrity", is accepting what one has become, what one has done and what human existence is in general, without grandiosity. At existential level, integrity is accompanied by serenity in the face of old age and death. Its opposite is "despair" and fear of death with all possible avoidances of its reality.[4]

The sense of Self and the Child, Parent and Adult systems

1. The three systems, with their different strata and their interaction modes, take part in the construction of the sense of Self. Sense of Self comes from the intimate overlay of three components which exist in evolution and interaction, though not always in conjunction, and even more rarely in integration.

    a. In the Child component, the person is satisfied or frustrated with themself in terms of what they *would like to* be or not to be. It does not matter whether this desire obeys reality or ethics. If the person follows the promptings of their Child system, they may, for example, consciously or unconsciously, devalue themself because of a failure to cure a parent's depression, save the world or be a father's or a mother's favourite child. Conversely, the person may derive excessive value from being better loved than a sibling, being richer or smarter than a father, bossing subordinates around or having "all" the men or "all" the women falling for them. The person may also experience a great and profound acceptance of Self, of others and of life, whether it has been anchored in this attitude for a long time or whether it has acquired it in the overcoming of transforming crises.

    b. The Parent component is mostly made up of elements that others have given to the person in the past or today: judgements, attributions[5] or narratives. Its more recent strata add what the person "must be", "should be" or "should have been" according to principle, tradition, ethics or values. In addition, the social parent includes judgements or narratives about groups the person belongs to: gender, family, age group, social class, profession, religion or philosophical affiliation, nation, race, etc.

    The person's greater or lesser vulnerability to others' judgements lies at this level: are their boundaries too penetrable and give others power over their sense of Self? Or too rigid and cut them off from any feedback? Or are they able to sort out what to accept and reject, both for positive and negative feedback? And how do experiences today resonate with the earlier strata of the psyche?

    c. The Adult system seeks lucidity; it directs the person's sense of Self towards self-awareness; of course, it never achieves complete objectivity because it is neither omniscient nor impervious to the other systems' inhibitions. It plays, however, a great role in overcoming the Child illusions or the Parent judgements to accept the human condition in a never-ending gradual process.

2. These three components can be in disjunction, inhibition, conjunction, collusion or integration. The fact that one component is dominant does not imply that the others are absent or resolved. To think that one's sense of Self is unified and coherent is a mistake: disjunctions and collusions at this level are probably more frequent than we think.

    Here is an example. A woman displays a realistic self-image, with a good awareness of her qualities and limitations (Adult component). However, she secretly retains her father's message in her Parent system: "You are brilliant, but you will never satisfy me".[6] This Parent influence at times induces in her Child system the experience of being a desperate, "worthless" little girl, incapable of meeting any expectation, which ends in episodic bouts of depression. Internal devaluation lies behind this woman's rather positive and realistic sense of Self. Whatever the context, it may be useful to identify, analyse and at least partially resolve this devaluation.

3. *Sense of body* is a particularly sensitive aspect of sense of Self. The person's body stores pleasure or pain and is the person's "home", but it is also "the first thing others perceive". The body *is* the person, it belongs to the person and is their primary territory, but it is also what others can see and touch. From the subjective Self's stratum, we know that others' bodies provides us with a lot of information about who they are and what they experience; the same is true in reverse, in a way that we can only partially control: "you cannot not communicate".[7] The body keeps traces of the earliest strata of our script and experiences,[8] among other things, in the form of "character defences" developed by Reich, bio-energetic and bio-script approaches.[9]

    a. The Child component in the person's sense of body bears traces of experiences from the very beginning of life, often embedded in several overlaying and interacting strata. Experiences of:

    - physical well-being, pleasures, games, pleasant movements;
    - illnesses, deprivations, death risks perceived clearly or not, perhaps traumas;
    - the way we have been physically stimulated since early childhood;
    - "vitality affects",[10] according to Stern, i.e., everything that concerns the intensity and rhythm of these stimulations.

    As the Child system is marked by subjectivity, imagination and desire or aversion, it can distort the person's perception of their body and make it appear beautiful or ugly, resistant or vulnerable, sick or healthy, depending on its strata's dynamics.

    b. The Parent system, in its earliest strata, has recorded the ways in which the person's body has been treated since birth, as well as the emotions of those who have touched it and cared for it: did they feel pleasure, embarrassment, disgust, desire, indifference or something else? These emotions, which often parental figures did not clearly perceive themselves, or dared not face, nevertheless mark the person's sense of body in its conscious and unconscious dimensions. To this will be added later the physical, emotional and verbal reactions of other people (peers, relatives, partners, etc.), moral conceptions and "taboos", recommendations concerning food, health, etc. The Parent system, like the Child system, can distort the person's perception of their body in different ways.

c. The Adult system is more lucid: this is its specific contribution. If it is not inhibited by the other two systems, it will tend to give the person a more realistic view of their body and its needs: food, health, sexuality, etc.

As above, this or that element may appear to be dominant, but this does not exempt the practitioner from being attentive to what may be present in the background: they would risk reinforcing disjunctions, inhibitions or collusions.

Sense of Other

1. The sense of Other works on symmetrical lines. The Child system considers the other according to its subjective experience, needs and desires.[11] The Parent system sees the Other primarily in terms of who they should be: family, social and professional roles are very important here. The Adult system seeks to meet the Other as they are, then adjusts the relationship accordingly. Here again, these three components, with their superimposed strata, combine or collide according to their interactions.
2. What about the *Other's body?* It relates to mine in many ways: through social gestures such as shaking hands, through physical signs of friendship or tenderness, in sexuality, in aggression, but also in the occupation of space, in the joint performance of a physical task, in physical interactive play (sports), in arts such as dance, etc. The sense of the Other's body is a dimension of the sense of Other and implies all three personality systems' overlaying strata.

The Other's body is particularly important in the earliest social experiences, especially from the "self-regulating Other" who becomes the Parent pole in the resulting ego state trio.

Sense of existence

"Human existence" is an abstract concept. Initially, as first representations derive from social experiences, the person's sense of existence is only a result of their sense of Self and sense of Other. This does not mean that any practitioner can ignore this representation: it is sometimes a very revealing gateway to the person/group's needs. As for the sense of Self and the sense of Other, what is most apparent should not make one neglect what is hidden, under a mask or in the shadows.

Here is an example. A generous woman is committed to the service of others, without being a rescuer. She usually shows conjunction and often high-level integration between her three systems: her generosity harmonizes with her parental values, which have evolved within a personal elaboration; in its implementation, the Adult has an important and regulating place; with this activity, her Child system receives justified gratifications that contribute to her global balance. In middle age, after a time of bereavement then separation, she discovers her "demon"[12]: a deep sense of futility with a faint rage against the whole universe. She realizes this experience has been with her for a very long time, although she always discounted it. In contrast to her conscious convictions, it kept inducing barely perceptible tension and a subtle depressive tone. Coming from the Child and Parent's deepest strata, the "demon" usually operates in disjunction: it acts in a hidden way, away from the interacting evolving strata. For this woman, however, its manifestations become increasingly clear, omnipresent and disturbing; they invade the whole of her existence and gradually undermine its coherence, to the point of giving rise to suicidal thoughts. To provide a holding environment, to make sense of them and to think about them, she first had to be helped to look them in the face, to bring them out into the open and to accept her "demon" as part of herself.

It is often when a "crisis" leads us to feel the limits of human existence, our own or others', that we perceive most acutely the need for change in our sense of Self, our sense of Other and our sense of existence. Achieving such a transformation brings us closer to "integrity", as described by Eric Erikson.[13]

The Self and the Ego

Although "Ego" and "Self" have each been signposts for psychoanalytic currents with divergent tendencies,[14] *the "Self"*, in the sense of the person's subjective perception of themselves and their actions, *cannot be separated from the "Ego"*, in the sense of the centre for solving internal conflicts and adapting to external reality: the two aspects reinforce or undermine each other.[15] This does not imply these two notions have to be identified, for the person does not always act in conformity with their sense of Self, and the sense of Self may prevent them from adapting. But when both are sufficiently free of imbalance, inhibition or chaos, they often motivate the person to continue to grow, to change and to use their creativity to do so.

An integrated sense of Self, or rather a sense of Self on its way to an ever-changing integration, is by no means incompatible with several personality systems in the Ego, provided that their possibilities of conjunction and integration are highlighted, and integration is understood as *between systems*.[16] A theory that includes both aspects and shows their articulation is adapted to approaches where it is important the persons should build themselves from the resources of their past and present situation. This applies to non-therapeutic areas, but also to therapy, because therapy cannot be reduced to solving pathologies; encouraging the person towards autonomy and creativity is an essential aspect of it, and in practice it is impossible to achieve one without the other.

TRANSACTIONAL TEXTS: THE SELF

Berne

What does Berne think about the Self? Of course, there is his text on the "real Self",[17] which deals with the person's perception of themself. Although this topic comes from Federn, who investigated how continuous the sense of Self is in various situations, it is very close to Self psychology. The same is true of the term "ego-syntonic", which seems, despite the words used, to be about the person's sense of Self (see below). In fact, Berne, like many psychoanalytic and psychotherapeutic theorists of his time, does not distinguish between Ego and Self; more precisely, *he reduces the Self to the Ego.*

1. In a paragraph entitled *"Ego [internal] boundaries"*, he writes:

> During therapeutic sessions, "Mrs. Tettar was aware of certain obsessions, phobias and compulsions which were ego-dystonic. At such times, her obsession with cleanliness (...) were usually perceived by her as not part of her real Self".[18]

But what Berne has in mind is, above all, the distinction between *ego* states, in this case the Adult and Child systems in the sequential or descriptive perspective. He continues:

> In this kind of thinking, her mind was divided into two systems: "real Self" and "not real Self".
>
> (...) Real Self knew things about sanitation (...) which an infant would be incapable of appreciating, while "not real Self" was guided by magical thinking in a way characteristic of an infant at a certain specific phase of development. Thus "real Self" was characteristically Adult, and "not real Self" was characteristically Child.[19]

This brings the author back to boundaries and allows him to present the three-circle diagram not as a simple schematic representation, but as a structural representation.

> Mrs Tettar's own view of these two different aspects of her personality implied the existence of a boundary between them (...). Hence a set of circles [the ego-state diagram] may be taken as a fair way of representing the structure of personality[20].

The impact of this graphic representation on ego state theory in classical TA has been extensive. It encourages the representation of personality systems in the form of three "places"; it makes it easy to place a phenomenon that would belong to only one of them (which is the case only in the repetition

perspective); it also makes it difficult to draw collusions, conjunctions or integrations, or even multiple interactions between systems. As a result, the practitioner might think, might even be biased, in a particular direction.
2. Ms Tettar's "real Self is unstable", however. Berne adds a new paragraph entitled "The Problem of the Self":

> When it was said that Mrs. Tettar's hand-washing was ego-dystonic, this meant specifically Adult-ego dystonic. In her overt psychotic state, however, when her "real-Self" was the Child, the hand-washing became ego-syntonic (...). The problem now revolves around what determines "real-Self". Evidently, this does not depend upon executive power, since when she was reluctantly washing her hands or hunting for specks, in her non-psychotic condition, her Child had the executive power, but the Adult was still experienced as "real Self".[21]

Note that if the Adult "real Self" is uncomfortable with the externally predominant Child behaviours, *it is because the person goes on being aware that they are doing these acts.* If one is thinking from the privileged point of view of Ego psychology, i.e., competence in action, it is indeed "a system that was outside of (the system of the real Self)",[22] and there are indeed three distinct Ego personality systems. But if one is thinking from the privileged point of view of Self psychology, i.e., sense of Self, the person's experience is continuous. At the very least, continuity goes on when the real Self remains in the Adult, even in cases of acute disjunction (like Ms Tettar's). However, continuity is broken in dissociation where the person loses consciousness of their reactions and actions in their previous states: this is the case in some borderline or psychotic states, in acute alcohol or drug intoxication, or in dissociative personality disorder. But from these pathological states, one cannot build a complete personality theory, certainly not of a healthy personality.

3. Immediately after this passage, Berne introduces the metaphor of three types of psychic energy and a comparison with the monkey (the Self!) jumping from branch to branch. The metaphor clearly shows what Berne assumes: since the monkey can only be on one branch at a time, *the Self is at all times carried entirely by one personality system.* The person says "I" in only one system at a time. The following text is from *What do you say after you say hello?*:

> Clara's Parent was listening to her son with motherly respect, and that was her active Self at the moment. Meanwhile, her Child was reacting to what he said in quite another way, but neither her Parent nor her Adult was aware of her facial movements because she could not "feel" them. Her son, however, was fully informed of her Child's reactions because they were right in front of his eyes. [...] Along with the biological principle of the Plastic Face, the psychological principle of the Moving Self is equally important in keeping the script going and is based on a similar defect of awareness. The

feeling of "Self" is a mobile one. It can reside in any of the three ego states at any given moment and can jump from one to the other as occasion arises.[23]

Is it truly impossible for a mother to be aware, not of her facial movements, but of her feelings when she listens to her son, even if they are unpleasant? Not at all. This text actually shows us how, when it comes to the Self, Berne builds his argument on examples of disjunction conceptualized along the lines of dissociation; taking it to the extreme, it is as if the three personality systems gave rise to a multiple personality disorder! For Berne, "the Self is a mobile feeling" and not the result from an integration of multiple experiences as in Self psychology and in Erskine and Trautmann's ego state theory. Once again, we see how his thinking tends to separate the three personality systems from each other instead of emphasizing their interactions and integrative aspects.

TA recent trends

Erskine and Trautmann's ego state theory, taken up by most recent trends of transactional analysis,[24] does not refer explicitly to the Self; however, Self integration holds a central place there. The integrated Adult is seen as the unique locus of integration, as opposed to the Child and Parent composed of "isolated", i.e., disjunctive elements; it has become the *symbol of the person, more precisely of their only growing aspects and in contact with the here and now.* In a sense, it can be said to have taken the place of the Self, for it contains all the elements in which the person recognizes.

Hargaden and Sills' relational TA[25] has a more explicit connection to Self psychology. Many concepts describing transference characteristic of "borderline states" are inspired by its leader, H. Kohut,[26] mainly because empathy holds an important place in his work. This is probably not accidental, because the sense of Self can neither be built nor evolve without understanding and respecting others' sense of Self.

Notes

1   See ERIKSON, E., 1950.
2   STERN, D., 1985.
3   ERIKSON, E., 1950, pp. 247–251.
4   ERIKSON, E., 1950, pp. 268–269.
5   An attribution is a script message attributing a quality or a defect to a person: "You are intelligent, mean, good at music, bad at maths", etc. See HOLTBY, M.E., 1976.
6   LOOMIS, M., and LANDSMAN, S., 1980, apply the same paradoxical juxtaposition to manic-depressive dynamics; similar dynamics are found, to a lesser degree, in many people.
7   WATZLAWICK, P., HELMICK-BEAVIN, J., and JACKSON, D., 1967.
8   See WALDEKRANZ-PISELLI, C.K., 1999.

9   See LOWEN, A., and LOWEN, L., 1977. CORNELL, W.R., 1998. CORNELL, W.F., and HINE, J., 1999.
10 STERN, D., 1985, pp. 53–61.
11 Kohut uses the term "self-object". This term refers to "any experience of another person (object) as part of, rather than as separate and independent from, one's self". (*Dictionary of APA*, art. Self-object.) Kohut insists on the normal and healthy character of persisting "self-objects" in the adult person. See KOHUT, H., 1971. In terms of transactional analysis, we would say that the adult person possesses a Child system which is a resource and without which they cannot be.
12 See BERNE, E., 1972, pp. 122–123.
13 ERIKSON, E., 1950.
14 Psychoanalysis trends in Berne's time can be classified into four main groups: Freudian psychoanalysis, based on the concept of drive; the theory of object relationships; Ego Psychology, which is concerned with the dynamics that allow the person to function in the world and to which Federn and Berne belong; and the Self Psychology. See GRÉGOIRE, J., 2007c[ES], pp. 14–16.
15 See pp. 162–163.
16 See the quotation from Piaget in Chapter 8, p. 160. PIAGET, J., 1968, p. 14.
17 BERNE, E., 1961, pp. 20–21. BERNE, E., 1972, pp. 248–255.
18 BERNE, E., 1961, p. 20.
19 BERNE, E., 1961, p. 20.
20 BERNE, E., 1961, p. 20.
21 BERNE, E., 1961, pp. 20–21.
22 BERNE, E., 1961, p. 22.
23 BERNE, E., 1972, pp. 248–249.
24 See GRÉGOIRE, J., 2007c[ES].
25 HARGADEN, H., and SILLS, C., 2002[ES].
26 Although Kohut was at this time president of the American Psychoanalytical Association in 1964–1965, Berne never mentions his works nor Self psychology.

11
INTEGRATION AND RELATIONSHIPS

Here are two themes that imply both a relational dimension and a high degree of integration between personality systems:

- intuitive perception of others' experiences, which preludes empathic relationships;
- autonomy, which, according to Berne, includes awareness, spontaneity and intimacy.

These two notions, with which our research on intrapsychic system interactions ends, lead to relational dynamics, which is the subject for the next two chapters.

Intuitive perception of others' experiences

One of Berne's major steps was working on intuition. In Chapter 7, we discussed this research in relation to the Adult earlier strata. For Berne, intuition was a resource for children and for the Child system; he also saw it as a neopsyche manifestation. We know he solved this theoretical problem by introducing the "Professor" into the Child second-order structure. Working chiefly from the repetition perspective, he studied repetitive ego states in the grown-up person and found that their *contents* include *the former child's* three personality systems; this is logical, since an ego state includes the whole of the person's experience at a given time. In the former child's case, Berne considered the three personality systems together, which is characteristic of the interaction perspective.

Intuition, as we know, perceives others' experience by questioning the role played by the *three* personality systems. The Child component is essential. Unlike the Adult system, the Child does not have to consider whether new discoveries are coherent with previous ones. That means it can perceive new things with excitement. Unlike the Parent system, the Child is not concerned by conformity with acquired values or models. Furthermore, it is open to imagination: the Child can use it, for example, to "be in somebody else's shoes" without worrying about boundaries between people; it can take advantage of the possibilities this imaginary experience reveals. The primal images and primal judgements Berne analysed are examples of this.[1]

Taken on its own, however, this Child perception has its downside. It remains aimed at the person's own experience and inhabited by their subjective yearnings, desires or fears; it perceives things from a biased angle. *We cannot therefore speak of a second mode of "reality testing"*[2] as Berne said. The Child system may be seduced by the Other or by its own desires, or it may seek to strengthen its sense of Self by "saving" the Other. If it "is in the Other's shoes", it is unable to make the essential distinction between "how I would feel if I were in the Other's shoes" and "how the Other actually feels with their own reactions".[3] Or the Child may have no initial experience to relate to the Other's experience; worse, it may perceive its representation of that experience as a threat to itself or to its own sense of Self, leading it to view the Other as "crazy" or "evil". Many of the worst aggressions are subjectively "justified" in this way.[4]

The Child system can also inhibit intuition when it follows its own desire. For example, a person may be quite capable in their professional life of knowing intuitively and, quite to the point, who to trust or not. But they do not use this skill in their love life because their Child system is dominated by passionate desire. Afterwards, the person would sadly say, "Now that I think about it, I don't understand how I could have been tricked like that!"

In any case, if the Child system were on its own, intuition would not be very different from projection. It is up to the Adult, via its multiple processes, to keep us in touch with "reality" because it stands by regularities that are independent of anyone's desires. One can think that, in the presence of a Child intuitive idea, the Adult's first reaction is to check it quickly for coherence and plausibility, on a provisional and merely probable basis. It also plays a role in the wording of that intuition, somewhat like a dream's secondary elaboration. Then, if necessary, it can play a role in choosing between several divergent intuitions aroused by one situation.

The Parent system cannot be reduced to the role of intuition inhibitor ("It's not OK to look at what grown-ups don't want to show you"), as Berne sometimes does. Models that the person internalized and transformed in interaction with the other two systems can in fact include both intuition reinforcements (permissions) and inhibitions.

But, more importantly: *the Parent system itself is a source of representations for the other's internal experience.* It contains internalizations of this experience, admittedly more or less distorted ones. There is no reason to deny to the Parent what is granted to the Child: intuition can use these representations under the same conditions, i.e., with the Adult quick check for coherence and plausibility. There is no need to sift through all Parent contents: there are countless elements in everyday life that we do not need to question. The Adult's intervention consists in sorting out which of Parent's and Child's contents should or should not be critically examined and, if necessary, modified or changed.

To conclude, integrating Child, Parent and Adult is essential in intuition. Like emotion and relationship, intuition involves the three systems' different strata. The whole intuitive process can bring up and into words perceptions of earlier strata of the psyche, establishing interactions between deeper and newer strata. With Adult intervention, it makes it possible to elucidate unconscious phenomena, notably transference and counter-transference; it is also essential for empathic relationships, as we see in the following chapter.

Autonomy

From the interaction perspective, it is impossible to describe autonomy as resulting from only one of the systems. In TA history, this role was once given to the "Free Child": therapy was then conceived as liberating the Free Child from the influence of the "Parent" considered only in its limiting aspect. This overly black and white view, whose practical usefulness is often questionable, leads to a theoretical misunderstanding of Parent structuring aspects and interactions between systems.

First, Parent influences cannot be reduced to inhibitions, as they have a reinforcing and permissive side. Second, the "Free Child" metaphor is problematic if used in an absolute way: a part of the Child system without any Parent influence is as inconceivable as a human being without having received any education or belonging to any culture. Such freedom without reference would be meaningless. Removing obstacles that hinder or block development and creativity is only a prerequisite; freeing oneself means to move in the space opened by a personally chosen project that is part of a human and inter-human world.

For this reason, Oller Vallejo suggests that the word "Free" (in the expression "Free Child") should be understood as "free *in the presence of an* internal or external *Parent*": "The child must also express himself or herself without the adapting care of the caregiving figures, although these figures will still care for him or her with protective limits when it is occasionally necessary. They also are a secure base (…) from which to explore and to which to return if the child needs care or simply to feel secure. These first protected manifestations to be oneself characterize the function of the Free Child (…)".[5]

This makes "Free" a relational term applicable to manifestations the same way other descriptive terms are. In classical TA, it tends to become a kind of intrapsychic structure that orients the person's whole development dynamism. In this, it is similar to Erskine and Trautmann's "Integrated Adult" in their ego state theory.

From the interaction perspective, mentioning personality systems' function or specific contribution is tantamount to saying *each system* contributes to the person's survival and development, followed by autonomy. It would be better to speak of "autonomy process" rather than "autonomy" because autonomy, like integration, is not a once-and-for-all outcome. What counts is the motion by which the person conquers and plays an acting role in their own existence, directs their own creativity in a direction that they have chosen and expresses this creativity in their relationships and projects.

Therefore, autonomy, or rather "the autonomy process", can only be conceived as an operation to which each personality system contributes, but which is *always evolving and does not belong to any system*. The Child system contributes its ability to desire and direct energies towards something other than what already exists, to appreciate what is missing and to encourage the person to find it by continuing to grow. The Adult system brings its lucidity and its panoramic point of view, and the Parent system its reinforcing and structuring capacity. These three components combine in being able to act creatively in one's life. Then, the autonomy process rebounds on the three interacting personality systems: it frees the Child expression, which Berne calls "spontaneity"; it frees the Adult ability to see things as they are and not just as it has always seen them, which Berne calls "consciousness"; and it frees the Parent to keep elaborating more flexible patterns and increasingly personal values. In the relational field, it opens paths towards true intimacy.

TRANSACTIONAL TEXTS

Berne's intuition as knowledge of others' experiences

We already discussed Berne's articles on intuition in Chapter 7 about the Adult system.[6] Below is additional material on personality systems' interaction and intuitive knowledge of others' experiences.

1. Berne's first article on intuition[7] is based on a World War II experience when Berne, then a military psychiatrist, tried to guess soldiers' civilian occupation at first contact. The more he did it, the more his scores improved. Wondering how this was possible, he observed that, without being aware of it, he had started to look at the person's hands, obviously an important source of information. Berne credited this to the primary process. From our point of view, this is a trial-and-error process that should be credited mostly to the Adult system, although it largely took place at the subconscious level.
2. In his 1952 article, Berne examines intuition's role in psychiatric diagnosis. He rightly maintains that all decent practitioners make accurate diagnoses without being able to justify them by exclusively deductive procedures; he concludes that they go beyond the Adult ability. From the interaction perspective, we will go a step further and argue that this complex process requires *integration of the three personality systems.*
3. In his discussion of *primal image, primal judgement,* and *ego-image,*[8] Berne is in fact talking about being aware of and using specific forms of counter-transference. He expresses this kind of perception in terms of erogenous zones, in other words in a vocabulary centred on Freud drive concept. We can add to his reflection other sources of awareness and use of counter-transference: emotional, cognitive, imaginary or sensory reactions, insofar as they are aroused by the person or the group and not by the practitioner's own script. This is one of the central themes for psychoanalytic TA,[9] Erskine and Trautmann's integrative psychotherapy[10] and relational TA.[11] Elements from the earlier strata of the psyche play an essential role; in the perspective discussed here, the process that gives them holding and meaning and provides parameters for thought results from *the combination of the three personality systems,* as analysed above.[12]

4. In *Transactional Analysis and Psychotherapy*, intuition gets a new name: Berne, full of admiration and tenderness, talks about the "Little Professor", the child's Adult which becomes the "Adult in the Child" (A1). Berne describes with great pleasure – and irony aimed at "great psychiatry professors" – children insight into others' internal reactions, especially grown-ups. The same is true of patients, especially schizophrenics. This does not surprise Berne, since, in his conception, their Child earlier strata manifest themselves as they are, without influences from other systems.

The Child system is particularly good at detecting another Child system in communication, particularly in its non-verbal and unconscious aspects: "it takes one Child system to understand another one". For Berne, the Adult and Parent intervention is rather likely to curtail how sharp the Child is, but we do not have to follow him on this point.

However, this wonderful intuition, when it exists, only works if it is free of projective elements; this is the Adult role. The Child system reacts to the other person according to its needs and desires: do they like me or not? how can I get them to do what I want? will they keep me safe? etc. If the Child believes that the other person will fulfil its desires, it is vulnerable to seduction and can be manipulated. To avoid this, the person needs the Parent structuring elaborations. Available Adult and Parent are crucial to check intuition content and to give it sound limits once it has been formed; they should not direct its content in advance or to prevent it from developing, which Berne saw very well.

Autonomy

1. To define autonomy, classical TA uses three words: *awareness, spontaneity, intimacy* from Berne's Autonomy chapter[13] in *Games people play*, Part III- Beyond Games.[14] Before we get to this text, here is an extract from the following chapter "The Attainment of Autonomy", which begins *ex abrupto* with:

> Parents, deliberately or unaware, teach their children from birth how to behave, think, feel and perceive. Liberation from these influences is no easy matter since they are deeply ingrained and are necessary during the first two or three decades of life for biological and relational survival. Indeed, such liberation is only possible at all because the individual starts off in an autonomous state, that is, capable of awareness, spontaneity, and intimacy, and he has some discretion as to which part of his parents' teachings he will accept.[15]

This calls for two comments:
- *Autonomy is projected back into childhood.* This is childhood as "lost paradise", dear to Berne. This description needs to be stripped of its idealization of children; in the same way, other texts that insist just as

one-sidedly on children's powerlessness to be stripped of their pessimism. Coming between these two positions, D. Stern provides a more balanced view, based on observation. He talks about an "infant" living in its "interpersonal world"[16] where, from the start, it acts as a person in a world of persons. However, if this infant enjoys from early on the beginnings of autonomy (which belies notions such as "original fusion" or "normal autism"[17]), the *rest of the way towards development still needs to be covered.* Interactions' generalized representations and psyche's successive strata will serve this life-long task. Berne, on the contrary, often presents the attainment of autonomy as *a return to the past*, a deconstruction of what has been added to an ideal starting state. Yet, returning to a golden age, and golden age itself, are mythical illusions. If there is autonomy, or rather autonomy process, it can only be in the form of a progressive construction, given that this necessarily involves crises and stages of deconstruction, as we saw earlier.[18]

- *Autonomy is conceived as a release* from external limitations, *rather than as an opening* to meaningful possibilities. In philosophical language, Berne sees freedom only in terms of "freedom *from*" and leaves aside "freedom *for*": it is all very well to free oneself *from* constraints, but *for what actions and projects* will this freedom be used? Using N. Symor's terms, Berne conceives autonomy as "independence" rather than "interdependence".[19]

The rest of *Games people play*'s Chapter 17 confirms this:

The attainment of autonomy, then, consists of the overthrow of all those irrelevancies discussed in [previous] chapters. And such overflow is never final: there is a continual battle against sinking back into the old ways.[20]

And Berne lists all the things that should be rejected:

The weight of a whole tribal or family historical tradition (…); the influence of the individual parental, relational and cultural background (…); the demands of contemporary society at large; the advantages derived from one's immediate relational circle (…); the rewards of being a Sulk or a Jerk (…). Following this, the individual must attain personal and relational control so that all the classes of behaviour described in the appendix[21] (…) become free choices, subject only to his will. He is then ready for game-free relationships, such as that illustrated (…) in Chapter 15.[22] At this point he may be able to develop his capacities for autonomy. In essence, this whole preparation consists of obtaining a friendly divorce from one's parents (and from other Parental influences) so that they may be agreeably visited on occasion but are no longer dominant.[23]

This is quite significant because it implicitly conveys Berne's idea about what psychotherapists and practitioners in guidance, education and organization have to do. There is no doubt that autonomy requires a substantial reduction in psychological games and dependence on parental influences and the deconstruction of many defence mechanisms. However, Berne gives the impression that an autonomous person would ideally no longer belong to their family or to any relational group, and that they would somehow be like a "Martian"[24] on Earth. Able to decide everything in their life, "except perhaps dreams",[25] they would enjoy a superhuman freedom, unfettered, but unattached. Ultimately, the past would no longer have any impact on them. But how could a human being define their identity without talking about their past? Besides, is this really what we wish for the people and groups we accompany?

This is dreaming of pure freedom unburdened by the past, dreaming of "a self-made man" who owes nothing to anyone, nor to their culture. Yes, this is a dynamic challenge, but it is also full of illusions and narcissism. This absolute autonomy dream is an unreachable ideal. This is precisely the important point: this myth is a trap that is often tragic and full of violence. Besides, should not TA practitioners encourage as much as possible the person to meet human condition as it is, with its resources and its limits? And is theory development not concerned with this task, as if its beliefs and myths had no impact on practitioners and, through them, on individuals or groups?

2. Here is now the Chapter on Autonomy, traditionally cited by classical TA: it begins with a first capacity, *awareness:*

> Awareness means the capacity to see a coffee pot and hear birds sing in one's own way, and not the way one was taught (...). A little boy sees and hears birds with delight. Then the "good father" comes along and feels he should "share" the experience and help his son "develop". He says, "That's a jay and this is a sparrow". The moment the little boy is concerned with which is a jay and which is a sparrow, he can no longer see the birds or hear them sing (...). A few people, however, still can still see and hear in the old way. But most of the members of the human race have lost the capacity to be painters, poets, or musicians, and are not left the option of seeing and hearing directly (...); they must get it second hand. The recovery of this ability is called here "awareness" (...). Awareness requires living in the here and now, and not in the elsewhere, the past or the future (...). The aware person is alive because he knows how he feels, where he is and when it is. He knows that after he dies the trees will still be there, but he will not be there to look at them again so he wants to see them now with as much poignancy as possible.[26]

Berne emphasizes human development's essential themes: contact with the here and now, awareness of being mortal. He offers two examples.

First, *the child before words*, which raises the question: how will we "see and hear birds sing" once we know some are jays and others are sparrows? Should we forget it? Can we forget it? When engrossed by landscape, nature, or artwork,[27] do we lose all knowledge? No! A gardener knows a lot about flowers, has planted them, observed them, helped them grow: does he sense flowers less because of this? Is a mother less able to sense her children "as they are" because she knows a lot about them? No, provided of course they do not let themselves be trapped by intellectualization, which cuts them off from their experience's deepest dimension.[28]

The second example is the *artist*. Examples for integrated activities in Chapter 8[29] show that any complex and meaningful activity can be elevated to the level of art. Artists, who know what a long road they have travelled to get where they are, would probably be surprised to see it as a return to childhood. Yet there is some truth in this statement if we strip it of its chronological aspect. True art, in any field, as well as any activity "raised to the level of art" (i.e., any activity involving a high degree of integrating personality systems), does not concern only the psyche's most recent strata. True creativity, while making full use of recent strata's resources, requires at the same time contact with the earliest deepest strata. A painter, a musician, an enthusiastic teacher, are said to be working "with their guts", guts being the earliest strata symbol. Without holding provided by the most recent strata or by an equally deep relationship, this contact can only result in primitive acts. Early strata are necessary for creativity and *their present state is the inspiration*, not a hypothetical and illusory "state of grace" that has mysteriously persisted in some corner of ourselves, as if our past were only the past of a part of us.

3. The second autonomy capacity is spontaneity. Here Berne gives importance to feelings and presents them as a choice between ego states:

> Spontaneity means option, the freedom to choose and express one's feelings from the assortment available (Parent, Adult and Child feelings). It means liberation from the compulsion to play games and have only the feelings one was taught to have.[30]

However, from the interaction perspective, one does not need to choose *between* several feelings from different personality systems. Allowing each system's resources to contribute according to its own role in our emotional life and to our choices is enough.

4. The third autonomy capacity is intimacy, or rather the capacity to choose intimacy. Strangely enough, Berne reduces intimacy to awareness and paradoxically says relatively little about its relational aspect. He considers it as an activity restricted to the Child system alone, free from Parental influences.

> Intimacy means the spontaneous, game-free candidness of an aware person, the liberation of the eidetic perceptive[31] uncorrupted Child in all its naiveté living in the here and now (…). Because intimacy

is essentially a function of the natural Child (...), it tends to turn out well if not disturbed by the intervention of games. Usually the adaptation to Parental influences is what spoils it, and most unfortunately this is almost a universal occurrence. But before, unless and until they are corrupted, most infants seem to be loving, and that is the essential nature of intimacy (...).[32]

The same year *Games people play* was published, Berne wrote in *TAB* two articles about the "intimacy experiment". In this, two persons looked at each other without speaking during several minutes. According to Berne, this situation "tends to diminish the Parental influence and partly free the expressive Child, so that intimacy can be achieved".[33]

Autonomy's three components are viewed from the same perspective:

1. unilateral emphasis on the Child system, without intervention from the other systems;
2. desire to reach a mythical and impossible "Free Child", because no human being exists outside of their history and culture;
3. correlative vision of the Parent system as "the one through whom misfortune happens";
4. intimacy and autonomy become regressive phenomena limited to very particular experiences, which are after all only interludes in a person's daily life.

In *What do you say after you say hello?*, Berne seems to follow a different, relational, present-life perspective:

Bilateral intimacy is defined as a candid, game-free relationship, with mutual free giving and receiving, and without exploitation.[34]

Notes

1 See pp. 131–132.
2 BERNE, E., 1961, p. 53.
3 Being able to imagine what a person, whose frame of reference is fundamentally different from one's own, might feel and do comes from a lucid knowledge of the Other that can only be obtained through sufficiently prolonged contact. This is an essential part of the professional training for practitioners in any field.
4 This ties in with the concept of "murderous identities" to which A. Maalouf has devoted a book. MAALOUF, A., *In the Name of Identity: Violence and the Need to Belong*, 1998.
5 OLLER VALLEJO, J., 2002[ES], p. 179.
6 See pp. 131–133.
7 BERNE, E., 1949.
8 See p. 132. BERNE, E., 1955. BERNE, E., 1957a.
9 For example, NOVELLINO, M., 2005.

10   ERSKINE, R.G., and TRAUTMANN, R., 1996.
11   HARGADEN, H., and SILLS, C., 2003[ES].
12   See pp. 207–210.
13   BERNE, E., 1964a, pp. 178–181.
14   BERNE, E., 1964a, p. 169
15   BERNE, E., 1964a, p. 182.
16   STERN, D., 1985. This is the title of the book: *The interpersonal world of the infant.*
17   See the discussion in STERN, D., 1985, pp. 135–137, pp. 295–296, and passim.
18   See pp.183–186.
19   These terms coming from group dynamics were probably introduced into TA by SYMOR, N., 1977. The "dependence cycle" (perhaps better called the "autonomy process" cycle) has four steps: dependence, counter-dependence, in-dependence and interdependence.
20   BERNE, E., 1964a, p. 182.
21   BERNE, E., 1964a, pp. 185–186. This appendix is a simple listing of the following classes of behaviour: Class I. Internally programmed: dreams, fantasies, fugues, delusional behaviour, involuntary actions, others; Class II. Probability programmed: activities, procedures, others; Class III. Relationally programmed: rituals and ceremonies, pastimes, operations and manoeuvres, games, intimacy.
22   This chapter 15 is a transcript of a dialogue between a therapist and a patient. One might expect a dialogue where intimacy is prominent. However, it is almost exclusively Adult-Adult in tone, where this has such a small place that it is almost impossible to guess. Berne does not underline it, because his conclusion is short: "In summary, the proceedings given constitute an activity" (structuring of time dominated by the Adult) "enlightened with some pastime". BERNE, E., 1964a, p. 175–177.
23   BERNE, E., 1964a, pp. 182–183.
24   BERNE, E., 1972, pp. 100–104. See HOSTIE, R., 1980.
25   BERNE, E, 1964a, p. 183.
26   BERNE, E., 1964a, pp. 179–180.
27   MASLOW, A.H. (1968), who calls this type of experience "peak experiences", is close to Berne's description, but he uses the term overcoming, not going back.
28   See Stern's text on the advent of the Verbal Self. STERN, D., 1985, pp. 209–210.
29   See pp. 160–162.
30   BERNE, E., 1964a, p. 180.
31   Eidetic perception refers to the kind of experience described in relation to awareness as "seeing or hearing birds sing". It is close to Maslow's "peak experiences". MASLOW, A.H., 1968.
32   BERNE, E., 1964a, p. 180–181.
33   BERNE, E., 1964b, p. 14. BERNE, E., 1964c, p. 15.
34   BERNE, E., 1972, p. 25.

12
CO-CREATIVITY AND RELATIONSHIPS

Personality systems are open to internal and external events. Internally, they perceive each other and interact. However, *this interaction depends in several ways on how they relate with external events*:

- many of their contents are directly related to external events, the most important of which are relational;
- their evolutionary processes are very often initiated, promoted or frustrated by relationships. Most of what needs to be done to achieve autonomy, make and unmake successive integrations, and implement evolving creativity, can only be accomplished in a relational frame of reference;
- creativity is expressed in a world full of relationships: even an artist working alone mentally addresses potential spectators or readers.

All that has been said above about the person, their three personality systems, their internal and external competence, and their sense of Self, must therefore be placed in the broader context of relationships, whatever the field of application considered.

The psyche's successive strata also leave their mark on relationships. On this point, D. Stern diverges[1] from the object relations theory and the Self psychology theory. These theories, focused on pathology, observe two main strata: in the earliest stratum, the Other is "an object for the Self"[2] and is perceived as a way to satisfy the person's needs and desires; in the most recent stratum, the Other is recognized and accepted as a "separate" distinct and different being. D. Stern, who focuses his work on the healthy infant, observed that the infant is in an interpersonal position from the very beginning: from its emerging Self, the infant needs the "Self-regulating Other"; however, it does not mean they are in a fusional or undifferentiated relationship.[3] According to Stern, development's earliest strata are not primarily sources of painful or destructive "eruptions"; on the contrary, they are the foundation of our entire later social life; without them, our adult relationships would have neither intensity nor variety.

The three personality systems have always coexisted, each with its own specific contribution. At the deepest strata's level, they preserve the implicit memory of first relationships in ego state trios, where the Child records the person's experiences and the Parent records the others' experiences as the person perceived them; as for the Adult system, D. Stern states that rudimentary lucidity, awareness that the Other is "another" and not an extension of oneself, exists from birth. Thanks to this, the relationship can become more varied and complex, as the three interacting systems play their organizer role connected to distinct dimensions of experience. The Other is then increasingly perceived *both* as a separate entity (Adult), as a source of gratification (Child) and as a person with rights and needs which we respect as much as we expect them to do the same for us (Parent). Of course, this is not done once and for all: it is an ongoing process interacting personality systems and their strata. This is where relational creativity or relational deadlock come from.

The role of the relationship

What is at stake in a relationship? There are three levels:

1. *Providing a holding environment*
   Even if the person can hold themselves in a situation, the relationship enriches or modifies the holding environment. "Holding" *is* a central theme in D. Winnicott's theory: he uses it for the relationship between mother and child, but also for any deep relationship. "Providing a holding environment" takes roots in the earliest strata of development; among other things, this is what the "Self-regulating Other" does from the beginning of life.[4] From there, "providing a holding environment" extends in more recent strata: for example, frame of reference and rules for a process or group provide a holding environment.

   Our impulses, emotions and sensations (especially at their most brutal, archaic or intense) need "holding", either by ourselves, or by ourselves and someone else, or by ourselves and a group. *"Holding" is neither repressing nor being overwhelmed*; it is ensuring that the impulse, emotion or sensation can resonate in an internal and external *space* without losing all reference points, as happens in panic, terror, destructive acts, madness, etc. This leads to another meaning of the expression *"holding"*: holding *on*. Primitive, violent or destructive dynamics can only be "held" if there is someone who "holds on" without breaking contact. When holding is provided by someone else, they must find the right distance: neither too far away, which would cause the person to lose contact and feel abandoned or run away, nor too close, which would risk overwhelming both partners and pushing them into defensive reactions or acting out.[5]

   This is not to say that "providing a holding environment" is only useful during emotional turmoil! As soon as two people engage in a close relationship, they provide each other "holding"; this is a co-creation of their own, a "co-holding" if you like, which underlies the relationship and continues as long as it exists. A practitioner, whatever their field of application, may bring it to the foreground and make it the theme of a specific intervention. In the private sphere, perception, hope or fantasy of "available holding" probably plays an important role in relationships with lovers and friends, even groups which are, or should be, "holding environments".

All three systems, Child, Parent and Adult, are needed to "provide holding": without the Child, it would be no more than fake appearance or defensiveness; without a flexible yet firm Parent, it would turn into acting out; and without the Adult, the process would not be grounded in reality.

The "holding provided" has different modalities: its extremes can be symbolized by the "cocoon" and "armour" metaphors.[6] Both extremes are usually harmful; neither allows for change: the armour is too rigid; the cocoon leads to listless lethargy.

2. *Giving meaning together*
This level is not reduced to the definition of the word "meaning". The foundations for "meaning" are established as soon as the person perceives, through the Other's or the group's reaction, that what they are experiencing can be "held" and is therefore neither abnormal,[7] nor crazy, nor absurd.[8] As we know, this does not necessarily imply content approval.[9]

While "giving and getting a holding environment" is more about the person's competence to manage their external and internal life, their sense of Self takes a more important role in co-creating meaning. The person "enters into the co-created meaning" with their three systems: they internalize with the Parent, perceive another aspect of reality with the Adult and live another way with the Child. In a situation of "mourning" (letting go), the person's reactions must of course be given holding initially; however, bitterness usually continues well beyond that because they cannot "give meaning". As for trauma, much of its destructive mental impact is linked to a lasting inability to both provide a "holding environment" and to "give meaning" to what happened, without the victim being able or willing to find another person to do this with them.

3. *Communicating and thinking together.*
This is the relationship's verbal level: each partner (or members of the group) can contribute with their own resources and personal frame of reference. One should not speak or think for the other person: one should accompany them in the relationship as a distinct person with their own resources, judgements and emotional, cognitive and creative capacities. This verbal level clarifies the previous levels' contents and makes them more easily usable to restore the person's or group's sense of Self and competence, when necessary, then to open the space for decisions and action. Here too, co-creativity comes into play: what is elucidated by joint words or joint thought is not equal to the sum of what each partner would bring separately.

It is through these three levels that, in every TA field,[10] the practitioner, the person and the group can direct their relationship towards change together. This dimension has been highlighted above all by H. Hargaden and C. Sills'[11] relational TA, but also by all the approaches inspired by object relations theory, such as Erskine and Trautmann's integrative psychotherapy, "transactional psychoanalysis" and co-creative TA.[12]

Relational interactions

The same applies to relationships as to internal dynamics: they can bring about disjunctions, inhibitions, conjunctions, collusions or interpersonal integrations.[13] In contrast to the intrapsychic dynamics we have discussed so far, these are based on a relationship between the person and another, or a group, which is at least temporarily inscribed in external reality.

In fact, this is the very foundation of how we build ourselves and our personality systems, for this begins in and via the relationship. In healthy development, the Other's presence is continually internalized and personalized through a lifelong evolutionary process, so that our existence is based on an endless to-and-fro between the relational and the intrapsychic. When this situation brings about successful conjunctions or integrations, it gives all partners the opportunity to build and internalize *resources that would never have existed without their having met*. Each can keep these resources within themselves when the other is not physically present[14]; each can let go when the relationship ends. The Parent organizes this process of internalization and plays an irreplaceable role as an "checkpoint" between the person and the Other, including into adult life; of course, this process will only lead to true creativity if freed from bare repetition, in other words, if it has sufficiently evolved in interaction with the other two systems.

But if this process of going to-and-fro between the inside and the outside is deficient, the person falls into *loneliness* or "yearning" for the Other. Or they continue to need the Other in order to make sure that their own intrapsychic processes function, to make use of the Other's competence or to strengthen their own sense of Self: the relationship turns into *dependence*. Temporary dependency can be where autonomy develops, for example children dependent on "good enough" parental figures. Dependency can also be temporary and partial, allowing a common task or learning to be done. But dependency can prevent autonomy: what occurs then is a more or less fixed collusion, no longer between elements of the person's personality systems (as in intrapsychic dynamics), but between a part of them and a part of someone else's.

Relational collusions

These are of different types, depending on their structure and the context in which they occur.

1. *Fusional relationship.* This is a symmetrical relationship in which collusion happens in the concurring aspects of the personalities involved, while the others remain inhibited or unrecognized; usually the partners feel strongly valued in their sense of Self. When this type of relationship gives way to a more realistic perception (for example, when the "honeymoon" fades), this valorization can be a powerful motivation for the partners to continue to deepen their connection and to put energy into maintaining and developing the relationship.

Alternatively, one of them may, in order not to "let go", move from one relationship to another in an attempt to recapture the initial sparkle.

2. *Clinging relationship.* In contrast to the fusional relationship, the clinging relationship is dissymmetrical, so that one can observe a high and a low position.[15] One partner clings to the other like ivy growing on a tree, to the point of risking suffocating the other, as the comparison would suggest. The relationship is built on the illusion that, on the competence level, one partner is able to deal with not only their own life's internal and external events but also the other's. On the sense of Self level, though, it is often the partner in the high position who values themself by taking charge of the other (often by devaluing the latter), so that they would feel threatened if it stopped or if the other were to take effective autonomy.

3. *The symbiotic relationship*[16] is a particular case of a clinging relationship. One partner's Parent and Adult are ignored, as well as the other partner's Child.

    - As a result, the partner in the "high" position (Parent and Adult) avoids investing their own Child; except for gratifications from their sense of Self, they ignore their own needs and desires. This apparently unacknowledged Child is complicit in the situation (relational collusion), as it allows it to obsess over the partner, to shift the responsibility onto them and to value itself as a useful person.
    - The other person behaves like a passive child,[17] ignoring their own capacity for autonomy and leaving it to their partner to decide and think for them. The Child benefits from the illusory security and the rejection of responsibilities, and the Parent has internalized the strategy of letting the partner act in their place. When this occurs, we can say that "two (or more) individuals behave as though between them they form a whole person".[18]

    This type of dependency often conceals collusion at the psyche's deepest levels, whereby the person apparently in the Child position unconsciously seeks to provide "holding" for an unspoken, usually archaic need or suffering of their parental figure(s).[19] Processes of this type convey unconscious beliefs and strategies such as: "The Other needs me to need them so that they don't feel bad or abandoned, and I will make sure to be what they need", "I will make myself bad so that they can love me, care for me or feel useful, because otherwise they will be the one to die, feel abandoned, get sick, etc.". Underneath the symbiotic relationship's apparent dissymmetry, there is a hidden reciprocity; more precisely, this dependency covers another dependency in reverse. These paradoxical dynamics are, of course, likely to reappear in transference.

4. *Dominant relationships.* Here, one partner's defences push them towards pseudo-autonomy where true emotional contact with the Other is avoided. This allows them to strengthen an apparently unshakable, but secretly fragile sense of Self,[20] while the Other, whose sense of Self is greatly devalued, desperately seeks an illusory "holding environment". This results in relationships of domination, control, seduction, devaluation or exploitation.[21]

5. *Family, group, and institutional systems.* Relational collusion is not limited to two people. They include family, group and institutional systems studied by different systemic approaches.

Relational integrations

The empathic relationship

Rogers defined empathic understanding this way: "To perceive the internal frame of reference of another with accuracy, and with the emotional components and meanings which pertain thereto, as if one were the other person, but without ever losing the 'as if' condition".[22]

This refers to understanding the Other's experience, whether this understanding comes from intuition, as discussed in the previous chapter, or from explicit communication.

However, this is not enough for an *empathic relationship to take place*:

- The practitioner has to provide a holding environment for all this and not become absorbed in the person's world, to the risk of social collusion.
- To perceive that someone else understands what is going on inside oneself can be felt by some people as terrifying, a source of shame, etc.; therefore, empathy also implies *communicated respect*.[23]

This attitude alleviates two fears linked to this kind of situation: fear of devaluing one's sense of Self and fear of being taken over. Empathy is not limited to professional relationships; in different ways and to different degrees, it is an essential element of friendship, love and any collaboration that is humanly successful, i.e., free from undue competition, exploitation or devaluation.

Empathy is not a unilateral process to perceive the Other's experience: empathy is *registering this perception in a relationship*. On my side, I perceive with respect what the other person is experiencing, and I accept the fact that they are experiencing it; on the other side, the other person knows and accepts that I perceive their experience and does not feel either threatened or devalued. This type of relationship is established and deepened through empathic transactions,[24] in which the practitioner communicates and verifies what they have perceived and receives confirmation from the person or group.

In empathy, the Child provides the ability to "resonate" with the Other's experience,[25] but for this resonance to be truly empathic, personality systems integration and contact with the person are both necessary. The Parent system provides the models of respect, acceptance, suspension of judgement, etc., and in its earliest strata, internalizations of long-standing or deeply experienced empathic relationships. The Adult system verifies that this resonance comes neither from a dynamic specific to the speaker, nor from a less evolved Parent's projection or internalization. This is how we move from the imaginary position of "putting oneself in the other's shoes" to the integrated position of "picturing the reactions of someone else who has different reactions, thoughts and feelings from mine".

At the theoretical level, this presentation of empathy differs from B. Clark's,[26] which is constructed from a sequential or descriptive perspective. In H. Hargaden and C. Sills' relational TA, it holds a central place.

Intimacy

From the interaction perspective, intimacy is an integrated relationship source of creativity between people or in a group, without collusion between personality systems. Like empathy, intimacy is an integrated relationship at a double level: integration *in each person concerned* and integration *in the relationship*. Like all integration, it is in constant evolution: it is neither everlasting nor acquired once and for all but can be either reinforced or demolished according to 1) external *circumstances*; 2) the partners' *emotional life*; 3) the stability of their mutual *bond*; 4) their conscious *decisions* to invest or not their energy and creativity to preserve and strengthen the relationship. These four dimensions are important in relationship therapy and counselling.

In general, the intimacy core is less about the partners' competence than their sense of Self: this is often where each partner draws the most resources from. But there are also powerful synergies where partners share in the accomplishment of a task done together.[27]

Integrated collaborative relationships

In the integrated collaborative relationship, the emphasis is the other way round: the partners support each other primarily, but not only in terms of competence and external effectiveness. Conjunctions and integrations between their personality systems are focused on a common task's achievement. Most of these relationships are limited to this frame of reference; a few, however, can blossom into relationships such as certain professional friendships, where people also feel recognized in their sense of Self.

Co-creative and transferential dimensions

1. All psyche strata usually manifest themselves in relationships if these are intense enough. Some earlier strata dynamics are powerful resources, while others appear to be deterrents or potentially destructive. During change processes in any field of application, one has to pay particular attention to dynamics likely to cause them to fail or to divert them from their objective. Among these, transference and counter-transference have been studied extensively, although unconscious dynamics can manifest themselves indirectly in many ways: 1) chronic body tensions[28]; 2) relational attitude biased in one way or another (transference in the narrow sense); 3) projective

identifications, where the practitioner feels constant pressure to confirm the person's or group's script; 4) parallel processes[29]; 5) unconscious communication; 6) dreams[30]; 7) acting out, 8) counter-transference in the practitioner and in the group, etc.

We discussed already what happens in personality systems when processing these dynamics. Their perception and identification are a special case of perceiving others' experience through intuition[31] as we saw in Chapter 11. In order to benefit from them later on, partners need to co-create, if not already done, a "holding environment" and a meaning, and to think together. This does not only concern potentially destructive elements: certain essentially positive dynamics show inertia that can subtly but permanently hinder progress. The practitioner needs to bring them to light through respectful inquiry and reflection on the process.

2. The concept of transference has covered variable ground in the history of psychoanalysis and psychotherapy.[32] Originally, transference was analysed mainly from Freud's and followers' repetition perspective: they defined it as a reiteration of past desires or relationships. Repetition implies a particular type of projections: the person perceives the Other through what they experienced in the original scene and reacts accordingly.

According to R. Little, however, "since Freud, our understanding of transference has expanded. Klein and her followers insist that transference is much more than a repetition of relational patterns about important past figures. They see it as enacting internalized object relations in the here and now. In contrast to Freud, many contemporary therapists understand it as a process where some current emotions and parts of the Self are externalized in the therapeutic relationship. This includes projecting object relations with both positive and hostile feelings, and fantasies".[33] When applied to each person's or group's transference, this invites us to go beyond strict repetition perspective and to consider them from an evolutionary point of view, within the relationship frame of reference with the practitioner and their counter-transference. There is more to transference than an imaginary projection the practitioner must "avoid": it implies understanding and questioning how and in what way their own way of being and acting encourages this undesirable process.[34] Transference, in this perspective, is not a simple projection on a cinema "screen" which is not fundamentally modified by the screened film, but a real relationship, more precisely *a relational collusion.*

C. Moiso[35] has analysed the most frequent of transference types, where the person projects a past parental figure onto the therapist. Most importantly for therapeutic practice, he distinguishes two transference types according to the Parent's evolution degree:

- transference of a Parent pre-verbal stratum[36] (P1), beyond the reach of verbal investigation;
- transference of a more evolved stratum (P2), accessible to verbal, narrative or emotional techniques.

Transference elements may also come from the Child system. Erskine[37] mentioned a process (from an evolutionary perspective) where the Child has created an imaginary parent for survival, "Bogeyman" or "Fairy Godmother",[38] who meets all the child's needs in an imaginary life, usually in sharp contrast to real life, and which the child projects into the therapeutic situation. Kohut studied the idealizing transference which "mobilies an all-powerful object" ("You are perfect, and I am part of you"), and the mirror transference which "remobilizes the grandiose Self" ("I am perfect and I need you to confirm it"); both are common in narcissistic personality disorder.

There are also relationships poisoned by projections from a "diabolical" imagination into racism, extreme nationalism, sects, traditionalisms or fundamentalisms (which, in one way or another, consider the outside world as Satan's domain), etc.

3. When the psyche deeper strata's manifestations have been held and given meaning, they can be resources that partners, or group members, can use co-creatively. G. Summers and K. Tudor's[39] co-creative TA has highlighted this aspect very well.

However, co-creative TA uses an ego state theory close to Erskine and Trautmann's, where the Child and Parent systems are exclusively considered as repetitive and connected by transference; the Adult, the only system neither transferential nor repetitive, becomes the only place where creativity happens. This angle risks reducing the ego state theory to a dichotomous opposition between transference and absence of transference, without any proper transactional content; it leaves aside the idea of three evolving personality systems in interaction.

Furthermore, no doubt under Gestalt influence, the opposition between *contact* with the "sterile" past and *contact* with the "solely creative" present easily becomes dichotomous.[40] The risk is then to reinforce the opposition and to give the impression that, in order to be "in the present" or "in the here and now", one needs a "chemically pure" distilled relationship, free of any trace of the past; and that is impossible. Yes, there is no creativity in repetition, but outside repetition, we only ever create as a complete person, from the contents of the interacting and integrating Child, Parent and Adult.

Groups and institutions

We are in relation not only with people but also, although in a different way, with groups and institutions. These are important dimensions in TA fields of application, whether in education, guidance or especially in organization. Group dynamics, institutional or corporate culture, etc., may be as important to consider as individual dynamics even if the intervention direct beneficiary is an individual, as in coaching. As for therapists, they are obviously concerned by therapy group dynamics; however, they should not forget that some client problems come out of institutional contexts and power games within groups or between groups. For example, it would be a mistake, probably fraught with consequences, to direct the therapy of a person who is a victim of professional harassment as if it were only a problem of self-assertion.

What dynamics link a person to a group or institution of which they consider to be a member? It is useful to distinguish between different types of groups and belonging.

1. Berne describes group *affiliation* process in great detail when he sets out his *group imago*[41] theory, i.e., the personal, conscious and unconscious representation that each member makes of the group and of themselves in the group. This is one of the very few instances where Berne describes development from a healthy functioning perspective. Clarkson[42] combined this description with observations on group dynamics developed at the Tavistock Institute. Here is the data from the interaction perspective:

    a. Even before the person comes to the group, they have a "*provisional imago*" which is the result of previous experiences; in other words, of all personality systems' strata: in addition to more or less realistic information and expectations at verbal stratum level, it also includes various defence mechanisms or transference fantasies.
    b. In the group's early stages, the imago becomes "*adaptive*" and then "*operative*". Berne links the first to a cautious and defensive commitment to feeling safe and finding one's place by adapting[43]; with the "operative" imago, the person begins to express themself more personally. At this stage, their personality systems' energy is directed towards their "sense of Self in the group"[44]: the Child calms down its fantasies, the Parent gradually frees itself from the group's real or imaginary expectations, and the Adult forms an increasingly realistic representation of the group. On the one hand, these processes are part of structuring a healthy group; on the other, they make the group vulnerable to the unconscious "basic assumptions" described by Bion.[45]
    c. With the *activity* phase,[46] the group can work on its task and become a "working group", where the person can manifest and use their interacting personality systems for the group benefit and its task, as well as for themself and other members.
    d. Tudor[47] recalled how important the end of the group is, with its "mourning" or *letting go*.

2. Berne's analysis of group imago phases does not apply to *constraint groups*: penitentiary institutions, refugee or prison camps and ghettos of all kinds. This also applies to people who are victims of professional harassment, of a violent environment, of a couple or family where they are abused, etc., if they do not have the objective or subjective possibility of leaving these groups.
3. The group imago theory does not apply to groups *to which the person has always belonged without any choice on their part*: family, social, religious,

institutional, national or cultural affiliations. These are often surprisingly long-lasting, even if the person has undergone many changes in their life. This is because, well beyond dependence on strokes, the Child system tends to place great value on them, often because it perceives them as an essential element of its sense of Self or identity. The Parent, in its primitive strata, adds a dimension of duty or loyalty[48] which can go as far as sacrificing one's own life and that of one's loved ones, blind allegiance to leaders or active hatred for those outside.[49] The Adult system, even evolved, is often quite late in taking a stand on these contents, if it ever does: these contents remain unquestionable evidence for a very long time, if only because no one has ever contested them or even stated them clearly.

But if the person has belonged or belongs to different cultures or environments,[50] the Parent may have internalized contradictory models, and the Child may experience this potential uprooting as painful. The person may react with various strategies[51]: moving from one culture to another according to circumstances, retreating into an opportunistic individualism or constructing their personal integration from elements of their different environments or cultures.

4. Without falling into "group illusion", i.e., without considering a group as a "supra-person", it cannot be denied that being in a group or belonging to an institution induces convergent subconscious or unconscious reactions in its members. These dynamics can be compared to *resonance*: members tend to share a certain range of mutually reinforcing internal and external reactions. These group, institutional and cultural "resonances" can be analysed according to the three personality systems: what are the imaginary elements, conscious and unconscious wishes and desires that resonate in the group (Child system)? To which characters do their usual role models refer? What values or priorities are considered intangible or implicit criteria for judgement (Parent system)? How clear is the group about itself and the relationships within it (Adult system)? And above all, how well do these elements integrate? Are there partial and opposite integrations like splitting ("pairing groups" according to Bion)?

With a few differences, this presentation is similar to Berne's[52] group culture theory: a Parent element, the group "etiquette" – an Adult element, the "technique" – and a Child element, the "character". However, his description only considers certain elements and strata of the three personality systems.

TRANSACTIONAL TEXTS

Berne and relationship

Berne, when talking about change, thinks in terms of intervention rather than relationship, as chapter 19's title "The Decisive Intervention" in *What Do You*

Say After You Say Hello? This does not mean he was not aware of the relationship's importance in his practice. Here are clues scattered at various points in his work:

1. Berne is convinced that it is essential the therapeutic relationship is lived in mutual respect and transparency. This is visible in his experiences on staff-patient meetings[53] or in statements about an Adult presence in every human being:

   > Every grown-up, no matter how disturbed or functionally deteriorated, has a fully formed Adult which under proper conditions can be re-cathected (…).[54]

2. In his practice as a therapist and a practitioner, Berne tracks down anything that resembles a psychological game that would transform the relationship into a power relationship, whether this dynamic comes from the therapist or the patient.
3. The "I'm OK–You're OK" relationship, which belongs to the script theory, also describes in TA a type of attitude necessary for the relationship between the practitioner, the person and the group.
4. Berne's "three Ps" (protection, permission and potency) described in *What do you say after you say hello?*[55]: the emphasis on "decisive intervention", unfortunately, risks giving the impression that "the therapist is doing something to the patient' and leaving what we now call the co-creative aspect of the relationship in the shade. R. and M. Goulding made the essential distinction clear: while the therapist and the patient each have potency, "the power is in the patient"[56] and must belong to the patient.

However, every healthy relationship includes a secure frame of reference (protection) and space for creativity and personal experimentation (permission). Potency applies when it comes to "providing a holding environment" by "holding on". When engaging in discussion and looking for meaning, both partners' resources (potency) must be combined and put at the service of co-creation.

After Berne, C. Steiner emphasized with "potency" that any relationship, especially the therapeutic relationship, deserves this name only insofar as it is free of power games.[57]

Intimacy

1. We saw in the previous chapter that Berne, in *Games people play*, does not really emphasize the relational aspect of intimacy. He does, however, in *What do you say after you say hello?*:

   > Bilateral intimacy is defined as a candid, game-free relationship, with mutual free giving and receiving, and without exploitation.[58]

2. There is a description of intimacy in TA which, unusually for its time, is made from the interaction perspective: L. Boyd and H. Boyd[59] wrote it in 1980. To the proximity of the two persons' Child systems, as emphasized by Berne, they added a necessary condition for intimacy: the presence of Parent systems feeling "concern for the Other"[60]:

> We believe that for intimacy to occur, each party must experience the elements of closeness and caring *simultaneously* and with each other. Therefore, we offer the following formal definition of intimacy: Intimacy is a simultaneous and mutual set of transactions consisting of both caring (P2-C2) and closeness (C2-C2). (...) During intimacy each participant receives caring from the other, sends caring to the other, and shares closeness with the other. The complexity and richness of intimacy is the result of each individual operating from two ego states simultaneously.[61]

And why not the Adult, whose lucidity is entirely appropriate... the authors would certainly not disagree? At the time, it was already a great deal to conceive a dynamic integrating two personality systems!

L. and H. Boyd follow Berne in classifying intimacy as a structuring of time; but remarkably, they describe it as a potentially lasting *relationship*:

> It is commonly believed[62] in TA circles that intimacy is necessarily short-lived and brief. We suggest that there is nothing inherent in the intimacy transactions that requires that intimacy be brief, other than the individuals' more or less limited tolerance for intense emotional experience and their more or less limited willingness to value and protect the intimate relationship. In preserving an intimate relationship, it is necessary that all participants provide for and protect opportunities for caring and for closeness. An initial experience of intimacy between two people is not nearly so difficult as the maintenance of an ongoing intimate relationship.[63]

This change of perspective, which leads us to consider the relationship in its duration and history rather than through snapshots or brief episodes, announces the shift to come in the relational approach. Before leaving the relational field, however, we need to examine one of its essential factors: communication.

Notes

1 STERN, D., 1985.
2 Kohut says: a "Self-object". This term refers to "any narcissistic experience in which the Other serves the Self". According to Kohut, this type of relationship is neither the prerogative of borderline and narcissistic personality disorders, nor of any pathology, but is part of healthy functioning. See Chapter 10, note 11.

3   STERN, D., 1985, p. 101.
4   See p. 72, p. 110, etc. STERN, D., 1985.
5   See the description of script protocol dynamics and its narrative given by CORNELL, W.R., and LANDAICHE, M., 2006.
6   The character body-armour that Reich and bioenergy speak of also has a "holding" function, see REICH, W., 1933. LOWEN, A., and LOWEN, L, 1976 and others.
7   "To normalize" is part of giving meaning. See ERSKINE, R.G., and TRAUTMANN, R., 1996.
8   Reframing can be one of many other ways of co-creating meaning.
9   The "narrativist" approaches work above all to "give meaning" to events in the person's life. See ALLEN, J.R., and ALLEN, B.A., 1997. The work on fairy tales also includes an implicit aspect of "giving meaning". See BERNE, E., 1972, pp. 111–116.
10 See van BEEKUM, S., 2005.
11 HARGADEN, H., and SILLS, C., 2002.
12 See GRÉGOIRE, J., 2009.
13 Cornell and Landaiche introduced the concept of "relational" impasse. CORNELL, W.F., and LANDAICHE, M.N., 2006.
14 This is, for example, the case of Stern's "evoked companion". STERN, D., 1985, pp. 111–122.
15 See RUBBERS, B., 1998.
16 This concept is often used imprecisely for all supportive relationships and even for fusional relationships.
17 On passivity, see SCHIFF, A.W., and SCHIFF, J.L., 1971. The four forms of passivity are: doing nothing, over-adaptation to the Other's assumed expectations, agitation, violence/incapacitation.
18 SCHIFF, J., and others, 1975, p. 5.
19 This is one of the possible interpretations of the "second order symbiosis" mechanism. SCHIFF, J., and others, 1975, p. 9.
20 See the concept of "blameless" attitude: ERSKINE, R.G., 1994.
21 In his article on mystification, Martorell highlighted one of the mechanisms inherent in these relationships: the repetitive definition of one person's external reality and internal reality by another, which very often takes the repetitive form of: "You're the one with the problem". MARTORELL, J., 1994.
22 ROGERS, C., 1959, p. 210. In: TUDOR, K., 2011, p. 40.
23 ERSKINE, R.G., and TRAUTMANN, R., 1996, have specifically emphasized respect in the practitioner questioning of the person or group with their concept of "respectful inquiry".
24 HARGADEN, H., and SILLS, C., 2002[ES], pp. 167–198.
25 It is increasingly accepted that "mirror neurons", also known as "empathic neurons", play an essential role in this type of relationship and, more generally, in interpersonal relationships. See IACOBONI, M., 2009.
26 CLARK, B.D., 1991.
27 Synergy is presented as the most developed phase in the evolution of a couple by BADER, E., and PEARSON, P., 1983.
28 This is the approach of trends originating from Reich and his disciples, Lowen and Pierrakos. REICH, W., 1933. LOWEN, A., 1976. PIERRAKOS, J., 2005.
29 See CLARKSON, P., 1991c.
30 In TA, see, for example, THOMSON, G., 1987, and recent articles by BRÉCARD, F., 2005. GHIRINGHELLI, H., 2005. GUICQUÉRO, A.M., 2005.

31 See pp. 207–210.
32 See CLARKSON, P., 1991b.
33 LITTLE, R., 2006 ES, p. 8.
34 See LITTLE, R., 2006ES.
35 MOISO, C., 1985ES.
36 The development theory detailed above (Chapter 4) explains why replacing chronological connotations by strata considerations.
37 ERSKINE, R.G., 1988.
38 It is sometimes called P1+ but it is not really a Parent ego state: it does not result from the internalization of a parental figure, but from a Child creation.
39 SUMMERS, G., and TUDOR, K., 2000ES.
40 The same is true of Erskine and Trautmann's ego state theory.
41 BERNE, E., 1963, pp. 220–226.
42 CLARKSON, P., 1991a.
43 Some personalities do not adapt, because their defence mechanism pushes them to seek to impose themselves or to monopolize.
44 The term "operative imago" should not be misleading: the energy is not yet directed towards action, but towards the sense of Self in the group. This, according to Berne, depends on how the person believes they are perceived by others, and especially by the leader(s).
45 BION, W.R., 1961. The basic unconscious assumptions of a group are, according to Bion, fight/flight and pairing, which often takes the form of a split between two parts of the group.
46 Berne's expression is "secondary adjusted imago". BERNE, E. 1963, p. 226. Clarkson P., 1991, uses the less ambiguous term "clarified imago".
47 TUDOR, K., 1997.
48 See de GAULEJAC, V., 1987.
49 See MAALOUF, A., 1998.
50 See the contribution of the sociologist B. Lahire, whom we have discussed in relation to the Social Parent: see pp. 115–116. LAHIRE, B., 2001. MOUNIER, P., 2001, pp. 208–210.
51 See what Shea Schiff calls "deviant parenting systems". KOUWENHOVEN, M., 1983.
52 BERNE, E., 1963.
53 BERNE, E., 1968b.
54 BERNE, E., 1961, p. 82., see also p. 164.
55 BERNE, E., 1972, pp. 371–376.
56 The power is in the patient: this is the title of Goulding's first book: GOULDING, R.G., and GOULDING, M., 1978.
57 STEINER, C., 1981.
58 BERNE, E., 1972, p. 25.
59 BOYD, L., and BOYD, H., 1980.
60 *"Caring"* can mean, depending on context, caring for the other or taking care of the other.
61 BOYD, L., and BOYD, H., 1980, pp. 281–283.
62 Following Berne himself.
63 BOYD, L., and BOYD, H., 1980, pp. 281–283.

13
COMMUNICATION WITHIN THE RELATIONSHIP

Communication embodies the relationship. It is like a wave on a river: it embodies how strong the river is, but when it has gone, the river is still there, and another wave can form. Communication also structures the relationship, makes it evolve and transforms it in depth: without communication, the relationship remains blurred and implicit, and therefore vulnerable to all subjective projections. Problems raised by what is not said, and even more so by family or institutional secrets,[1] provide ample proof. In short, communication clarifies or obscures the relationship, inspires creativity or inhibits it; in any case, it lays the foundations for what will follow.

Like most of our actions, communication has different interacting levels for each person. The *inner side* of communication comprises the three systems' action and their reciprocal interactions; it includes conscious and unconscious elements. From the interaction perspective, this inner side is analysed the same way previous dynamics have been, i.e., according to the three personality systems, superimposed growth strata and interactions.

The *outer side* deals with external manifestations, the analysis of which first comes from a sequential or descriptive perspective. That is beyond the scope of this book, but it is important to emphasize how structures and manifestations are articulated with one another. This is the purpose of this short chapter.

The outer side of communication

The *outer side* comprises the verbal, the paraverbal[2] and the non-verbal; while non-verbal communication takes place without interruption for all participants, its verbal and paraverbal aspects imply distinguishing between a *speaker*, i.e., the person who speaks, and one or more *listeners* to whom communication is addressed. This differentiates communication from relationship, which can be defined as a "relational field" that does not belong to any particular participant but is the result of a shared co-creation.

In addition, the outer side carries at least three simultaneous elements:

1. *Content*, usually explicit and verbal: this is what the speaker wishes to convey. Its meaning does not only depend on words, but also on context, on each

person's expectations and on previous exchanges,[3] which brings us back to the relationship.
2. *Intention*, which concerns the reaction that the speaker wishes to obtain from the listener. This is closely related to the external message's *form*[4]: it can be informative, interrogative, imperative, permissive, expressing an emotion, etc. There is no such thing as "neutral" communication in which the speaker does not seek in any way to direct how the listener will react, whether in terms of external content (e.g., giving an order or information), internal experience (helping the listener to become aware of an emotion or belief) or process (encouraging lateral communication in a group).

   It would be a mistake to understand this intention as necessarily manipulative. Practitioners in all TA fields and other approaches are familiar with "intentions" such as: opening space for the listener's expression, fostering a sense of understanding and acceptance, helping the listener to formulate and achieve their goals, facilitating emotional expression, stimulating Adult thinking, managing group process, lightening the mood, etc. Each of these approaches, which are an integral part of the practitioners' art, seeks a specific effect and has no meaning outside of it.
3. Finally, all communication shows *the way the speaker conceives and experiences the relationship*[5] *with the listener*. This aspect, usually implicit though always present, reveals itself in outer attitudes: respect, openness, competition, distance, etc.

From the inner to the outer side

At the verbal self's stratum, the speaker seeks to be "congruent", i.e., to reduce to a minimum any inconsistencies between outer side elements of the communication. The speaker seeks to give it a form that is as adequate as possible with regard to their *intention* (see point 2 above), in order to foster the reaction they want as much as possible. However, they cannot control all parameters: to some degree, their internal tensions or conflicts, their disjunctions, inhibitions or intrapsychic or social collusions, or simply their uncertainties or hesitations are expressed externally and are more or less consciously perceived by the listener.

When participants' personality systems are at least in *conjunction*, they are more likely to be congruent enough to either avoid long-lasting gaps between what each believes to be communicating and what the other understands, or to clarify in a relatively short period of time any failure in the process. A fortiori, a speaker whose personality systems are in *integration* is likely to develop a more powerful communication, as seen with the integrated activities' examples quoted in Chapter 8.[6] These internal qualities will enable them to react effectively to external blocks due to context or different frames of reference. In these cases, outer side communication will be highly coherent and more easily analysed in a sequential perspective, using any set of descriptive categories, for example with Berne's descriptive terms. This is particularly useful for an objective within the sequential perspective limits, like the search for options.[7]

However, if either speaker's or listener's personality systems are in *disjunction*, *inhibition* or *collusion*, whether these interactions are *intrapsychic* or inherent in the partners' *relationship*, there is a good chance these inconsistencies or undercurrent dynamics will "spill over" to the outer side of communication and result in incongruent, even contradictory, confused or paradoxical communication. Berne expressed this phenomenon in two conceptualizations that do not entirely overlap:

- through the idea of non-verbal communication, as in Clara's example in Chapter 10[8];
- through the double transaction concept,[9] which include an apparent or "social" level and a psychological level. This notion combines an external manifestation with an intrapsychic dynamic, which brings us back to one of TA's strong points, i.e., the articulation of these two dimensions. However, this articulation will only be fully grasped if one keeps in mind that these two elements are not of the same nature, despite the impression created by the transposition in the diagrams of an intrapsychic dynamic into a verbal communication, the "psychological message".[10]

The frame of reference's role

Frames of references play an essential role in how each participant experiences the relationship and its communication (see point 3 above). The speaker formulates communication according to their own frame of reference, but the listener perceives and understands it according to their own and may therefore receive it in a different way than the speaker intended. The sooner the participants become aware of this "misunderstanding", the easier it will be for them to remedy it, and the more this return to a common "wavelength" will deepen their mutual trust. Open reformulating ("This is what I interpreted; did I understand correctly?") is one of the many ways to achieve this.

In a frame of reference, the three interconnected personality systems come into play: the Child's hopes and fears, the Adult established data and the Parent models, including expectations connected to participants' role. In addition, the participants' sense of Self often plays an important part in how they perceive, understand and experience communication.

If the *common area* between the speaker's and the listener's frame of reference is initially very small, then there are initially few possibilities for communication. But if things go well, communication builds on this common area and gradually increases its scope. This does not exclude conflict, on the contrary, because a conflict can only be clearly perceived, let alone dealt with, when it has been expressed, which implies a sufficiently large common area between frames of reference.

There are three cases:

1. The speaker and listener have similar enough representations and expectations at a given moment: communication can carry on smoothly in terms of process, and their joint attention will be focused on content.

2. The listener's verbal and non-verbal reaction shows that their representations or expectations of the relationship and communication are at odds with the speaker's at that moment: it is usually difficult for both of them to continue a genuine exchange in terms of content without first re-establishing sufficient agreement, regardless of their positions on the content. It may also be that both implicitly agree not to talk about this or that thing, either as a conscious strategy or through unconscious collusion.
3. The communication process manifests inconsistent expectations and representations in at least one of the participants: the less explicit and more unconscious aspects will have the greatest influence, since no regulation is possible as long as these aspects have not been clarified internally and/or externally.

These three statements and Berne's communication laws are very much alike. Let us specify that they are *not* a reformulation of the latter: they are expressed in terms of ego states in a transaction at a given moment and, apart from that, do not involve neither the frame of reference nor the relationship.

About the transaction diagram

The diagram traditionally used to represent simple transactions belongs by right to the sequential and descriptive perspective, as it describes external manifestations of personality systems. It is based on several simplifications that reduce communication to a process where a single ego state addresses another's single ego state. How useful this perspective is within its own frame of reference has been highlighted earlier.[11]

From the interaction perspective, almost all transactions are "triple", for three reasons at least: 1) the three personality systems usually have their impact on communication; 2) communication is not addressed to a particular ego state, but to the person as a whole; 3) the transaction is part of the wider and deeper flow of the relationship.

No matter how rich the interaction perspective may be, the practitioner cannot neglect communication's concrete aspects. Contact with intrapsychic dynamics among individuals and groups is not established, maintained and evolved by some kind of magic ignoring concrete words and gestures, but *through them*. Subsequently, if the approach focuses on awareness and use of conscious and unconscious dynamics, the task will not be carried out successfully either if external communication is not good enough. These perspectives and approaches therefore complement each other, and it would be harmful to lock oneself in any one of them.

TEXT: TRANSFERENCE TRANSACTION

Here is a text whose theme, transference transaction, lies at the crossroads between communication and relationship. What Berne tells us about it is almost allusive in its brevity, as we shall see.

A note: In *Transactional Analysis and Psychotherapy*, Berne uses the concept "transaction" in a very particular way. Although this concept describes manifestations, falling by right under the sequential or descriptive perspective, Berne makes an intuitive and metaphorical use of it which inserts it directly into the repetition perspective. More precisely, he treats ego states as real people: the Child "is" the little boy or girl of yesteryear who bursts into today's conversation, the Parent "is" their father or mother who comes to interfere in the group's exchanges:

> The other members (...) perceived clearly that it was not Magnolia but her mother who sat with them and who, as they expressed it, putting a "ceiling" on the proceedings. They did not want any "parents" in the group. When the "real Magnolia", that is, her Adult and Child, emerged in the course of therapy, she was quite different and was well received.[12]

In the text on transference transactions, Berne, as is often the case, does not explain the theory but provides an example:

> One day Camellia (...) announced that she had told her husband that she was not going to have intercourse with him anymore and that he could go and find himself some other woman. Rosita asked curiously: "Why did you do that?" Whereupon Camellia burst into tears and replied: "I try so hard and then you criticize me".
>
> There were two transactions here (...). [In the second], Rosita's question (...) now constituted a new transactional stimulus and was intended as one adult speaking to another. Camellia's response, however, was not that of one adult to another, but that of a child answering a critical Parent. Camellia's misperception of Rosita's ego state, and the shift in her own ego state, resulted in a crossed transaction (...)
>
> This particular type of crossed transaction, in which the stimulus is directed to the Adult while the response originates from the Child, is probably the most frequent cause of misunderstandings in marriage and work situations, as well as in social life. Clinically it is typified by the classical transference reaction. In fact, this species of crossed transaction may be said to be the chief problem of psychoanalytic technique. (...). The point was that this sort of thing happened regularly to Camellia.[13]

The last sentence shows the link between this transfer transaction and Camellia's script. In fact, Berne's most important text on transference is probably his first script description:

> A script does not deal with a mere transference reaction or transference situation[14]; it is an attempt to repeat in derivative form a whole transference drama, often split up into acts, exactly like the theatrical scripts...[15]

Berne roots the script, i.e., the whole of a person's life, in their first relationships. Given how important the script is in his thinking, there is a major convergence with the object relations theory and with social TA.

Following Camellia's example, Berne briefly mentions countertransference:

> The reciprocal [cross-transaction] occurs when a stimulus is addressed to the Adult and it is the Parent who responds (…). The diagram [of this type of transaction] may be used, *mutatis mutandis*, to represent a countertransference reaction.[16]

Notes

1. Destructive secrecy, linked to often unconscious inhibitions, is different from ethical secrets, for example professional secrecy or simple discretion.
2. Paraverbal: everything that is heard but not words: tone of voice, rhythm, etc.
3. This point is studied by the "interactional" branch of linguistics; see KERBRAT-ORECCHIONI, C., 1986–1987.
4. Which is not to be understood as the grammatical form: "Tomorrow you will go to this place" can be just as imperative as "Go to this place". And "Could you give me that hammer?" is just as much a request as "(Please) give me that hammer".
5. See WATZLAWICK, P., HELMICK-BEAVIN, J., and JACKSON, D., 1967. LE GUERNIC, A., 2004, pp. 10–11.
6. See pp. 158–159, examples 2 and 4.
7. KARPMAN, S., 1971[ES].
8. See p. 203.
9. See ÉVRARD, B., GRÉGOIRE, J., MAQUET, J., and QUAZZA, J.P., 2009.
10. This transposition is based on a metaphor (a process is not a sentence) and implies an interpretation. The same applies to the translation of script dynamics into verbal "messages".
11. See pp. 253–254.
12. BERNE, E., 1961, p. 153.
13. BERNE, E., 1961, pp. 66–69.
14. We could say "relationship" instead of "situation".
15. BERNE, E., 1961, p. 86.
16. BERNE, E., 1961, p. 68.

14
THE PRACTITIONER AND THE INTERACTION PERSPECTIVE

The interaction perspective does not aim to introduce new techniques, but to offer a transactionalist theoretical outlook that allows the practitioner to manage their relationship with the person, their attention and, consequently, their interventions in a more open and consciously chosen way. The interaction perspective goes beyond divisions between classical TA and TA recent trends, between the conscious and the unconscious, between working through in the past and working in the present: it opens diversified possibilities which adapt to multiple contexts and types of intervention. In this, TA fully manifests its integrative character.

In each application field, it means the practitioner can use the deeper understanding offered by a structural view (the three personality systems as organizers), defined in terms of here-and-now dynamics,[1] without being automatically drawn into the repetition perspective which is more geared to psychotherapy work. The interaction perspective is particularly useful to understand relational processes that cannot be analysed using only one of the Child, Parent and Adult systems and their superimposed dynamics. It gives room to the past without confining itself to repetition and is open to the present, and the future to be built; it keeps within sight access to autonomy and creativity for the person, the group or the institution. It answers the need for an approach that makes room for multiple levels of intervention, according to W. Cornell's description of the therapist's stance referred to above.[2]

Relationship, availability, intervention

In their enlightening study on therapeutic relationship, most of which is also valid for all TA fields with the necessary modifications, R. Erskine and R. Trautmann[3] consider three elements to be necessary: 1) respectful inquiry, which means that the practitioner does not presume to know what the person is experiencing independently of what they are expressing about their own experience; 2) "attunement" with the person and 3) the practitioner's personal commitment.

H. Hargaden and C. Sills,[4] in relational TA, use the concept of empathic relationship instead; M. Novellino[5] insists on the analysis of counter-transference and unconscious communication. W. Cornell and M. Landaiche[6] used the "therapeutic couple" metaphor to describe the closeness that characterizes the therapeutic relationship.

These different conceptualizations encourage the therapist or the practitioner to develop a relationship of personal commitment in which they accept to be affected by the person, group or institution's concerns, as opposed to a position exclusively confined to external observation.

In short, from the interaction perspective, *the person(s)'s personality systems or groups of ego states, with their different strata and interaction modes* (disjunction, inhibition, collusion or integration), *inevitably exert multiple influences on the practitioner's personality systems. Conversely, insofar as the practitioner provides a holding environment for these influences, gives them meaning and thinks them through, they will function as an excellent resource to understand the dynamics at play.* From there, the practitioner will be able to guide the relationship so that members of the group can best contain their individual or collective reactions, make sense of their situation and think about solutions, first with their practitioner, then increasingly in autonomy and creativity.

Each perspective has its own particular sensitivity

In the field, each perspective corresponds to a type of sensitivity chosen by the practitioner at a given moment: their perception, reactions and choices are going in a particular direction, without blocking the possible emergence of other aspects. The practitioner curbs possibilities if they confine themself to one only. On the contrary, it is in this wide-open availability that they will have the best chance of choosing an effective intervention.

When the focus of the practitioner's attention is on the ego states' descriptive characteristics, they are at this point in time in the sequential or *descriptive* perspective; often this is a gateway to the relationship's early stages. If they turn inward to the connection of these ego states with the person's past, they are in the origin perspective, which they may choose to restrict to the repetition perspective. From the interaction perspective, their relational sensitivity is primarily directed towards the three personality systems' entity and their interactions.

Of course, however open their availability and attention are, the practitioner does not have to deal explicitly with every element they perceive. They must nevertheless maintain an overall view, broader than the specific field targeted by their intervention; otherwise, they would lose their overall perspective, lack the necessary hindsight and run the risk of falling under the control of their own script or their own unconscious. They may momentarily focus on one personality system or on a particular group of ego states, but they need to be aware they are using an intuitive simplification, often useful though not a comprehensive description.[7] Of course, a positive change in one personality system usually leads to changes in the others, so that an intervention focusing on one system can be a real step forward. However, the overall personality development is not split into three watertight areas, so the practitioner should not be caught off guard when, having worked on one of the systems, they are led to take the others into account because of collusion or resistance, or simply because it is appropriate to strengthen their conjunction.

This ego state theory aims to provide the practitioner with a "map" of this space and the multiple possibilities it offers. Each possibility is based on one or more specific conceptual tools:

- all three Child, Adult and Parent personality systems defined in the here and now as always present and interactive;
- the consideration given to systems or groups of ego states that are not dominant in the person's perception (real Self) or behaviour (executive power);
- the overlapping strata of their evolution;
- their interaction modes and
- the dialectic between competence and sense of Self.[8]

This dialectic often provides a useful heuristic key[9] to identify hidden or unconscious dynamics in a given situation. A block concerning the person's internal and external competence, in other words their ability to "manage" their internal experiences and external life, often stems from a sense of Self problem and vice versa. It is therefore often useful to look in this direction. Here is an example, the case of a man who internalized the injunction "Don't get angry" (subjective experience inhibition in the Child system by Parent injunctions and models): at the first level, his problem concerned his internal competence, the management of his emotions. However, his therapeutic work was hindered by strong resistance, which only eased the day he became aware of a belief held by both the Parent and the Child in collusion: "Getting angry is not worthy of you". The work was then fruitfully directed towards the sense of Self.

Opening receptivity and attention to the three systems

When positioned in the interaction perspective, the practitioner lets their attention wander on all personality systems. They do not allow themself to be obsessed by the dominant ego state but leave room for ego states in the background, whether in disjunction, inhibition or collusion. They not only remain vigilant to possible future influences, but they question themself in order to spot as lucidly as possible influences that perhaps *these ego states now already exert* on their own personality systems.

Each system is present and "observing"

To start with, let us examine Berne's warnings, one version of which reads: "The trichotomy [of the three systems Child, Adult and Parent] must be taken quite literally. It is just as if each patient were three different people. Until the therapist can perceive it this way, he is not ready to use this system effectively".[10]

Here is an example: if the practitioner has started work on one personality system symbolically, such as the interview with the parent,[11] they must remain aware that everything said to the personified "Parent" is also heard by the Child, and that it is very often in the Child that the most important changes take place. At the same time, the Adult starts considering the parental figure's past actions in a new, more "panoramic" light, i.e., better able to grasp the difference between positions without taking sides.[12] Referring to the empathy concept, the practitioner should not only have empathy for the person's Parent, but also and at the same time for what the person subjectively experiences in their Child and discovers in their Adult.

This leads to a gradual opening to the person, group or institution's frames of reference, not so much as a unified "world view" but as a juxtaposition of several views according to each personality system and its superimposed strata.[13] If the person's personality systems are in conjunction, and even more so in integration, getting to know this person is enough to make contact with their frame of reference. But if there are disjunctions or inhibitions,[14] several divergent elements must be taken into consideration. The practitioner's personality systems perceive influences from the person's personality systems that are contradictory or in tension. If the practitioner is not careful, the process will become unconscious and beyond their control; but if they are open and able to provide a holding environment for such tensions or contradictions, they can benefit from them in a conscious and empathetic way.

A specific application of this is considering how each personality system *might* understand, and possibly distort, a specific intervention. The way the Child may perceive and, in a sense, distort certain verbal statements has been described above[15]: in general, it tends to understand sentences literally and to give them a broader or different meaning than the speaker intended, because the Child constantly refers what is said and done to its previous experiences, desires and fears. But the Child is not the only one. The Parent system constantly compares communications to rules and models it has internalized and reacts accordingly. The Adult system, however lucid and objective it may be, is not immune to distortion either, since it tends to confirm what it thinks it knows rather than admit to an event that is sufficiently new to surprise it.

Here are some examples that directly concern practitioners:

- In the case of alcohol-dependent people, if the practitioner says: "I'm really glad you're not drinking any more", the person's Child system may react like this: "You are happy and I am frustrated, just you wait…!"
- Saying "I am worried about you" is not at all the same as "I haven't heard from you and was wondering what was going on": it could be understood as "My therapist thinks it's serious".
- If a teacher warns about a sanction, then does not enforce it without explaining why, the Child system will conclude: "These sanctions are meaningless, there is no need to take them into account".
- A sentence like "You are not responsible for your thirty-year-old daughter's divorce" can be understood by the Parent as "For my therapist, divorce is not serious", or by the Parent and Child systems as "My therapist is telling me to abandon my daughter".

What happens behind the scenes?

When it comes to unsatisfactory, restricting or painful dynamics, *personality systems that are briefly unable to manifest themselves* (inhibition) *go on not only existing but also being active in an underground or clandestine way*. Practice confirms Berne's examples here. With the interaction perspective, the practitioner remains receptive to all three personality systems, and a significant part of their attention remains focused on the systems that do not determine the person's external conduct (executive power) at this point or are not included in the person's sense of Self (real Self).

The main point here is no longer which personality system will prevail on the internal or external stage, as this is a concern that belongs to the sequence perspective, according to which Berne developed his energy theory.[16] The point is to perceive the person's resources and vulnerabilities in their three personality systems' entity. Personality systems that have remained in the background of the internal or external scene have an impact that can be left out only in a limited number of cases. If the therapist wants to understand symptoms, defence mechanisms or resistances, they must identify the dynamics in which they are involved and relate to them.

Here is an example: a teacher has problems with authority in the classroom. In supervision, he is invited to turn his attention to what is happening in his Child system; he realizes that, although he has effective strategies at his disposal, he does not dare to implement them in fear of becoming a teacher he knew as a child who used to terrorize his class. The adequate authority models he elaborated and registered in his Parent recent strata are inhibited (overgeneralization[17]) by contents that belong to the Child earlier strata and do not seem to have received a sufficient holding environment.[18] Let us note that the problem manifests itself as external competence ("exercising authority"), but that the element at the source of the block is connected to the sense of Self: "I don't want to be like…". This is not all: the interaction perspective, in fact, invites us to look beyond a single "cause". Further exploration revealed that this inhibition was reinforced by a Child's secret sympathy for his pupils' rebellion, which went back to his adolescence. For this man, change only really began when both elements, his childhood fear for his sense of Self *and* his complicity, were brought to light.

Opening up to various strata and the unconscious

As seen in the previous example, the interaction perspective provides openings to the psyche's early still active strata. In fact, it very often opens the opportunity to identify early or unconscious dynamics that are by definition "in the background", including transference dynamics. As they are neither recognized nor accepted by the person, they never take centre stage internally; nor do they take centre stage externally, except if acted on, in which case it is the link between the act and the internal life that is unconscious: "It suddenly took hold of me, I don't understand what happened to me!" To consider systems "in the background" is therefore a gateway to grasp unconscious dynamics, provided of course that the practitioner is able to perceive them, to provide a holding environment for them and to put them to good use.

Establishing conjunction

Time has come to establish conjunction between the three systems when what is called for is encouraging dynamics towards development and creativity, or when several changes in various personality systems and strata have been made. Their mutual inhibitions need to be reduced and their tendencies made convergent enough, though not perfectly homogeneous, which would close the way to creativity. For the person as well as for the therapist in counter-transference, inner tensions become much more bearable, unless new resistances reveal previously uncontained dynamics.

Here is an example. A person is about to take an important decision, which is the result of a relatively long period of work and which they consider in good conscience to be liberating. Will the practitioner emphasize the Parent which has now integrated the idea that it is legitimate for the person to make this decision? Or the Adult which will enable them to think about their means? Or the Child which needs to be reassured while looking forward to the opening prospects? Even if each point may previously have been the focus of specific work, time will come when the practitioner needs to put the three systems' resources together in the service of the person, instead of limiting their work to ruling out pathologies.

Therapy work is focused on the person's early or recently acquired resources, on the person's representation of the future and on multiplying and stabilizing conjunctions and integrations between personality systems. It establishes new connections between the psyche's early and more recent strata, so that, as far as possible, it no longer considers the early strata's contents as dangerous or "monstrous"; instead, having pushed the work of "making sense" to the limit, the person has become aware of the resources and useful energy these contents contain, and perhaps has even come to consider them as potential allies.[19]

Establishing sufficient conjunction concerns all TA fields or other approaches. Two specific applications are the related fields of motivation and decision making.

C. Ramond[20] analyses *motivation to learn* through three components: for the Parent, conforming to values; for the Adult, being convinced of how useful what one learns is and how valid the learning method is; and for the Child, wanting to learn. More generally, human motivation must be based at least on a *conjunction* between personality systems, i.e., each must be involved, and none can be neglected. If one personality system does not take part in it, or works in the opposite direction, motivation will be partial or deficient. The same will be true if the person's competence or sense of Self is not considered. Of course, a certain amount of integration is desirable, as this is where the person's creativity is released.

The same considerations apply to important *decisions*: they must be made with the three personality systems in mind, each in conjunction with the others.

Note that motivation can be at a "meta" level: the person's Child, Parent and Adult systems may be in disagreement, or even at an impasse in a given area, and yet together generate a powerful motivation to seek a yet unknown solution, because, for example, the pain generated by the impasse is too strong (Child component), the consequences are destructive (Adult component) or they clash with the person's values (Parent component). Such motivation is usually at work when a person or a group asks for help.

Collusion between systems

Classical TA considers script dynamics in terms of Parent "message(s)" and Child "decisions". Despite the importance given to decision, which is a relational process, it very often remains in a unilateral representation of what happened originally: relying on power imbalance between the parental figures and the young child, it willingly fits into a dominant vision where "children are born princes and princesses, then parents turn them into frogs".

The interaction perspective invites the practitioner to help the person to consider, if they can, the Child conscious and unconscious motivations that have helped to set up their script and that perpetuate it. This implies not just seeing the child of old as a powerless victim: even if they were in reality, that was probably not the whole reality; in any case, the child was not powerless in the person's own fantasies. What did the child actually or symbolically or magically try to do *to* or *for someone else* in making its decision and later sticking to it? According to Berne themself, "A child's job is to find out what his parents really mean. This helps to maintain their love, or at least their protection, or in difficult cases, his mere survival. But beyond that, he loves his parents, and his chief aim in life is to please them (if they will let him), and in order to do that he has to know what they really want".[21] The notion of "unconscious loyalty"[22] often helps the practitioner to understand the person's dynamics and to enter the right relationship with them.

Why speak of collusion here? Because of the hidden relationships, these early situations induce later in personality systems. Often unconsciously, they make the Child an accomplice in the script that brings it so much suffering. The person wants to change their life, but without "abandoning" the parental figure, whom they continue to want to excuse, change, heal, make better, make more loving, etc.; or they don't want to change because they have the hidden belief that if they do, it will harm the parental figure, who in their fantasy will be destroyed, die or feel abandoned.[23]

With required modifications, the same dynamics are found in the person's relationships today. An extreme example is how strong the ties are that bind a person to the spouse who beats or abuses them, or to the institution where they are harassed. These are dynamics which, although recent, awaken early personality strata and which cannot be dealt with at the behaviour level alone. Conversely, there is no need to look for an "early" event that would foreshadow the current event: the psyche's early strata remain active and vulnerable throughout life. Such "early" elements may or may not exist, but it seems inappropriate to build an approach based on the prejudice that the best strategy is necessarily the one attached to the earliest event.

There are also collusions linked to aggressivity, either unrecognized or turned against oneself. The person may be possessed by jealousy or hatred; as a child, they may have hoped to destroy the parental couple, the family, a sibling; if the traumatic event occurs in adulthood, they may want to take revenge on an ex-spouse, make their boss pay for what they have suffered or destroy the family, society or the world. Collusion comes from a conscious or unconscious sense that resolving their problem and "letting go" of their rage or hatred would be tantamount to vindicating those who abused them, "accepting" what was done to them and destroying what is left of their sense of Self.

In many cases, this type of collusion is compounded by guilt, which is regularly denied by exaggerated expressions of love: this is the "reversal into its opposite".

There is no way out if the underground elements are not taken into account. The person must learn to distinguish between hate and anger, cognitively and emotionally: hate is based on anger, whether or not rooted in reality, on which the person's sense of Self has been made dependent; consequently, to stop harbouring it would be tantamount to abandoning oneself and, in a sense, reproducing the trauma. The person must learn how and to what extent they can, without giving up their justified anger, and especially without having to keep the relationship with the abuser, 1) *stop hurting* themselves, because hatred is self-destruction; 2) *live with the fact* that what happened did happen, without filling their whole existence with destructive emotions; 3) redirect their energies and creativity towards a personal future. This is, as we can see, a real "letting go" process.[24]

In other cases, collusion is maintained by the sense of Self, to be understood as "the sense of Self with others in existence"[25]: the person does not want to give up the image of the wise child, the Saviour, the qualities they are proud of. It is true that changing one's script often involves giving up an unrealistic or impossible representation of oneself: being perfect, being strong, being the source of well-being for everyone, enduring suffering, being the hero or the righter of wrongs, being faithful or loyal against all reason, etc. This sense of Self is often repressed in the unconscious because the mere fact of expressing it would force the person to perceive its "grandiose" character. There will be little change if they do not let go of this representation, which brings us back to "letting go". Sometimes this is accomplished in the wake of other work, but often stubborn resistance requires explicit support.

An example: a patient who, in her own opinion, "works too hard", sincerely wants to give herself permission to take time for herself, but something is blocking her; after looking into it, she comes to express that she has always considered herself "brave" and that she is very attached to this sense of Self. Discussing what can reasonably be classified as "bravery" (moving into the Parent through interaction with and decontamination of the Adult), and analysing script messages such as "Work hard" or "Never say no" (Parent component), proved insufficient. This client had to "let go" of her attachment to this Self-image and invest in another image at the Child level that she initially perceived as mundane, less exciting and unrewarding: "being a helpful person without being overwhelmed".

Along similar lines, one may wonder about the Parent secret complicity in behaviours that are at first sight opposed to it. How is it that the formidable Parent of some alcohol addicts is not strong enough to put an end to their behaviour, while it constantly harasses the Child with reproaches and guilt? Given the inescapable physical dimension of the addiction and the fact that, for the Child system, it is perhaps the only way to feel a little freedom from this omnipresent Parent, what complicity can the internalized parental figure have with the addiction? There are numerous hypotheses. Has a parent figure subtly sent the paradoxical message "I don't like wimps, I think you show character when you resist me, that's how much you look like me"[26] Did the addiction, or the failure, evoke for the person someone who was shunned in the family, but for whom they secretly felt an attraction, so that in the message "You'll end up like Uncle George (notoriously considered a 'drunk')", the contempt and exclusion were tinged with a subtle secret sympathy, which the child nevertheless perceived? Do the person's problems and rebellion meet a repressed desire: "My son or daughter is doing what I never dared to do myself?" Or, more seriously, did the parental figure need the person to have problems or to be used as a "scapegoat" to restore a deficient sense of Self? Would the parent have felt abandoned if they no longer had to deal with a problem in their children, even if it was only by berating them? Did they ask too much of a "parentified child" who eventually collapsed under the task?

The practitioner who encounters collusion will feel the often contradictory or paradoxical impact within themself. The person may alternately try to convince them that their parents were excellent and complain bitterly about their emotional absence. In transference, the person may take the therapist as a target for their repressed aggression or rage, as a witness to the unfairness of what they have suffered, or may seek their therapist's approval for the behaviours they cling to while waiting for the permission to let go.

If, however, the practitioner provides this dynamic with a "holding environment" in themself and in the relationship, the first result will undoubtedly be that their empathic relationship with the person will become much deeper. A person experiencing internal conflict does not feel truly understood by someone who takes sides with one pole of the impasse (or collusion) *against* the other; they need to be understood and accepted *in their own contradiction* and in *each of its* poles, before they can face the paradox in which they find themselves trapped. This approach is at the opposite of any approach where the practitioner is conceived as unilaterally supporting the Child *against* the Parent.[27]

The practitioner who engages in this process is not left with their first impression of the collusion impact. They provide a holding environment for it and makes sense of it by getting out of the confusion induced; they do not confound opposing or contradictory elements. In short, they deconstruct the collusion within themself so that they can help the person to do so, initially with them and later without them.

Integration

Integration differs from mere conjunction and collusion in its link to autonomy and creativity. Consequently, it cannot be the result of specific interventions. The practitioner can only accompany the person, the group or the institution, to create integration. Their role is neither to guide it in a directive manner, nor to lose interest in it under the pretext that it is outside their mission, but to *open a space for* it through the authentic relationship they co-created with their participants and to welcome its development with joy. There is a big difference between pointing out a possible option to their Adult, respectfully giving advice (which involves pointing out without bias possible consequences of various options) and manipulating or imposing a solution. For while the practitioner can be an invaluable aid to the three-character play that the Child, Parent and Adult systems create at any given time, they are ultimately neither the stage manager directing the production nor the author devising the plot.

Notes

1 A structure gives coherence and continuity and exists by definition in the present. From the repetition perspective, the "structural model" deserves its name only because it describes three personality systems *in the person's present life*, although two of them (the Parent and the Child) may be defined as *today's* repetitions of the past.
2 See p. 13. CORNELL, W.F., 2006.
3 ERSKINE, R.G., and TRAUTMANN, R., 1992.
4 HARGADEN, H., and Sills, C., 2003.
5 Novellino, M., 2005.
6 CORNELL, W.R., and Landaiche, M., 2005.
7 See Grégoire, J., 2007c.
8 See pp. 163, see pp. 204–206.
9 Heuristic: a lead that is followed to explore its validity, without deciding on it at the outset.
10 BERNE, E., 1961, p. 185. Except that it is a single person where the three systems are interconnected.
11 McNEEL, J., 1976.
12 See Chapter 7.
13 See Chapter 10.
14 See examples in Chapters 9 and 10.
15 See pp. 95–96.
16 BERNE, E., 1961, pp. 20–21. How to formulate this point is inherited from Federn, see FEDERN, P., 1952. Graham Barnes (BARNES, G., 1999a, 1999b, 1999c) considers that the use of the quantitative concept of energy implies a competitive conception of internal dynamics and relationships (which system or which interlocutor will win?). He argues, on the other hand, that R. Goulding and the redecision school have created a therapeutic solution to the problem posed by Berne's concepts. BARNES, E., 1999c, p. 69.
17 See pp. 67–68.
18 This is not a sufficient reason to declare that this situation falls within the psychotherapeutic field, although some of its intervention modes cannot be implemented in the situation described. Awareness, the search for different options drawing on the current resources of the person or the group, and the expression of feelings in the here and now are not contradictory with TA fields of education, guidance or organization. See GRÉGOIRE, J., 1994. CORNELL, W.F., and HINE, J., 1999.
19 Jung's Senoi dreamwork is an example of this approach. This form of encounter with the "Shadow" (the part of oneself that one does not want to meet) takes place through

a succession of symbolic actions such as "staying in the presence of the inner 'monster'", "seizing the 'monster'" and finally "demanding from it the gift that it keeps for oneself"; this gift is seen as a very important and eminently personal resource and, when obtained from the "monster", it becomes a valuable ally. KAPLAN-WILLIAMS, S., 1985.
20 RAMOND, C., 1995, pp. 153–160.
21 BERNE, E., 1972, p. 101.
22 See HEIREMAN, M., 1989.
23 In this case, the relational collusions of the past have been internalized and have become intrapsychic. See pp. 233–234.
24 See pp. 183–186.
25 See pp. 191–192.
26 Berne would call this the 'come-on' script. BERNE, E., 1972, pp. 114–115.
27 The notion of "potency" must not be misunderstood in this way.

CONCLUSION

The approach taken in this book offers a way to expand TA's theoretical framework and to make it even more fluid, so that the theory can help practitioners in all TA fields to make more conscious, more independent and more informed choices, without diminishing either their overall view of the approach or their awareness of links uniting its multiple dimensions.

The *theory* to which practitioners refer plays an essential role in their work. Through what it describes, it guides their attention, their perception and their intuitive search. It cannot describe everything, but it must at least show the general characteristics of the space in which choices are made. A theory that leaves out whole sections of human dynamics and intervention is like a map with a missing piece; it deftly distracts practitioners from what it leaves out by giving them the impression of an illusory one-dimensionality. Advocates for the necessarily integrative nature of psychotherapy have made this abundantly clear.[1]

It is damaging to reduce theory to a simple juxtaposition of operational methodologies, as if it were not useful to consider the link between various interventions and the relationship that makes them possible. It is also damaging to include nothing more than the description of the early dynamics at the origin of various pathologies, as if practitioners had no other task than working through pathogenic archaic material[2] and could lose interest in the ever-developing autonomy and creativity of those they accompany.

Of course, theory is not the only external reference point available to the practitioner: they also benefit from supervision and experience, among other things. They might feel able to rely on these, or on the relationship itself, to guide them in areas that theorists have neglected to map out. In practice, this is what happens to some extent. But this kind of sailing without bearings under poor weather cannot be set up as an ideal. Theory as a resource is underemployed: it performs the function that gives it meaning only in a mode both partial (it describes only part of what it is supposed to describe) and biased (it surreptitiously gives some elements an exaggerated importance at the expense of others). This entails a risk not only for the person, the group or the institution, but also for practitioners and trainees, especially as it tends to shape in its image the framework of reference of an entire professional group, including tutors and supervisors.

The practitioners' choices are also guided by what they learn in the relationship itself, in direct contact with those they accompany, by their intuition, empathy, personal resources and even their unconscious. This is only possible if two conditions are met:

- They work on themself, which allows them to take advantage of these resources without becoming a plaything for their own script's projections or dynamics.
- They commit to a co-creative relationship in their practice. There is no need to be perfect (many would say not!); but it is essential that they be an autonomous, creative and conscious person.

Finally, the quality of such a relationship is nourished by all participants' deep personal qualities. As we have seen, Erik Erikson, when referring to the life stages of the human journey, describes the two possible outcomes as "ego integrity" or "despair and fear of death".[3] He sees integrity as a lucid, serene and loving look at one's own life "as an experience which conveys some world order and spiritual sense, no matter how dearly paid for. It is the acceptance of one's and only life cycle as something that had to be (…): this means a new, a different love of one's parents".[4] He concludes: "It seems possible to further paraphrase the relation of adult integrity and infantile trust by saying that healthy children will not fear life if their elders have integrity enough not to fear death".[5]

This personal integrity is reflected in the various dimensions of life and includes "professional integrity". People in all TA fields or other approaches who have accompanied individuals, groups or institutions in their journey, with the joys and disappointments it entails, gradually go through human development's successive strata in their professional as well as their personal lives. This leads them to ever new, always evolving, modes of integration and creativity. In this way, without lasting discouragement during powerlessness, or excessive exaltation during success, practitioners can accept more deeply the value and abundance of their own persons, their resources and the work done, together with the joys and limitations inherent in human existence. If they enter a relationship as committed and conscious as they can with the people they accompany, the latter will be helped, if they so wish, to develop lucidity and confidence in their own resources and to build their own future with creativity. Along the way, practitioners will value as a priceless gift the development and integrity they encounter in the people they work with.

Notes

1 See, for example, PAGES, M., 1993. FOURCADE, M., 2007.
2 See CORNELL, W., 1988.
3 ERIKSON, E., 1950, pp. 268–269.
4 ERIKSON, E., 1950, p. 269.
5 ERIKSON, E., 1950, p. 269.

AFTERWORD
Ego states in Transactional Analysis (May 2017)

Berne's theoretical journey

Background and motivation

Any new theory or theoretical advance comes from an encounter between tendencies that enliven or disturb existing theories and the active motivation of a person, a group or an institution. In Berne's case, the 1950s and 1960s were marked by important cultural changes and saw the birth of several new therapeutic methods, most of which belonged to the "humanist" current. Individual or collective motivations generally involve various aspects: curiosity, passion for research, first intuitions of how beneficial a new perspective will be, but also dissatisfaction with the established theory and practice, a feeling of incoherence or the perception of a gap between resources and needs.

Berne's motivations prior to his first transactional analysis publications are of course only indirectly accessible to us: they come from what Berne told us and from what transpired in his written works, especially *Transactional Analysis and Psychotherapy*.[1] Nevertheless, it is possible to pinpoint some key elements, most of which will last until his final work.

One can identify at least four interconnected elements in Berne's work, which for him are Parent values and have undoubtedly guided his thinking from the outset.

- Ambroise Paré's "First, do no harm",[2] especially do not extend the suffering of patients and their relatives unnecessarily: this sheds light on Berne's desire to "heal" people as quickly as possible, rather than "improve" them.[3]
- The effort to reduce the *distance* between therapist and patients as much as possible, so that patients could truly take part in their therapy. A striking example is the staff meeting in the patients' presence.[4]
- The idea of a "*phenomenological*" therapy,[5] guided by the person's conscious experience rather than by "orthodox conceptual forms".[6] This undoubtedly plays a part in Berne's reticence towards sterile, intellectual and theoretical complications, which "obscure facts"[7] and are a counterproductive waste of time.
- The aspiration to a "*social* psychiatry"[8] that is attentive to the person in their individual or group relationships, rather than limiting itself to their internal dynamics.

These Parent-dominated aspirations are certainly coupled with Child reactions such as a taste for observing interactions between people, impatience with the length of psychiatric treatment or irritation with the "superior beings" aspect of the profession. It can be assumed that these Child and Parent reactions are mutually reinforcing and are therefore in conjunction, or even integration.

First conceptualization

Strong as they may be, Parent and Child motivations alone are not enough to create a new theory or practice. The intuitive and conceptual Adult must also create a coherent conceptualization that serves the project and takes experience into account. This is usually done in stages: each stage inspires experiments that will test the developing theory and guide subsequent reflection and action. In this way, a back-and-forth process between theory and experience begins; over time, the two components become more and more inseparable, but they never merge.

The ego state theory does not escape this rule. As far as the *"phenomenological"* aspect is concerned, the starting point on the experience side is Penfield's discovery.[9] On the conceptual side, we find Federn's idea[10]: psychotic patients' ego goes through complete and discrete "states"[11]; the same process happens in the transition from dreaming to waking. Federn only distinguishes between an "adult" and a "child" state; his disciple Weiss[12] mentions the "psychic presence" of others but does not link these three notions. Berne, for his part, notes that "voices" heard by some psychotics are very often literal repetitions of what parental figures once said. He therefore added a third state, which would become the Parent.

Many theory authors demonstrated genius in bringing together, into a structured whole, elements which before them seemed to have no link between them. Berne brought together previous elements in a conceptual system structured in three "ego states": the structural model was born.

On a practical level, his hypothesis, soon confirmed by cases such as Ms Enatosky's,[13] is that these three ego states can be re-experienced in a favourable setting, and that this is a rapid and effective therapeutic tool. However, the patient's Adult must remain conscious and remember these states, which rules out hypnosis with induced amnesia, drugs and electrical stimulation. Reconnecting with the "early scene" and bringing it into consciousness is a powerful resource for Berne in treatment. For this, he relies mainly on the patient's information and insight, and very little on emotion.[14]

But his project, as we have seen, is not limited to this "phenomenological" aspect: it also includes the idea of a *relational* theory and approach to the psyche. This orientation fits perfectly with the structural model, since all its terms are relational. More precisely, these terms develop a metaphor of an "internal family", a kind of inner re-enactment of the relationships within the family of old.

As early as *Transactional Analysis and Psychotherapy*, he associated a new experience element with this relational aspect: R. Spitz's studies on sensory deprivation,[15] on which basis Berne developed his theory of stimulus-hunger.[16]

On the practical side, relational concern translates into "social control". It is not so much a matter of the person controlling their internal reactions, but rather of establishing the Adult's dominance in *social* situations. Berne defines it as: "control of the individual's own tendency to manipulate other people in destructive or wasteful ways, and of his tendency to respond without insight or option to the manipulation of others".[17]

Experience shows that relational and phenomenological aspects are *not independent*. Not only is social control a preparation to explore internal conflicts, but it is already effective on this level: "The assumption is made, usually correctly, that the resulting improved social experiences will lead to a diminution of archaic distorsions and anxieties, with some relief of symptoms"[18]; moreover, it often leads to beneficial changes in close relatives' reactions. Berne, who likes clear distinctions, divides treatment into two stages: separate ego states or decontaminate the Adult, then "deconfuse the Child".[19] For a long time, he left the second stage to psychoanalysis[20]; then he increasingly explored transactional possibilities: studying the script gave him ample means to do so.

Initial extensions and clarifications

In theory development, first conceptualizations are most often like a painter's sketches: from the very beginning, they will be worked on in more details or modified according to whether they make sense and what impact first experiments have.

As far as the ego state structural model is concerned, one important modification is the introduction of *psychic organs*, or *personality systems*. This book shows[21] how the sequential perspective naturally leads to the interaction perspective: for example, when one ego state takes centre stage, the other two "witness" it and react accordingly. The concept of personality systems[22] is the theoretical expression of this fact, as it implies that the three ego states coexist and interact continuously. The "internal dialogue" is a metaphor for these interactions.

The ego state model becomes truly *structural*, in the first sense of the term. A structure is "the arrangement of elements constituting a constructed whole, which makes it a coherent entity and gives it its specific aspect".[23] The three psychic organs are structures because they are *permanent* centres of reactions and actions, which accounts for the psyche's continuity and cohesion.

Another structural model extension is the *second-order structural model*. This is not in fact a separate model: it is both a logical and partially experience-based development of it. In the case of the *Parent*, the Triss sisters' case[24] shows the "experience" side. They are twins whose behaviours are very different, even opposite, which Berne logically explains by the grandparents' influence. In the case of the *Child*, Berne begins by reasoning in a similar way: if we consider that the child of old already had three ego states, we can consider their Child, Adult and Parent of that time as sub-structures of the present Child ego state.[25]

In this form, however,[26] this conceptual tool has few practical applications: Berne only cites Aaron's case,[27] which is a dream analysis. As for the Adult three-fold subdivision, whose artificial character we have noted,[28] Berne, who considers it initially as "a tentative formulation" "for academic purposes", clarifies it within the same book through the concept of programming: "The ethical Adult may be regarded functionally as the Parent-programmed Adult. [...] The feeling Adult may be understood as a Child-programmed Adult".[29]

Finally, notions of *transaction* and *internal dialogue* follow directly from the ego state structural model. Given its social character, the simple transaction[30] is an obvious extension. The double transaction, on the other hand, implies the simultaneous activity of two ego states, one of which operates "behind the scenes": this is not a novel idea, since phenomenological experience already combines two ego states, the one that is "relived" and the Adult who plays the role of an active witness. Berne adds that two ego states can also influence each other in the internal[31] dialogue, the study of which is initiated with the Influential Parent[32] concept.

Descriptive terms

In the field of accompanied psychological change, a theory would remain abstract and difficult to implement if it did not give at least heuristic indications on its concepts' concrete manifestations. Berne collects *clues for a behavioural and social diagnosis* of ego states, at least of the Child and the Parent, under the title "The complete diagnosis".[33] In accordance with this purpose, these terms remain strictly in line with the structural model: they are elaborated from the metaphor of the "internal family" and, therefore, are intrinsically relational. For Berne, this list is not an explanatory model: it indicates neither the meaning of the experience nor any underlying structure. It only takes a more or less systematized form in Berne's last book[34]; he makes no reference to it as a systematic tool in the rest of his works.

Double transactions

However, the transition from perceptible clues to experiences of change encounters detours and obstacles in all approaches. Concepts located at these two levels are not enough to confirm a theory: it needs intermediate concepts referring to *underlying mechanisms*. With them, many situations that are at first sight incoherent or incomprehensible become intelligible and acquire at least the beginnings of a meaning; they provide the practitioner with indications on what should or, more importantly, should not be done. Here is an example: setting up to fail. It seems absurd at first sight, but it becomes clearer and takes on a different meaning once we work with the psychological game's concept.

Double transactions[35] belong sometimes to descriptive concepts, sometimes to underlying mechanisms. In some transactions, psychological stimuli and responses are "hidden" only for form's sake: implications, undertones, insinuations, etc., only make sense if they are understood by the listener. At other times, as in psychological games, the underlying level is truly "hidden" to all partners; decoding the ulterior motive requires an interpretation that goes beyond direct perception. Berne hardly studies the first type of transactions. He rarely explores double transaction resources in humour, illustrations, metaphors, interventions addressed to several ego states at the same time,[36] indirect transactions,[37] etc. On the contrary, when he talks about double transactions, he clearly wants to move quickly to games. The term *"ulterior"*[38] he uses has a manipulative connotation itself.

Games and time structuring

Game is the concept that Berne probably used most to understand underlying mechanisms. Prior to his extensive research on script, he states that the most time in therapeutic groups is taken up with games and their analysis.[39]

Berne first defined the game in terms of complementary ulterior transactions. In the case of games, they "progress towards a well-defined, predictable outcome. Descriptively, [a game] is a recurring set of transactions, often repetitious, superficially plausible, with a concealed motivation".[40] It is only in Berne's last book[41] that the formula G appears. The game course is always transcribed by him in a linear mode: one partner is the initiator, while the other is drawn or trapped into the game because they have a "weak point" corresponding to the "trigger".[42]

From the outset, Berne includes games in his description of time structuring. Its classification is undoubtedly the result of a long observation of human interactions, coupled with a conceptualization in terms of transactions. In this framework, Berne inserts the notion of intimacy, considered as a rare event, which occurs when games "give way".[43]

The script

Berne's thinking has led him to focus on the concept of script. He describes it in his last book as having two sides: a narrative side (the earliest) and a concurrent side. From the *narrative* point of view, the script is a story, with "prologue, climax and catastrophe".[44] It is the conscious and unconscious representation that the person makes of their life, from birth to old age and death. Experience shows that everything happens as if, unconsciously or not, the person tends to adapt their existence to this narrative, which brings to mind fatality in myths, classical tragedies and fairy tales.

According to Berne, script analysis aims to relate "…the current life-drama (…) to its historical origins so that control of the individual's destiny can be shifted from the Child to the Adult, from archaeopsychic unconsciousness to neopsychic awareness".[45] It is therefore logical for Berne to question influences in the person's past that have committed or precipitated them to this "destiny". To do this, Berne transcribes the script's main aspects in the form of "messages" which come from past parental figures whose impact is still current: this is the *concurrent* side. A loop is closed, as the early scene becomes once again the fundamental aim of the process.

It is in this context that the Steiner-Berne matrix[46] was developed. Steiner's contribution is probably the important concept of counter-script: it refers to mechanisms that sometimes protect the person from the most destructive aspects of their script and sometimes only serve to "postpone the inevitable".

Note that in script theory, concepts of the Child second-order structure take on new meaning. The P1 becomes the receptacle of parental programming.[47] The A1 is the "Little Lawyer" or "Little Professor" who finds loopholes "in order to find more ways for the Natural Child to express himself". And E1, in one passage at least, serves as a marker for the "demon",[48] the person's unpredictable spontaneity. The whole script drama is transposed to the Child.

Classical TA

Most theories, if they survive long enough, undergo internal transformations. Sometimes these are slow and almost imperceptible mutations, and sometimes they are upheavals like T. Kuhn's "paradigm shifts".[49] As far as classical TA is concerned, the changeover took place almost silently, as it had already started among Berne's students during his lifetime; he encouraged their creativity, while imposing strict limits[50] on conceptual simplicity and conciseness. These restrictions certainly influenced the "theoretical style" of Berne's students.[51]

After his death, Berne's colleagues and students pursued his work by describing other script aspects, such as drivers[52], impasses,[53] and other underlying mechanisms: racket feeling,[54] passivity, discounting and redefining,[55] racket system,[56] etc. As for ego states, some major aspects have already been pointed out in this book[57]; a more technical description can be found in *Les orientations récentes de l'analyse transactionnelle*.[58]

The so-called San Francisco school

1. *"Something else than psychoanalysis"*. Berne, it is said, began elaborating TA with a view to "do something else than psychoanalysis". He did not really integrate analytical concepts into his theory, even if in many passages he shows that he considers them to be founded and established.[59] His immediate successors shared this attitude, which could be described as "para-psychoanalytic". Transference and counter-transference were not integrated into transactional theory until recent TA trends brought them to the forefront.

   However, some authors such as C. Steiner and S. Karpman developed a downright anti-psychoanalytic attitude based on two positions close to Berne's own values: the first, in line with the "radical therapy" movement,[60] considers the psychoanalytical approach as a mystification that distracts people from real change, that of political awareness and action; the second sees it as an unnecessarily complex intellectualization. These positions are attributed to Berne without taking into account how intricate his thinking is; it is as if these authors had retained only Berne's initial Parent motivations and isolated them from the rest of his journey, and from cultural and theoretical evolution after him.

C. Steiner developed his "stroke economy" theory.[61] From this point on, *strokes* and the ways to seek, obtain, even extort them,[62] play an important role in transactional theory and practice. However, most practitioners do not put the political reference in the foreground, whereas in Steiner's case, cultural prohibitions and parental restrictive messages are closely intertwined.

2. *The descriptive "model" becomes quasi-structural.* In classical TA, diagnostic clues (the descriptive "model") take on a much greater importance than for Berne. They are used as a *classification* of external relational interactions, both stimuli and responses, especially in Karpman's "options list".[63] Like any classification, this way of thinking has positive and negative aspects: it helps to find one's way quickly among multiple facets of experience and to make temporary connections with other experiences; but its categories easily turn adamant and become "labels" that obscure the practitioner's mental availability.

Furthermore, the descriptive model increasingly takes the structural model's place and role in classical TA. For example, the article on "options" analyses transactions as coming from "descriptive ego states", whereas Berne talks about transactions within the structural model.[64] The reference to the person's childhood is set aside, which brings transactions back into the here and now and make them a merely behavioural concept.

This makes sense as San Francisco's coaching process is conceived in a more behavioural mode. Besides, the explicit use of the structural model is not recommended if the person is not ready or if it is not compatible with the approach, as in non-therapeutic specialized fields.[65]

3. *The script concept undertakes the role previously assigned to structural ego states.* Classical TA is not shifting to a purely behavioural approach, as the script concept remains present and applicable: therapeutic work on early scenes is done through it. The script concept is considered above all from the point of view of "messages" and different script matrices. Consequently, TA increasingly focuses on the person's current problems; existentially important themes such as old age and death, i.e., the "fall" of the script as a story, lose their theoretical anchor.

Redecision and reparenting

The redecision and reparenting "schools" are not just "San Francisco" variants. Their name reflects what they are all about.

Unlike Berne's process, which focuses on the Adult, the *redecision* school rightly emphasizes the emotional aspect of psychological change and uses Gestalt and psychodrama techniques for this purpose.[66] Transference is not analysed, but its dynamism is redirected towards former parent figures: in other words, the relationship between the therapist and the person is not analysed, but the person is invited to enter a two-chair work with a parent figure and to express to this figure the feelings that are now directed towards the therapist. From the ego states' point of view, the Free Child, often referred to as E1, is of central importance as it is the bearer of awareness and of the expression of the person's true needs; the Adult, on the other hand, is viewed as devoid of feelings.

The *reparenting* school's concepts[67] focus on the detection and confrontation of passivity, symbiosis and their accompanying mechanisms. These concepts are widely used now, though they have mostly lost their reference to symbiosis and, in practice, have very often taken the place of Adult decontamination.

TA recent trends

In TA recent trends, the key element is the inclusion of transference and counter-transference. Working with repression has come back, compared to the San Francisco School, and in another way compared to Berne himself. The change this time was more abrupt than the transition from Berne to classical TA, and it gave rise to fiercer controversies.[68]

R. Erskine and R. Trautmann decisively contributed to this change with their theory which unifies ego states and *transference and counter-transference*. This is why their theory has been adopted by most recent trends. Taken together,[69] with the simplifications this implies, we can schematize these theories' general features in the following equivalences (the sign "$\rightleftarrows$" can be read as "goes together with"):

Parent and Child $\rightleftarrows$ transference and counter-transference
$\rightleftarrows$ dominated by the past $\rightleftarrows$ repetition
$\rightleftarrows$ not autonomous $\rightleftarrows$ lack of creativity

And on the other hand:

Adult $\rightleftarrows$ absence of transference and counter-transference
$\rightleftarrows$ contact with here and now and with the other
$\rightleftarrows$ autonomy $\rightleftarrows$ co-creativity

In this way, the approach's main starting point is no longer attention to behaviour as awareness of transference and counter-transference: this gives primary importance to relational diagnosis and to the practitioner's awareness of their own internal reactions and motivations.

Berne and classical TA thought of the relationship more in terms of instantaneous contacts than in terms of duration: this is visible in transaction theory. More generally, Berne's communication model is unidirectional, based on notions such as sender, message, receiver, contact, noise.[70] Hargaden and Sills' relational TA,[71] on the other hand, is based on a reciprocal, interactive and continuous relationship conception. The partners' global reactions are conceived as simultaneous and inseparable, especially transference and counter-transference. W. Cornell integrates TA and Reichian body therapy in the same relational perspective.

Transactional concepts: the big picture

What are TA concepts' general characteristics and resources? We saw in Chapter 14 how the interaction perspective offers possibilities to practitioners.

Attention to active ego states "behind the scenes" allows practitioners to *understand* how numerous and intricate internal dynamics are, not only their interlocutors', but also their own.

Novellino[72] gives us an example: "A therapist has realised that the person is avoiding talking about mother. Will he explicitly address this topic? Leaving aside layers untranslatable into words, each ego state provides the therapist with reactions for and against. On the 'for' side, the Child tells him that he is fed up with the person's endless and recurrent indictments of father; this reaction also makes him sense that 'something is wrong' with their communication. The Parent reminds him of his responsibility to steer the relationship in a productive direction; it perhaps even whispers to him that he has no right to get paid if the treatment does not progress. The Adult is aware that the process has been bogged down for some time and is even becoming repetitive. On the 'against' side, the Parent says: 'Be careful! Don't hurt this person: she is fragile…', and the Child adds: '…like my little brother once was', then, 'if she is shocked, she might leave you'; 'financially, that means less income'. The Adult, finally, recalls the negative consequences of a premature confrontation five sessions ago."

In a second step, the practitioner can wonder how each reaction *interacts* with the person or the group's ego states, and perhaps identify at which level and stratum these reactions might be located. Of course, and probably fortunately, the practitioner will only gradually discover the twists and turns of these multiple interactions, and the task of clarifying this ego state "tangle" will take time; but if the process is not inhibited, an ever-wider space will gradually open up for their thinking and interventions. The practitioner can then make a more informed *choice of* interventions according to what they can sense about the possible reactions of individuals or groups.

This space can be marked out in several ways. Depending on what emerges, the practitioner may turn to one or another *domain* of the patient's life, like "daily problems and relationships, as well as transference and counter-transference or other preconscious or unconscious issues".[73] They can also choose the *level*(s) of interventions: levels of aspects directly accessible to external and internal perception (behavioural and relational diagnoses); intertwined levels of underlying mechanisms; or levels of the deepest aspects, which are generally the most sensitive and the most defended, such as personality, or script, or, in another specialized field, the company's unconscious structures. When facing a psychological game, for example, will the practitioner confront it or deflect it (behavioural level), uncover the underlying motivation (mechanism level) or build on what is happening to respectfully explore[74] the person's or group's script?

This openness is one of TA fundamental strengths. TA concepts usually form a *"bridge"* between two or more levels, which distinguishes TA from approaches that intend to focus on only one; notably, the opposition between behavioural and psychodynamic approaches has no meaning in TA. The two main "bridges" are the script, and ego state theory, including diagnostic clues and interaction perspective. But they are not the only ones: a racket feeling,[75] for example, links behavioural aspects (racketeering) with mechanisms (getting strokes) and the script (repressing a forbidden feeling). Such concepts provide the practitioner with pathways from one level to the next in their thinking and interventions.

A most interesting aspect of this intervention freedom is that its power manifests itself in a way that is proportionate to the practitioner's *experience*, provided they do the corresponding self-work. According to Berne's aspiration, TA is not reserved for superior beings; but it is also a fact that well-trained and experienced professionals' practice is, with few exceptions, deeper, faster and more effective.

Acquiring this experience begins with realizing that transactional theory can only be used to understand others and their functioning if it is also used to become aware of both one's own resources and limitations. Once this prerequisite has been accepted, the practitioner becomes increasingly aware of how varied and intricate experience is. They feel from the outset that they cannot professionally manage a situation by examining the various parameters involved one by one,[76] nor by "applying" concepts one after the other. If they tried to do so, they would put themselves in the centipede's shoes:

> A centipede was living quietly, going about its business, until one day a toad, watching it come and go, asked: "Which leg moves after which?" The centipede went back to its hole, deeply disturbed by the toad's question. It tried to think of a possible answer but could not. So, it remained stuck in its hole, unable to move its legs, and died of hunger.[77]

But the toad is wrong! The practitioner is not stuck in "theorising theory" either.[78] They have the natural possibility of gradually integrating their ego states, concepts and actions. Integration, which is at the heart of the professional experience, and which represents in my opinion the training's ultimate goal, will enable them to emerge from this impasse, unless they slow down or stop the process. Integration means access to a progressive "panoramic" vigilance: unlike the walking centipede, this one is conscious, and the practitioner can always, if necessary, return safely to a careful examination of the situation.

At the same time, the practitioner can increasingly perceive the diversity of frames of reference and assess the consequences of each possible intervention at a given moment. Their style will become more personal, and their effectiveness more varied and intuitively immediate, at least outside the "blind spots" that remain in each of us. Moreover, this transformation can only have repercussions on the whole of their life. But of course, if they do not maintain it through training, study and work on themselves, there will be very little to integrate!

This journey, like Berne's, leads us ever further and deeper. Its stages are not always easy, many require "letting go", but each one is plentiful in interest and resources, including the last one, the end of the professional journey. In short, "what the experienced practitioner and the beginner have in common is that they are both on the same path".

As I conclude this chapter "ten years on", it remains for me to wish each of my readers a fulfilling journey along this path.

Notes

1. BERNE, E., 1961.
2. "*Primum non nocere*". BERNE, E., 1966, pp. 62–63.
3. STEINER, C.M., 1971a. CHENEY, W.D., 1971.
4. BERNE, E., 1968b.
5. BERNE, E., 1961, p. 2, p. 193.
6. See BERNE, E., 1961, p. 2: "It was easier for people to continue to think in orthodox conceptual forms than to shift over to a phenomenological approach".
7. BERNE, E., 1972, p. 400.
8. See, for example, BERNE, E., 1961, p. viii.
9. See p. 22.
10. FEDERN, P., 1952.
11. "Concrete" means: which includes the total recall of the cognitive and internal aspects of the experience. BERNE, E., 1961, pp. 1–2. R. Erskine describes well this global character of ego states.
12. WEISS, E., 1950. See BERNE, E., 1961, pp. 1–2.
13. BERNE, E., 1961, p. 196. The text is quoted in Chapter 1, p. 28.
14. Berne has strong reservations about therapy where emotions take centre stage. See BERNE, E., 1964a, pp. 142–143. BERNE, E., 1973, p. 70.
15. BERNE, E., 1961, p. 60. He will later add the experiences of H. and M. HARLOW. BERNE, E., 1963, p. 231.
16. Ibid, pp. 60–61.
17. BERNE, E., 1961, p. 6. Berne adds elsewhere: "This does not mean that the Adult alone is active in social situations, but it is the Adult who decides when to release the Child or the Parent, and when to resume the executive". Ibid, p. 65.
18. BERNE, E., 1961, p. 127.
19. BERNE, E., 1961, p. 176.
20. In 1966, Berne mentions the case of a phobic patient he invited to sit on the psycho-analytic couch after a two-year transactional treatment. BERNE, E., 1966, p. 293.
21. See pp. 27–37.
22. BERNE, E., 1961, p. 6.
23. C.N.R.T.L. (Centre National de Recherches Textuelles et Lexicales). *Dictionnaire*, art. "structure" (www.cnrtl.fr).
24. BERNE, E., 1961, pp. 159–160.
25. See pp. 84–88.
26. As we will see later, P1, A1 and E1 will be given a different meaning in the context of script analysis.
27. BERNE, E., 1961, pp. 149–150.
28. See pp. 153–156.
29. BERNE, E., 1961, p. 201.
30. At least those that Berne considers explicitly, to the exclusion of "oblique transactions" between the Adult and the Parent, or between the Adult and the Child, which are mainly "textbook cases".
31. In his early articles, Berne rightly spoke of a "trialogue". BERNE, E., 1957b, p. 127.
32. BERNE, E., 1961, p. 52
33. BERNE, E., 1961, pp. 51–53. This title (p. 51) shows the author's approach to this enumeration.
34. BERNE, E., 1972, p. 13. See pp. 17–18.

35 It should be noted that in Berne the apparent stimulus (called "social") is always Adult-Adult: he does not engage in the discussion of cases involving other possibilities, which in practise are very rare.
36 Nevertheless, it is worth mentioning Berne's "triple" intervention with the Hecht couple: BerneBERNE, E., 1961, pp. 187–188. See p. 255. This intervention has sometimes been referred to as "bull's-eye".
37 The indirect transaction begins with a stimulus apparently addressed to one person, but actually intended to influence another. BERNE, E., 1963, pp. 193–194.
38 *"Ulterior:* going beyond what is explicitly said or shown". MERRIAM-WEBSTER Dictionary, art. *"ulterior"*.
39 BERNE, E., 1966, p. 231.
40 BERNE, E., 1964a, p. 48.
41 BERNE, E., 1972, pp. 23–25.
42 Another concept was developed by HINE. J., 1990.
43 BERNE, E., 1961, p. 62. On Berne's conception of intimacy, see GRÉGOIRE, J., 2016.
44 BERNE, E., 1961, p. 86.
45 BERNE, E., 1961, pp. 86–87.
46 STEINER, C.M., 1966. BERNE, E., 1972, pp. 279–283.
47 BERNE, E., 1972, p. 104.
48 BERNE, E., 1972, p. 122.
49 KUHN, T., 1970.
50 BERNE E. and STEINER C.M., 1969.
51 However, that does not seem to have been a problem to an author like F. ENGLISH. See ENGLISH, F., 1977[ES].
52 KAHLER, T., and CAPERS, H., 1974.
53 GOULDING, R., and GOULDING, M., 1976. MELLOR, K., 1980. See pp. 83–85.
54 ENGLISH, F., 1971.
55 SCHIFF, J.L., and others, 1975.
56 ERSKINE, R.G. and ZALCMAN, M.J., 1979.
57 See pp. 7–9.
58 GRÉGOIRE, J., 2007c.
59 BERNE, E., 1972, pp. 400–401. See GRÉGOIRE, J., 2007a[ES].
60 STEINER, C.M., 1970. WILSON, J., and KALINA, I., 1978.
61 STEINER, C.M., 1971b.
62 See ERSKINE, R.G., 1974. The parasitic feeling includes in itself a reference to strokes. ENGLISH, F., 1971.
63 KARPMAN, S., 1971[ES].
64 See Magnolia's example, BERNE, E., 1961, p. 153.
65 This does not prevent expression of emotion nor work on underlying mechanisms, without which no significant change is possible. See CORNELL, W.F., and HINE, J., 1999.
66 GOULDING, R., and GOULDING, M., 1979[ES].
67 SCHIFF, J.L., and others, 1975.
68 See, for example, STEINER, C.M., and NOVELLINO, M., 2005 and their disappointing controversy.
69 For details, see GRÉGOIRE, J., 2007c[ES].
70 See EVRARD, B., GRÉGOIRE, J., MAQUET, J. and QUAZZA, J.P., 2009.
71 HARGADEN, H., and SILLS, C., 2002[ES].
72 NOVELLINO, M., 1990, p. 171.

73   CORNELL, W., 2006, p. 4.
74   ERSKINE, R.G., and TRAUTMANN, R., 1996.
75   ENGLISH, F., 1971. See above, pp. 181–183.
76   See GRÉGOIRE, J., 2015a.
77   Taoist tale. Quoted in CARRÈRE, J.C., 1998, pp. 315–316.
78   See GRÉGOIRE, J., 2015d.

BIBLIOGRAPHY

Notes on the bibliography:

- The date given is the date of first publication.
- This bibliography is divided into three parts:
    - Works by Eric Berne;
    - Books and articles about the ego state theory (when in footnotes, these show an ES acronym listed next to the year of publication); and
    - Other books and articles.
- *AAT* = *Actualités en Analyse Transactionnelle* (periodical). Editions d'Analyse Transactionnelle, 1977–2007.
- *SATAB* = *Selected Articles of the TAB*. TA-Press, 1976.
- *TAB* = *Transactional Analysis Bulletin.* 1962–1970.
- *TAJ* = *Transactional Analysis Journal* (periodical). ITAA, 1971–2007.

Works by Eric Berne

BERNE, E., 1948: *The Mind in Action*. Simon & Schuster.
BERNE, E., 1949: The Nature of Intuition. In: *Intuition and Ego States* (collection). TA-Press, 1977, pp. 1–31.
BERNE, E., 1952: Concerning the Nature of Diagnosis. *Ibid.*, pp. 33–48.
BERNE, E., 1953: Concerning the Nature of Communication. *Ibid.*, pp. 49–65.
BERNE, E., 1955: Primal Images and Primal Judgments. *Ibid.*, pp. 67–97.
BERNE, E., 1957a: The Ego Image. *Ibid.*, pp. 99–119.
BERNE, E., 1957b: Ego States in Psychotherapy. *Ibid*, pp. 121–144.
BERNE, E., 1958: Transactional Analysis: A New and Effective Method of Group Therapy. *Ibid.*, pp. 145–158.
BERNE, E., 1961: *Transactional Analysis in Psychotherapy*. Mockingbird, 2021.
BERNE, E., 1962: The Psychodynamics of Intuition. In: *Intuition and Ego States* (collection). T.A.-Press, 1977, pp. 159–166.
BERNE, E., 1963: *The Structure and Dynamics of Organizations and Groups*. Grove Press, 1975.
BERNE, E., 1964a: *Games People Play*. Ballantine, 2004.
BERNE, E., 1964b: The Intimacy Experiment (orig. *TAB*). *SATAB*, pp. 13–14.

BERNE, E., 1964c: More about Intimacy (orig. *TAB*). *SATAB*, p. 15.
BERNE, E., 1966: *Principles of Group Treatment*. Grove Press, 11th ed., 1977.
BERNE, E., 1968: *A Layman's Guide to Psychiatry and Psychoanalysis* (revised and expanded edition of BERNE, E., 1948). Penguin, 1976.
BERNE, E., 1968b: Staff Meetings with Patients. In: *SATAB*, pp. 98–99.
BERNE, E., 1969: Standard Nomenclature. In: *SATAB*, pp. 104–105.
BERNE, E., 1970: *Sex in Human Loving*. Penguin, 1976.
BERNE, E., 1972: *What Do You Say after You Say Hello?* Corgi Books, 1975.
BERNE, E., 1973[ES]: Transcription of Eric Berne in Vienna 1968. *TAJ 3*, pp. 63–72.
BERNE, E., 1977: *Intuition and Ego States* (collection). TA-Press, 1977.
BERNE, E., and STEINER, C.M. 1969: Writing for Publication. *SATAB*, p. 107.

Books and articles about the ego state theory

BARNES, G. (Ed.), 1978: *Transactional Analysis after Eric Berne: Teachings and Practice of Three TA Schools* (collection). Harper's College.
BLACKSTONE, P., 1993[ES]: The Dynamic Child: Integrating Second-Order Structure, Object Relations, and Self Psychology. *TAJ 23*, 4, pp. 216–234.
CLARK, B., 1991[ES]: Empathic Transactions in the Deconfusion of Child Ego States. *TAJ 21*, 2, pp. 92–98.
CLARKSON, P., and GILBERT, M., 1988[ES]: Berne's Original Model of Ego States: Some Theoretical Considerations. *TAJ 18*, 1, pp. 20–29.
CORNELL, W.F., 2003[ES], Brains and Bodies: Somatic Foundations of the Child. In: SILLS, C., and HARGADEN, H., – '
COX, M., 1999[ES]: The Relationship between Ego State Structure and Function: A Diagrammatic Formulation. *TAJ 29*, 1, pp. 49–58.
DASHIELL, S., 1978[ES]: The Parent Resolution Process: Reprogramming Psychic Incorporations in the Parent. *TAJ 8*, 4, pp. 289–294.
ENGLISH, F., 1977[ES]: What Shall I Do Tomorrow: Reconceptualize Transactional Analysis. In: BARNES, G., *Transactional Analysis after Eric Berne: Teachings and Practice of Three TA Schools.* Harper's College, 1978, pp. 287–347.
ERNST, F., 1971[ES]: The Diagrammed Parent: Eric Berne's Most Significant Contribution. *TAJ 1*, 1, pp. 49–58.
ERSKINE, R.G., 1974[ES]: Therapeutic Intervention: Disconnecting Rubberbands. *TAJ 4*, 1, pp. 7–8.
ERSKINE, R.G., 1988[ES]: Ego State Structure, Intrapsychic Function and Defence Mechanisms: Commentary on Eric Berne's Original Theoretical Concepts. *TAJ 18*, 1, pp. 15–19.
ERSKINE, R.G., 1991[ES]: Transference and Transactions: Critique from an Intrapsychic and Integrative Perspective. *TAJ 21*, 2, pp. 63–76.
ERSKINE, R.G., 1994[ES]: Shame and Self-Righteousness: Transactional Analysis Perspectives and Clinical Interventions. *TAJ 24*, 2, pp. 86–102.
ERSKINE, R.G., CLARKSON, P., GOULDING, R.L., GRODER, M.G., and MOISO, C., 1988[ES]: Ego State Theory: Definitions, Descriptions and Points of View. *TAJ 18*, pp. 6–14.
EVRARD, B., GRÉGOIRE, J., MAQUET, J., and QUAZZA, J.P., 2009[ES]: Autonomie des pratiques. Peut-on transiger avec la théorie? I. and II. *AAT 131*, pp. 38–56.
FOWLIE, H., 2005[ES]: Confusion and Introjection: A Model for Understanding the Defensive Structures of the Parent and Child Ego States. *TAJ 35*, 2, pp. 192–204.

GILBERT, M., 19 In: SILLS 96[ES]: Ego States and Ego States Networks. Presentation at the I.T.A.A. Conference on Ego States, Amsterdam, March 1996.

GILBERT, M., 2003[ES]: Confusion and Introjection: A Model for Understanding the Defensive Structures of the Parent and Child Ego States In: SILLS, C., and HARGADEN, H., *Key Concepts in Transactional Analysis : Ego States*. Worth Publishing, 2003, pp. 109–134.

GILDEBRAND, K., 2003[ES]: An Introduction to the Brain and the Early Developments of the Child Ego State. In: SILLS, C., and HARGADEN, H., *Key Concepts in Transactional Analysis: Ego States*. Worth Publishing, 2003, pp. 1–27.

GILLESPIE, J., 1976[ES]: Feelings in the Adult Ego State? *TAJ 6*, pp. 69–72.

GOULDING, R., and GOULDING, M., 1976[ES]: Injunctions, Decisions, and Redecisions. *TAJ 6*, 1, pp. 41–48.

GOULDING, R., and GOULDING, M., 1979[ES]: *Changing Lives Through Redecision Therapy*. Brunner & Mazel.

GRÉGOIRE, J., 2003[ES]: (Forum) Les modèles théoriques des états du moi et leur lien mutuel. *AAT 108*, pp. 45–58.

GRÉGOIRE, J., 2004[ES]: Ego States as Living Links Between Past and Current Experiences. *TAJ 34*, 1, pp. 10–29.

GRÉGOIRE, J., 2007a[ES], 2007b[ES]: Réflexions sur Berne, Steiner, les courants récents de l'A.T., et nous. I. and II. *AAT, 122*, pp. 1–29.

GRÉGOIRE, J., 2007c[ES]: *Les orientations récentes de l'analyse transactionnelle*. Editions d'Analyse Transactionnelle.

HARGADEN, H., and SILLS, C., 2002[ES]: *Transactional Analysis: A Relational Perspective*. Routledge.

HAYKIN, M.D., 1980[ES]: Type Casting: The Influence of Early Childhood Experience upon the Structure of the Child Ego State. *TAJ 10*, 4, pp. 354–364.

HINE, J., 1997[ES]: Mind Structure and Ego States. *TAJ 27*, 4, pp. 278–289.

HOLTBY, M.E., 1976[ES]: The Origin and Insertion of Script Injunctions. *TAJ 6*, 4, pp. 371–376.

HOSTIE, R., 1987[ES]: *Analyse transactionnelle, l'âge adulte*. InterEditions.

JAMES, M., 1974[ES]: Self-Reparenting, Theory and Process. *TAJ 4*, 3, pp. 32–39.

JAMES, M., and JONGEWARD, D., 1971[ES]: Born to Win. Da Capo, 1996.

JAOUI, G., 1992[ES]: Processus transférentiel et processus transactionnel. *AAT 64*, pp. 171–174.

JOINES, V., 1976[ES]: Differentiating Structural and Functional. *TAJ 6*, 4, pp. 377–380.

JOINES, V.S., 1991[ES]: Transference and Transactions: Some Additional Comments. *TAJ 21*, 3, pp. 170–173.

KAHLER, T., and CAPERS, H., 1974[ES]: The Mini-Script.. *TAJ 4*, 1, pp. 26–42.

KARPMAN, S., 1968[ES]: Fairy Tales and Script Drama Analysis (Orig. *TAB*). *SATAB*, pp. 51–56.

KARPMAN, S., 1971[ES]: Options. *AAT 1*, pp. 14–21.

KARPMAN, S., 1991[ES]: Notes on the Transference Papers: Transference as a Game. *TAJ 21*, 3, pp. 136–140.

KARPMAN, S., 1999[ES]: Letter. In: *Script*, August 1999.

KOUWENHOVEN, M., 1983[ES]: Systèmes parentaux absents, déficients et déviants. *AAT 28*, pp. 179–184.

LE GUERNIC, A., 2004[ES]: *Etats du moi, transactions et communication*. InterEditions.

LEVIN, P., 1982[ES]: The Cycle of Development. *TAJ 12*, 2, pp. 129–139.

LITTLE, R., 2006[ES]: Ego State Relational Units and Resistance to Change. *TAJ 36*, 1, pp. 7–19.

LOOMIS, M.E., and LANDSMAN, S.G., 1980[ES]: The Manic-Depressive Structure: Diagnosis and Development. *TAJ 10*, 4, pp. 284–290.
LORIA, B., 1988[ES]: The Parent Ego State: Theoretical Foundations and Alterations. *TAJ 18*, 1, pp. 39–46.
McNAMARA, J., and LISTER-FORD, C., 1995[ES]: Ego States and the Psychology of Memory. *TAJ 25*, 2, pp. 141–149.
McNEEL J. R., 1976[ES]: The Parent Interview. *TAJ 6*, 1, pp. 61–68.
MELLOR, K., 1980[ES]: Impasses: A Developmental and Structural Understanding. *TAJ 10*, 3, pp. 213–220.
MELLOR, K., and ANDREWARTHA, G., 1980[ES]: Reparenting the Parent in Support of Redecisions. *TAJ 10*, 3, pp. 197–203.
MOISO, C., 1985[ES]: Ego States and Transference. *TAJ 15*, 3, pp. 194–201.
NOVELLINO, M., 2003[ES]: On Closer Analysis: Revision of the Rules of Communication within the Framework of Transactional Analysis. In: SILLS, C., and HARGADEN, H., Key Concepts in Transactional Analysis: Ego States. Worth Publishing, 2003, pp. 149–168.
OLLER VALLEJO, J., 1997[ES]: Integrative Analysis of Ego-States Models. *TAJ 27*, pp. 290–294.
OLLER VALLEJO, J., 2002[ES]: In Support of the Second-Order Functional Model. *TAJ 32*, 3, pp. 178–183.
PHILLIPS, R.D., 1975[ES]: *Structural Symbiotic Systems. Correlations with Ego States, Behaviour and Physiology*. Author.
RAMOND, C., 1992[ES]: L'Adulte intégré. *AAT*, *63*, 1992, pp. 141–144.
RUBBERS, B., 1998[ES]: La symbiose: une relation de dépendance parmi d'autres? *AAT 87*, pp. 105–111.
SCHLEGEL, L., 1993[ES]: Die "psychische Organe" und ihr Verhältnis zu den Ich-Zustanden nach Berne. *Zeitschrift für Transaktions-Analyse 10*, 3, pp. 155–161.
SCHLEGEL, L., 1998[ES]: What Is Transactional Analysis? *TAJ 28*, 4, pp. 269–287.
SCHLEGEL, L., 2001[ES]: Gedanken zum "Erwachsenen-Zustand der integrierten Person" nach Berne. *Zeitschrift für Transaktions-Analyse 18*, 3, pp. 77–90.
SCHMID, B., 1991[ES]: Intuition of the Possible and Transactional Creation of Realities. *TAJ 21*, 3, pp. 144–154.
SILLS, C., 2004[ES]: Celebrating Differences. *Script*.
SILLS, C., and HARGADEN, H., 2003[ES]: *Key Concepts in Transactional Analysis: Ego States*. Worth Publishing.
STEINER, C.M., 2002[ES]: The Adult: Once Again with Feeling. *TAJ 32*, pp. 62–65.
STEWART, I., 2001[ES]: Ego States and the Theory of Theory: The Strange Case of the Little Professor. *TAJ 31*, 2, pp. 133–147.
SUMMERS, G., and TUDOR, K., 2000[ES]: Cocreative Transactional Analysis. *TAJ 30*, 1, pp. 23–40.
THUNNISSEN, M., 1998[ES]: The Structural Development of the Child Ego State. *TAJ 28*, 2, pp. 143–151.
TUDOR, K., 2003[ES]: The Neopsyche and the Integrating Adult Ego State. In: SILLS, C., and HARGADEN, H., Key Concepts in Transactional Analysis: Ego States. Worth Publishing, 2003, pp. 201–231.
TUDOR, K., 2011[ES]: Understanding Empathy. *TAJ 41*, 1, pp. 39–57.
WOODS, M., and WOODS, K., 1981[ES]: Ego Splitting and the TA Diagram. *TAJ 11*, 2, pp. 130–133.

Other books and articles

ALLEN, J.R., 2000: Biology and Transactional Analysis: A Status Report on Neurodevelopment. *TAJ 30*, 4, pp. 260–269.

ALLEN, J.R., and ALLEN, B., 1997: A New Type of Transactional Analysis and One Version of Script Work With a Constructionist Sensibility. *TAJ 27*, 2, pp. 89–98.

BADER, E., and PEARSON, P., 1983: The Developmental Stages of Couplehood. *TAJ 13*, 1, pp. 28–32.

BARNES, G., 1999a, 1999b, 1999c: Energy Metaphors: I. (a) *TAJ 29*, 2, pp.96–108. II. (b) *TAJ 29*, 3, pp.186–197. III. (c) *TAJ 29*, 4, pp.237–249.

BASCH, M., 1976: The Concept of Affect: A Re-Examination. *Journal of the American Psychoanalytic Association 24*, pp. 759–777.

BATESON, G., 1972: *Steps to an Ecology of Mind: Collected Essays in Anthropology, Psychiatry, Evolution, and Epistemology*. University of Chicago Press, 2000.

BATESON, G., 1979: *Mind and Nature: A Necessary Unity*. Hampton Press, 2002.

BION, W.R., 1961: *Experiences in Groups*. Tavistock.

BOURDIEU, P., 1980: *Le sens pratique*. Minuit.

BOYD, L., and BOYD, H., 1980: Caring and Intimacy as a Time Structure. *TAJ 10*, 4, pp. 281–283.

CARRÈRE, J.C., 1998: *Le cercle des menteurs: Contes philosophiques du monde entier*. Plon.

CHENEY, W.D., 1971: Eric Berne, Biographical Sketch. *TAJ 1*, **1**, pp. 14–22.

CLARKSON, P., 1991a: Group Imago and the Stages of Group Development. *TAJ 21*, 1, pp. 36–50.

CLARKSON, P., 1991: Through the Looking Glass: I. (b). *TAJ 21*, 2, pp. 99–107. II. (c) TAJ *21*, 3, pp. 174–183.

CONWAY, A., and CLARKSON, P., 1987: Everyday Hypnotic Inductions. *TAJ 17*, 2, pp. 17–23.

CORNELL, W.R., 1988: Life Script Theory: A Critical Review from a Developmental Perspective. *TAJ 18*, 4, pp. 270–282.

CORNELL, W.F., 1994: Shame: Binding Affect, Ego State Contamination, and Relational Repair. *TAJ 24*, 2, pp. 139–146.

CORNELL, W.F., 1998: If Reich Had Met Winnicott: Body and Gesture. *Energy and Character 28*, pp. 50–60.

CORNELL, W.F., 2000: If Berne Met Winnicott: Transactional Analysis and Relational Analysis. *TAJ 30*, 4, pp. 270–275.

CORNELL, W.R., 2006: Another Perspective on the Therapist's Stance. *Script 36*, 3, Apr. 2006, p. 4.

CORNELL, W.F., 2015: *Somatic Experience in Psychoanalysis and Psychotherapy: In the Expressive Language of the Living*. Routledge.

CORNELL, W.F., and HINE, J., 1999: Cognitive and Social Functions of Emotions: A Model for Transactional Analysis Counsellor Training. *TAJ 29*, 3, pp. 175–185.

CORNELL, W.F., and LANDAICHE, M.N., 2006: Impasse and Intimacy: Applying Berne's Concept of Script Protocol. *TAJ 36*, 3, pp. 196–213.

DAMASIO, A., 1994: *Descartes' Error: Emotion, Reason, and the Human Brain*. Putnam.

DAMASIO, A., 1999: *The Feeling of What Happens*. Berks, Cox & Wyman.

DILTS, R., 1995: *Strategies of Genius*. Dilts Strategy Group.

DOLLE, J.M., 1999: *Pour comprendre Jean Piaget*. Dunod.

EMDE, R., 1999: Moving Ahead: Integrating Influences of Affective Processes for Development of Psychoanalysis. *International Journal of Psychoanalysis 80*, pp. 317–339.
ENGLISH, F., 1971, 1972: The Substitution Factor: Rackets and Real Feelings I. *TAJ 1*, 4, pp. 27–32.
ERIKSON, E.H., 1950: *Childhood and Society*. Norton, 1993.
ERSKINE, R.G., 1974: Counterfeit Strokes. *TAJ 4*, 2, pp. 18–19.
ERSKINE, R.G., and TRAUTMANN, R., 1996: Methods of an Integrative Psychotherapy. *TAJ 26*, 4, pp. 316–328.
ERSKINE, R.G., and ZALCMAN, M.J., 1979: The Racket System: A Model for Racket Analysis. *TAJ 9*, 1, pp. 51–59.
FEDERN, P., 1952: *Ego Psychology and the Psychoses*. Basic Books.
FREUD, S., 1900: The Interpretation of Dreams. In: *Standard Edition of the Complete Works of Sigmund Freud*, vol. *IV and V* (STRACHEY, J., ed.). 2018–2014.
GOLEMAN, D., 1995: *Emotional Intelligence*. Bloomsbury.
GRÉGOIRE, J., 1994[ES]: Criteria for Defining the Boundaries of Transactional Analysis Fields of Application. *TAJ 28*, 4, pp. 311–320.
GRÉGOIRE, J., 2015a,b,c: Pensée et théorie dans l'accompagnement du changement psychologique, AAT, *150,*, pp. 7–8. GRÉGOIRE, J., I. (a) *AAT 150*, pp. 7–20. II. (b) *AAT 150*, pp. 22–33. III. (c) *AAT 150,* pp. 34–50.
GRÉGOIRE, J., 2015d[ES]: Thinking, Theory, and Experience in the Helping Professions. A Phenomenological Description. *TAJ 45*, 1, pp. 59–71.
GRÉGOIRE, J., 2016: Intimité: structuration du temps ou relation? In: *Journal d'Analystes Transactionnels*. Fibelys, pp. 173–180.
GRINDER, J., and DELOZIER, J., 1987: *Turtles All the Way Down*. Grinder & Associates.
HABERMAS, J., 1983: *Moral Consciousness and Communicative Action*. Blackwell, 2007.
HEIDEGGER, M., 1927: *Being and Time*. Harper & Row, 1962.
HINE, J., 1990: The Bilateral and Continuous Nature of Psychological Games. *TAJ 20*, 1, pp. 38–39.
HOSTIE, R., 1980: Eric Berne, the Martian. *TAJ 12*, 2, pp. 168–170.
HOUDÉ, O., 2004: *La psychologie de l'enfant*. Presses Universitaires de France. (Updating PIAGET, J., and INHELDER, B., 1966: *The Psychology of the Child*. Basic Books).
HYAMS, H., 2002: Dissociation: Definition, Diagnosis, Manifestations, and Therapy, With Special Reference to Cults/Sects. *TAJ 28*, 3, pp. 234–243.
IACOBONI, M., 2009: Imitation, Empathy, and Mirror Neurons. *Annual Review of Psychology*, pp. 653–670.
KAHLER, T., and CAPERS, H., 1974: The Mini-Script. *TAJ 4*, 1, pp. 26–42.
KARPMAN, S., 1968: Fairy Tales and Script Drama Analysis. *TAB 7*, pp. 51–56.
KEGAN, R., 1982: *The Evolving Self: Problem and Process in Human Development*. Harvard University Press.
KERBRAT-ORECCHIONI, C., 1986–1987: *L'implicite*, vol. *1 and 2*. Armand Collin.
KOHLBERG, L., 1984: *The Psychology of Moral Development, Vol.2: The Nature and Validity of Moral Stages*. Harper & Row.
KOHUT, H., 1971[ES]: *The Analysis of the Self: A Systematic Approach to the Psychoanalytic Treatment of Narcissistic Personality Disorders*. International Universities Press.
KÜBLER-ROSS, E., 1969: *Living With Death and Dying*. Scribner.
KUHN, T., 1970: *The Structure of Scientific Revolutions*. University of Chicago Press.
LAHIRE, B., 2001: *L'homme pluriel*. Nathan, 2001.

LAPLANCHE, J., 1987: *Nouveaux fondements pour la psychanalyse*. Presses Universitaires de France.
LAPLANCHE, J., and PONTALIS, J., 1974: *The Language of Psychoanalysis*. Norton.
LEVENSON, R.W., 1999[ES]: The Interpersonal Function of Emotions. *Cognition and Emotion 13*, pp. 481–504.
LOOMIS, M., and LANDSMAN, S., 1980[ES]: The Manic-Depressive Structure: Diagnosis and Development. *TAJ 10*, 4, pp. 284–292.
LOWEN, A., and LOWEN, L., 1977: *Bioenergetics*. Coward, McCann & Geoghegan.
MAALOUF, A., 1998: *In the Name of Identity: Violence and the Need to Belong*. Arcade Publishing.
MAHLER, M.S., PINE, F., and BERGMAN, A., 1975: *The Psychological Birth of the Human Infant*. Routledge.
MARIOTTI, M., SABA, G., and STRATTON, P., 2021: *Handbook of Systemic Approaches to Psychotherapy Manuals*. Springer.
MARTORELL, J.L., 1994: Mystification and Power Games in Couples Therapy. *TAJ 24*, 4, pp. 240–249.
MASLOW, A.H., 1968: *Towards a Psychology of Being*. Litton Educational Publishing.
MELLOR, K., and SCHIFF (SIGMUND), E.W., 1975a: Discounting. *TAJ 5*, 3, pp. 295–302.
MELLOR, K., and SCHIFF (SIGMUND), E.W., 1975b: Redefining. *TAJ 5*, 3, pp. 303–311.
MOUNIER, P., 2001: *Pierre Bourdieu: une I introduction*. Agora.
NATHANSON,, 1994: Shame Transactions. *TAJ 24*, 2, pp. 121–129.
NOVELLINO, M., 1984: Self-Analysis of Countertransference in Integrative TA. *TAJ 14*, pp. 63–67.
NOVELLINO, M., 1985: Redecision Analysis of Transference: A TA Approach to Transference Neurosis. *TAJ 15*, 3, pp. 202–206.
NOVELLINO, M., 1987: Redecision Analysis of Transference: The Unconscious Dimension. *TAJ 17*, 1, pp. 271–276.
NOVELLINO, M., 1990: Unconscious Communication and Interpretation in Transactional Analysis. *TAJ 20*, 3, pp. 168–172.
NOVELLINO, M., 2005: Transactional Psychoanalysis: Epistemological Foundations. *TAJ 35*, 2, pp. 157–172.
NOVELLINO, M., and MOISO, C., The Psychodynamic Approach to Transactional Analysis. *TAJ 20*, 3, pp. 187–192.
PAGÈS, M., 1993: *Psychothérapie et complexité*. Desclée de Brouwer.
PANKSEPP, J., 1993: Rough and Tumble Play: A Fundamental Brain Process. In: K. MacDONALD (Ed.), *Parent-Child Play: Descriptions and Implications*. pp. 132–173 Univ. of New York Press.
PARRY, A., 1997: Why We Tell Stories: The Narrative Construction of Reality. *TAJ 27*, 2, pp. 118–127.
PETRIGLIERI, G., and DENFIELD-WOOD, J., 2003: The Invisible Revealed: Collusion as an Entry to the Group Unconscious. *TAJ 33*, 4, pp. 332–343.
PIAGET, J., 1932: *The Moral Judgment of the Child*. Simon & Schuster, 1997.
PIAGET, J., 1936: *The Origins of Intelligence in Children*. International Universities Press, 1952.
PIAGET, J., 1968: *Le structuralisme*. Presses Universitaires de France.
PIAGET, J., and INHELDER, B., 1966: *The Psychology of the Child*. Basic Books.
PIERRAKOS, J., 2005: *Core Energetics: Developing the Capacity to Love and Heal*. Core Energetics Publ.

PINE, F., 1990: *Drive, Ego, Object, and Self.* Basic Books.
RAMOND, C., 1995: *Grandir* (2e ed.). Desclée de Brouwer.
REICH, W., 1933: *Character Analysis.* 3rd enlarged ed., Farrar, Straus & Giroux, 1987.
REUSS, H., 2003: Blocages, altérations et marchandage dans le travail de deuil. *AAT 106*, pp. 43–55.
ROGERS, C., 1959: A Theory of Therapy, Personality, and Interpersonal Relationships, as Developed in the Client-Centered Framework. In: S. KOCH (Ed.), *Psychology: A Study of a Science*, vol. 3. pp. 184–256, McGraw-Hill.
SCHIFF, J.L., SCHIFF, A.W., MELLOR, K., SCHIFF, E., SCHIFF, S., RICHMAN, D., FISHMAN, J., WOLZ, L., FISHMAN, C., and MOMB, D., 1975: *Cathexis Reader: Transactional Analysis Treatment of Psychosis.* Harper & Row.
SCHIFF, A.W., and SCHIFF, J.L., Passivity. *TAJ 1*, 1, pp. 71–78.
SCHIFF, J.L., SCHIFF, A.W., and SCHIFF (SIGMUND), E., 1975: Frames of Reference. *TAJ 5*, 3, pp. 290–294.
SHEEHY, G., 1976: *Passages: Predictable Crises of Adult Life.* Random House.
SILLS, C., 2003: Role Lock: When the Whole Group Plays a Game. *TAJ 33*, 4, pp. 282–287.
SILLS, C., 2004: Celebrating Differences. *Script*, 2004.
STEINER, C.M., 1966: Script and Counter-Script. *TAB 5*, pp. 133–135.
STEINER, C.M., 1970: Manifesto. In: *Readings in Radical Therapy*, Grove Press, 1976, p. 6.
STEINER, C.M., 1971a[ES]: A Little Boy's Dream. *TAJ 1*, 1, pp. 46–48.
STEINER, C.M., 1974: *Scripts People Live.* Grove Press.
STEINER, C.M., 1981: *The Other Side of Power.* Grove Press.
STEINER, C.M., 1984[ES]: Emotional Literacy Training: The Application of Transactional Analysis to the Study of Emotions. *TAJ 26*, 1, pp. 31–39.
STEINER, C.M., and NOVELLINO, M., 2005: Theoretical Diversity: A Debate about Transactional Analysis and Psychoanalysis. *TAJ 35*, 2, pp. 110–118.
STEINER, C.M., and PERRY, P., 1996: *Achieving Emotional Literacy.* Avon Books.
STERN, D., 1985: *The Interpersonal World of the Infant.* Basic Books.
SYMOR, N., 1977: The Dependency Cycle: Implications for Theory, Therapy, and Social Action. *TAJ 7*, 1, pp. 37–43.
THOMSON, G., 1983: Fear, Anger and Sadness. *TAJ 13*, 1, pp. 20–24.
VAN BEEKUM, S., 2005: The Relational Consultant. *TAJ 36*, 4, pp. 318–329.
VARELA, F., 1980: *Autopoiesis and Cognition: The Realization of the Living.* Reidel.
VON FRANZ, M.L., 1964: Individuation. In: JUNG, C.G., HENDERSON, J.L., von FRANZ, M.L., JAFFÉ, A., and JACOBI, J., *Man and His Symbols.* Aldus Books.
WALDERKRANZ-PISELLI, C.K., 1999: What Do We Do before We Say Hello? The Body as the Stage Setting for the Script. *TAJ 29*, 1, pp. 31–48.
WATZLAWICK, P., HELMICK-BEAVIN, J., and JACKSON, D., 1967: *Pragmatics of Human Communication. A Study of Interactional Patterns, Pathologies, and Paradoxes.* Norton.
WEISS, E., 1950: *Principles of Psychodynamics.* Grune & Stratton.
WIDLÖCHER, D., 1997: Article "Moi (Psychologie du)". In: *Encyclopaedia Universalis: Dictionnaire de la psychanalyse.* Albin Michel, p. 501.
WILSON, J., and KALINA, I., 1978: The Splinter Chart. *TAJ 8*, 3, pp. 200–205.
WINNICOTT, D., 1971: *Playing and Reality.* Tavistock, 1971.
WOODS, K., 2002: The Duplex Transaction and Pastiming. *TAJ 32*, 2, pp. 116–120.
XYPAS, C., 2001: *Les stades du développement affectif selon Piaget.* L'Harmattan.

ACKNOWLEDGEMENTS

For this English edition of *Conceptualizing Ego States in Transactional Analysis: Three Systems in Interaction*, I wish to thank the many people and institutions who devoted competence, time, energy and resources to it: Patrick Bailleau and the team of NORPPA; William Cornell (TSTA), for his wonderful preface and his encouragements and active part in the editing process; Katie Randall, Manon Berset and the teams of Routledge; Wren Haines and his team; Muriel Treharne, the translator; and Lise Small, for her discrete help throughout. I add all people and institutions who made the two French editions possible, as well as all those who taught me TA in different ways, including my students and my patients.

Finally, to all those who encounter this book through this new edition, I wish a fruitful and creative path in their implementation of TA for themselves and others. I hope they can find in it some ideas to carry on with our common task: developing transactional analysis theory and practice in a truly creative way.

José Grégoire

INDEX

Note: *Italicized* page references refer to figures, **bold** references refer to tables, and page references with "n" refer to endnotes.

action: external 7; impersonal 37; organ metaphor 13; superstitious 53; underhand 93
Adult ego states 1–9, 38, 77, 81, viii; Child ego state influences 17; and ego 25–26; functions of 19–21; and id 25–26; Parent ego state influences 17; primary and secondary processes 23–24; as resources for life and development 27–28; and superego 25–26
Adult system 47, 49, 52, 72–84; as computer metaphor 80–81; conscious and unconscious aspects 75–76; early strata 78–80; ego state theory 83; forming conclusions and strategies 76–77; impact on action 77; interaction perspective 150–151; and intuition 78–80; "Little Professor" 80; and lucidity 74; memorization 73–74; overview 72–73; perception 73–74; redecision school 81–82; reparenting school 82–83; role 81; and sense of Self 109–111; structural contribution 77–78; transactional texts 77–84; unconscious communication 83–84
Allen, J. xiii
American Psychoanalytical Association 116n26
archaeopsyche 5
attribution 115n5
autonomous forms of behavior 54
autonomy 60–61, 119–120, 121–125
availability: and intervention 148–149; and relationship 148–149
awareness 123–124, 157n18
awareness scale 106

Barnes, Graham 157n16
Basch, M. 100
behavior: adapted Child 54; autonomous forms of 54; of developmental phase 56; Parental ego state 7
Berne, E. 1–2, 17, 43–44, 45n31, 45n32, 48, 49, 51, 52, 53–55, 60, 68, 77–80, 81–84, 87, 90, 91, 99, 116n26, x–xi, xii; Adult innate process 76; background and motivation 161–162; computer metaphor 80–81; conscious and unconscious aspects 75; descriptive terms 164; double transactions 164–165; first conceptualization 162–163; games and time structuring 165; initial extensions and clarifications 163–164; integrated Adult after 96; integrated person for 94–96; interaction modes 92–94; interaction perspective 5–6, 8–9; intuition as knowledge of others' experiences 120–121; on phenomenological approach 73; and relationship 137–138; script 165–166; script evolution 41–42; on Self 113–115; situational determining factors 21–22; text on psychic apparatus 21; theoretical journey 161–166
bilateral intimacy 125, 138
Bion, W.R. 136, 137
Blackstone, Peg 57
Bourdieu, Pierre 63
Boyd, H. 139
Boyd, L. 139

causality 106
"character defences" 110

183

INDEX

Child early strata 78
Child ego state 1–9, 38, viii; and ego 25–26; functions of 19–21; and id 25–26; influences Adult system 17; primary and secondary processes 23–24, 51; as resources for life and development 27–28; second order structure of *42*, 42–44; and superego 25–26
The Child system 47–57, 70; association modes 51–52; conclusions/beliefs 52; debates 56–57; early transactionalists 55; fantasy 49; imagination 49; impact on action 52–53; interaction perspective 48, 54, 150–151; intuitive perception 49–50; language perception 50; memorization 50–51; organizer role of 51–52; overview 47; perception 47–50; perception mode 51; repetition perspective 53–54, 56; and sense of Self 52, 109–111; sequential/ descriptive perspective 54; strategies 52–53; subjective experience 48–49; transactional texts on 53–55
Clark, B. 133
Clarkson, P. 57, 62, 136
"classical TA" period 2, 7–8, 27, 40, 119, 166–168, xi–xii
clinging relationship 131
co-creative TA 133–135, xiii
co-creativity: and relationships 127–139; and transferential dimensions 133–135
collusion 87–88
communication 62; frame of reference's role 144–145; from the inner to the outer side 143–144; non-verbal 103; outer side of communication 142–143; within the relationships 142–147; transaction diagram 145; transference transaction 145–147; unconscious 75
confuse modal 50
conjunction 88, 93–94; establishing 153–154
constructivist philosophical perspective 72
content, and outer side of communication 142–143
Conway, A. 62
Cornell, W. 36, 80, 148, 168, xiii–xiv
counter-transference 27, 79–80, 120, 133–134, 153, 166, 168
creativity 51–52, 60–61, 89

Damasio, A. 73, 100
decisive' intervention xii
denial 104

"dependence cycle" 126n19
Descartes' Error: Emotion, Reason, and the Human Brain (Damasio) 100
descriptive terms 164
destructive secrecy 147n1
determinants level 21
development 35–40; Adult ego states as 27–28; of behavior 56; beyond childhood 39–40; Parent system 66; sense of Other 36; sense of Self 35–36; strata 40–41
differentiation 106
Dilts, R. 61, 70n5
discourse ethics 71n34
disjunction 86–97
displacement 23
dissociation 87
dominant relationships 131
double transactions 164–165
drama triangle 6
Dusay, J. xi

early Adult 82
early transactionalists 55
ego 75, 91–92; and Adult ego state 25–26; and Child ego state 25–26; and Parent ego state 25–26; and Self 112; state groups 86
ego-image 78–79, 120
"ego integrity" 160
Ego Psychology 91–92, 114, 116n14
ego states/ego states theory 27, 50, 83, 115, x; associated trios 30–31; combinations and inhibition 33–34; descriptive model xi; emotions as 99–101; evolving combinations of 30–35; generalized representations of events 31–33; from interaction perspective 24–25; meanings of x–xi; origin perspective 2–5; as personality systems 12–17; reinforcements and inhibitions *33*, 33–35, *35*; repetitive 33; sequential/descriptive perspective 1–2, 6–7; trios 96–97
"ego-syntonic" 113
eidetic perception 126n31
Einstein, A. 61
emergent Self 36–37, *37*
emotional chaos 106
Emotional Intelligence (Goleman) 100
emotions 99–106; awareness scale 106; as element of ego states 99–101; and feelings 105–106; "mourning"/letting go 103–105; overview 99; repressed 105;

substitute feelings 102–103, 105; and three personality systems 101–102
empathic neurons 70n6
empathic relationship 132–133
empathy 106
English, Fanita 105
Erikson, Eric 40, 91, 109, 112, 160
Erskine, R. 4, 26, 27, 40, 48, 49, 50, 51, 56–57, 70, 83, 115, 119, 120, 135, 148, 168, xiii
evoked companion 64–65
evolution perspective of ego states 2–5
existential life position 35, 44n10
experiences: intuition as knowledge of others' 120–121; intuitive perception of others' 117–119
explicit memory 38, 39, 68, 101
external action 7
external programming 22

fantasy 49, 83
Federn, P. 91, 113, 162, x–xi
frame of reference's role 144–145
free association 23
free attitude 54
Freud, S. 23, 49, 51, 55, 75, 91, 134
Freudian psychoanalysis 116n14
fusional relationship 130–131

games and time structuring 165
Games people play (Berne) 23, 26, 54, 77, 121–122, 125, 138
generalized representations of events 31–33
geniuses 70n6
Gilbert, M. 31
Gillespie, J. 82
Goleman, D. 100
Goulding, M. 69, 82
Goulding, R. 57, 69, 82, 157n16
group imago theory 136
groups 132, 135–137
guilt 104

Habermas, J. 71n34
Hargaden, H. 35, 91, 115, 133, 148, 168, xiii
Haykin, M. xii
Hine, J. 31
human motivation 97n20
holding environment 128–129

id: and Adult ego state 25–26; and Child ego state 25–26; and Parent ego state 25–26
identification 64

imagination 49
imitation 64
impersonal action 37
implicit memory 36, 38, 68
inhibition 87, 93
institutional systems 132
institutions 135–137
integrated activities 88–92; ego competence 91–92; notion of integration 90–91; sense of Self 91–92
integrated Adult 82
integrated collaborative relationships 133
integration 86–97, 117–125; defined 90; integrated activities 88–92; interaction modes 86–88; interaction perspective 156–157; as linear and accumulative process 90–91; process 90; transactional texts 92–97
integrative psychotherapy 26, 120, 129
Integrative Psychotherapy (Erskine and Trautmann) 26, xiii
intention, and outer side of communication 143
interaction modes 86–88, 92–94; collusion 87–88; conjunction 88; disjunction 87; inhibition 87; integration 88
interaction perspective 5–6, 8–9; Adult system 150–151; Child system 54, 150–151; collusion between systems 154–156; ego states theory from 24–25; establishing conjunction 153–154; integration 156–157; and its particular sensitivity 149–150; opening receptivity 150–153; Parent system 150–151; and practitioner 148–157; relationship/availability/intervention 148–149; strata and the unconscious 152–153
interactivity 106
internalized Parent ego state 65
internalizing: defined 64; relationship and communication 62; and rules/values 65–67; sources 63
internal programming 22
intervention: and availability 148–149; and relationship 148–149
intimacy 124–125, 133, 138–139; bilateral 125, 138; experiment 125
intrapsychic determining factors 21
introjections 64
intuition 49–50, 78–80; and Adult system 78–80; as knowledge of others' experiences 120–121
intuitive perception of others' experiences 117–119

INDEX

James, M. 82
Jongeward, D. 82
Jung, C.G.: Senoi dreamwork 157–158n19
Jung, G. 40, 59n51

Karpman, S. 166, 167, xii
Kegan, R. 65, 66
Kohlberg, L. 66
Kohut, H. 115, 116n11, 116n26, 135, 139n2
Kübler-Ross, E. 103
Kuhn, T. 166

Lahire, Bernard 63
Landaiche, M. 148
Laplanche, J. 23–24, 64
A Layman's Guide to Psychiatry and Psychoanalysis (Berne) xi
Levenson, R. 99
Levin, Pam 40
Little, R. 134
"Little Professor" 80
lucid consciousness 75

Martorell, J. L. 62
Mellor, K. 42
memorization/memorized experiences 50–51; Adult system 73–74; association modes for 51–52; The Child system 50–51; conscious and unconscious aspects 64; Parent system 64
memory: explicit 38, 39, 68, 101; implicit 36, 38, 68; organ metaphor 13
mirror neurons 70n6, 140n25
Moiso, C. 134, xii
"mourning"/letting go 103–105
Mozart 61
mystification 62, 73

neopsyche 4–5, 22, 23, 117
non-verbal communication 103
Novellino, M. 75, 83, 148, 169, xii, xiii
numbness 106

object relations theory 48, 57, 64, 75, 127, 129, 147
observer position 62–63
"operative imago" 141n44
organ metaphor 12–13; action 13; evolution and organization 13; memory 13; perception modes 12–13

origin perspective of ego states 2–5, 7–8; behavioural diagnosis 4; historical diagnosis 4; phenomenological diagnosis 4; relational diagnosis 4
"orthodox conceptual forms" 161
outer side of communication: content 142–143; intention 143; relationship with the listener 143
overdetermination 23
overgeneralisations 33–34

Paré, Ambroise 161
parental systems theory 66, 71n29
Parent developmental phase 66
Parent ego state 1, 3–6, 8–9, 28n5, 38; and ego 25–26; functions of 19–21; and id 25–26; influences Adult system 17; as resources for life and development 27–28; and superego 25–26
parent interview 62
Parent system 47, 60–70; according to redecision school 69; and autonomy 60–61; conscious and unconscious aspects 64; and creativity 60–61; development 66; early state of 69; evolution 64–67; impact on action 68; interaction perspective 150–151; internalizing sources 63; memorization 64; observer position 62–63; overview 60; perception in 61–63; relationship and communication 62; reparenting school 69–70; and sense of Self 109–111; sorting system 67; specific function of 68; and Stern's theory 64–65; theory of ego states 70; transactional texts 68–70
"peak experiences" 126n27, 126n31
perception modes 12–13
personality systems 5, 12, 35–40, 50, 56, xi; of child 44; and development strata 40–41; and emotion 101–102; evolution 16; genesis and evolution of *41*; memorization 15–16; mutual influences between systems 16–17; perception 15; in transactional texts 15–17
perspective and sensitivity 149–150
phenomenological experience 4
"phenomenological" therapy 161
physical sensations 106
Piaget, J. 65, 66, 90
Pontalis, J. 23–24, 64
practitioner and interaction perspective 148–157
prevailing concept 55

INDEX

primal image 120
primal judgement 120
Principles of Group Treatment (Berne) 26
probability programming 21–22
programming: existence 21; external 22; internal 22; probability 21–22
psychic organs 5, 12, 13–14, 21, xi
psychoanalysis 134, 163; Freudian 116n14; identification in 64; trends 116n14
psychoanalytic TA 120
psychotherapy 134
psychotherapy, integrative 26, 120, 129, 159

quantum mechanics 61

"radical therapy" movement 166
Ramond, C. 153
reality system 72–74, viii; *see also* Adult system
reality-testing 3, 81
real Self 6, 10n42, 113
rebelliousness 54
redecision/reparenting "schools" 167–168, xi
reframing 140n8
regression analysis 54
regulated improvisations 63
Reich, W. 110, 140n6
relational abilities 100
relational collusions 130–132; clinging relationship 131; dominant relationships 131; family/group/institutional systems 132; fusional relationship 130–131; symbiotic relationship 131
relational integrations 132–133; empathic relationship 132–133; integrated collaborative relationships 133; intimacy 133
relational interactions 130–133
relational needs 48, 96
relational TA 5, 115, 120, 133, 168, xiii
relationships 62, 117–125; and availability 148–149; and Berne 137–138; clinging 131; co-creative and transferential dimensions 133–135; and co-creativity 127–139; communicating and thinking together 129; communication within 142–147; dominant 131; empathic 132–133; fusional 130–131; giving meaning together 129; groups and institutions 135–137; holding environment, providing 128–129; integrated collaborative 133; and intervention 148–149; intimacy 138–139; relational interactions 130–133; role of 128–129; symbiotic 131
renaissance 61
re-parenting 5, 10n26
repetition perspective: The Child system 53–54, 56; of ego states 2–5
repetitive ego states 33
repression 87
respectful inquiry 51
Rogers, C. 132

San Francisco school 166–167
Schiff, Shea 66, 71n28, 71n30
script 165–166; elaboration 62; "protocol" 37, 39
script theory 35, 45n14, 52
Self: Berne on 113–115; and the Ego 112; TA recent trends 115; transactional texts 113–115
self-awareness 74
self-centred 49
self-confidence 108
self-dissatisfaction 108
self-distrust 108
"self-image" 108
self-indulgence 54
self-love 108
"self-object" 116n11, 139n2
Self psychology 57, 90, 91, 116n14, 116n26
Self-regulating Other 64–65, 68, 111
self-satisfaction 108
self-shame 108
sense of body 110
sense of existence 111–112
sense of Other 36, 111
sense of Self 35–37, 39, 47, 49, 52, 91–92, 103, 104, 108–115; and Adult system 109–111; and Child system 109–111; The Child system 52; and Ego competence 91–92; integration 91; integrity of 65, 90; and Parent system 109–111; positive 89; Self and the Ego 112; and sense of existence 111–112; and sense of Other 111; transactional texts: the Self 113–115
sequential/descriptive perspective: The Child system 54; of ego states 1–2, 6–7
Sills, C. 35, 91, 115, 133, 148, 168, xiii

situational determining factors 21–22
social Parent 63, 91, 109
social psychiatry 161
social unity 44n1
sorting system 67
Spitz, R. 163
splitting 87
Steiner, C. 82, 106, 138, 166–167, xii
Steiner-Berne matrix 166
Stern, D. 24, 31, 35–37, 38, 40, 45n35, 50, 55, 64–65, 76, 90, 122, 127, xiii
Stern's theory 64–65
"stroke economy" theory 167
structuring reinforcements 34
subjective experience 48–49
subjective Other 37
subjective Self 37
substitute feelings 102–103, 105
Summers, G. 135, xiii
superego: and Adult ego state 25–26; and Child ego state 25–26; and Parent ego state 25–26
symbiotic relationship 131

Tavistock Institute 136
Thomson, G. 102
Thunnissen, M. 35
transactional analysis (TA) 40, 57; classical 166–168; co-creative xiii; concepts 168–170; recent trends 115, 168, xiii; relational 4, xiii; transactionalists 55

Transactional Analysis in Psychotherapy (Berne) 4, 9, 10n48, 17, 21, 55, 68, 77, 80, 93, 94, 121, 146, 161, 163, xi
transactional psychoanalysis xiii
transaction diagram 145
transference 134, 167, 168; elements, and Child system 135; of a more evolved stratum 134; of a Parent pre-verbal stratum 134
transference transaction 145–147
Trautmann, R. 4, 26, 27, 40, 48, 50, 56, 70, 83, 115, 119, 120, 148, 168, xiii
Tudor, K. 135, xiii

unconscious communication 75, 78–84
unconscious loyalty 154

Vallejo, Oller 119
values 65–67
verbal Other 38
verbal Self 38

What do you say after you say Hello? (Berne) 54, 92, 98n23, 114, 125, 138
Wildlöcher, Daniel 91
Winnicott, D. W. 89, 128
Woods, K. xii
Woods, M. xii
World War II 120

Zalcman, M. 49